UNDERSTANDING THE TIMES®

A SURVEY OF COMPETING WORLDVIEWS

STUDENT MANUAL

UNDERSTANDING THE TIMES STUDENT MANUAL (5th Edition)
Published by Summit Ministries
P.O. Box 207
Manitou Springs, CO 80829

Contributors: Katelyn Brantley, Amanda Bridger, Jason Graham, Mike Hamel, David Knopp, Jeff Myers, and Stephen Sutherland

Editors: Louise Betelli, Linda Harris, Rachel Newman, and Scott Stewart

LCCN: 2017901537
ISBN-13: 978-0-9361-6321-5
ISBN-10: 0-936163-21-6

Printed in India
Seventh Printing (2022)

CONTENTS

Curriculum Overview

Our world revolves around *ideas*. Politicians, military leaders, CEOs, media moguls, and academics may think they are in charge of world affairs, but what they think—the ideas in their heads—actually control them. Ideas are the guiding force behind every twist and turn in public opinion. They determine what we accept or reject in the arts, media, business, science, education, politics, family, church, and the list goes on endlessly.

We cannot understand what's going on in the world until we look below the surface at the ideas that influence our beliefs and behaviors. These ideas can be grouped into six major worldviews.

This curriculum is about the *ideas* that construct our *worldviews*. Everyone has a worldview, which helps them interpret what is happening around them. Christianity has an explanation for reality, but so does Islam, Secularism, Marxism, New Spirituality, and Postmodernism. Each of these worldviews is founded upon a pattern of interconnected ideas. These worldviews dictate (consciously or unconsciously) how we interpret and respond to issues like stem-cell research, abortion, transgenderism, human rights, poverty, technology, etc.

Make no mistake, these worldviews are at war. This curriculum will open your eyes to the factions competing for your heart and mind. The stakes couldn't be higher. Because all humans are sinners (Romans 6:23), the worldviews developed apart from God will be sinful and flawed. But with the Christian worldview, we get God's perspective on the challenges we face and how best to deal with them.

Curriculum Sections

Before beginning this curriculum, it will be helpful to understand its structure and components.

1. **Syllabus:** What occurs each day and when assignments are due.

2. **Objectives:** Main learning goals for each chapter.

3. **Chapter Discussion Questions:** A review of the material read in each chapter.

4. **Classroom Activities:** Activities designed to reinforce content from each chapter.

5. **Readings:** Primary source materials, sometimes from non-Christian sources.

6. **Reading Discussion Questions:** A review of the material from the primary source readings.

7. **Reading Quizzes:** Multiple-choice and true/false questions for each primary source reading.

8. **Videos:** Lectures from experts, which dive deeper into key subjects.

9. **Video Outlines:** Notes from each video.

10. **Video Discussion Questions: A review of the material covered in each video.**

11. **Video Quizzes:** Multiple-choice and true/false questions for each video.

12. **Key Points:** Includes key questions, terms, verses, players, and works from each chapter reading.

13. **Writing Assignments:** Essay questions to answer at the end of each chapter.

14. **Tests:** A mixture of questions (matching, multiple choice, true/false, fill-in-the-blank, short answer, and essay) taken from each chapter's content.

College Credit

If you are interested in learning more about college credit for this course, please take visit summit.org/college-credit for more information.

Summit Alumni Network

This is a fabric of Christian thinkers and doers woven together by Summit Ministries' conference and curriculum grads. We gather—online and in-person—for ongoing study, strengthening community, and serving the cities in which we live. Join the network at summit.org/alumni.

WEEK 1

DAY	5-Day	ASSIGNMENT	PG
1	In Class	**START** UTT Chapter 01 Writing Assignment (p. 19)	
	In Class	**VIEW** UTT Chapter 01 Objectives	1
	At Home	**READ** UTT Chapter 01	
2	In Class	**DISCUSS** UTT Chapter 01 Questions	2
	In Class	**EXPLORE** UTT Chapter 01 Activities	2
3	In Class	**DISCUSS** UTT Chapter 01 Questions	2
	In Class	**EXPLORE** UTT Chapter 01 Activities	2
4	In Class	**DISCUSS** UTT Chapter 01 Questions	2
	In Class	**EXPLORE** UTT Chapter 01 Activities	2
5	In Class	**DISCUSS** UTT Chapter 01 Questions	2
	In Class	**EXPLORE** UTT Chapter 01 Activities	2

WEEK 2

DAY	5-Day	ASSIGNMENT	PG
6	In Class	**DISCUSS** UTT Chapter 01 Questions	2
	In Class	**EXPLORE** UTT Chapter 01 Activities	2
	At Home	**READ** "Plato's Cave"	9
7	In Class	**TAKE** "Plato's Cave" Quiz	
	In Class	**DISCUSS** "Plato's Cave" Questions	13
	At Home	**WATCH** "An Introduction to Worldviews"	15
8	In Class	**TAKE** "An Introduction to Worldviews" Quiz	
	In Class	**DISCUSS** "An Introduction to Worldviews" Questions	17
9	In Class	**STUDY** for UTT Chapter 01 Test	
10	In Class	**SUBMIT** UTT Chapter 01 Writing Assignment	19
	In Class	**TAKE** UTT Chapter 01 Test	
	At Home	**READ** UTT Chapter 02	

WEEK 3

DAY	5-Day	ASSIGNMENT	PG
11	In Class	**REVIEW** UTT Chapter 01 Test	
	In Class	**REVIEW** UTT Chapter 01 Assignment	
	In Class	**START** UTT Chapter 02 Writing Assignment (p. 37)	
	In Class	**VIEW** UTT Chapter 02 Objectives	21
	At Home	**READ** UTT Chapter 02	
12	In Class	**DISCUSS** UTT Chapter 02 Questions	22
	In Class	**EXPLORE** UTT Chapter 02 Activities	22
13	In Class	**DISCUSS** UTT Chapter 02 Questions	22
	In Class	**EXPLORE** UTT Chapter 02 Activities	22
14	In Class	**DISCUSS** UTT Chapter 02 Questions	22
	In Class	**EXPLORE** UTT Chapter 02 Activities	22
15	In Class	**DISCUSS** UTT Chapter 02 Questions	22
	In Class	**EXPLORE** UTT Chapter 02 Activities	22

WEEK 4

DAY	5-Day	ASSIGNMENT	PG
16	In Class	**DISCUSS** UTT Chapter 02 Questions	22
	In Class	**EXPLORE** UTT Chapter 02 Activities	22
	At Home	**READ** The Gospel of Mark 1–3 and 11–16	29
17	In Class	**TAKE** The Gospel of Mark Quiz	
	In Class	**DISCUSS** The Gospel of Mark Questions	30
	At Home	**WATCH** "The Christian Worldview"	32
18	In Class	**TAKE** "The Christian Worldview" Quiz	
	In Class	**DISCUSS** "The Christian Worldview" Questions	34
19	In Class	**STUDY** for UTT Chapter 02 Test	
20	In Class	**SUBMIT** UTT Chapter 02 Writing Assignment	37
	In Class	**TAKE** UTT Chapter 02 Test	
	At Home	**READ** UTT Chapter 03	

WEEK 5

DAY	5-Day	ASSIGNMENT	PG
21	In Class	**REVIEW** UTT Chapter 02 Test	
	In Class	**REVIEW** UTT Chapter 02 Assignment	
	In Class	**START** UTT Chapter 03 Writing Assignment (p. 55)	
	In Class	**VIEW** UTT Chapter 03 Objectives	39
	At Home	**READ** UTT Chapter 03	
22	In Class	**DISCUSS** UTT Chapter 03 Questions	40
	In Class	**EXPLORE** UTT Chapter 03 Activities	40
23	In Class	**DISCUSS** UTT Chapter 03 Questions	40
	In Class	**EXPLORE** UTT Chapter 03 Activities	40
24	In Class	**DISCUSS** UTT Chapter 03 Questions	40
	In Class	**EXPLORE** UTT Chapter 03 Activities	40
25	In Class	**DISCUSS** UTT Chapter 03 Questions	40
	In Class	**EXPLORE** UTT Chapter 03 Activities	40

WEEK 6

DAY	5-Day	ASSIGNMENT	PG
26	In Class	**DISCUSS** UTT Chapter 03 Questions	40
	In Class	**EXPLORE** UTT Chapter 03 Activities	40
	At Home	**READ** Sura 3–4	47
27	In Class	**TAKE** Sura 3–4 Quiz	
	In Class	**DISCUSS** Sura 3–4 Questions	48
	At Home	**WATCH** "A Closer Look at Islam"	49
28	In Class	**TAKE** "A Closer Look at Islam" Quiz	
	In Class	**DISCUSS** "A Closer Look at Islam" Questions	52
29	In Class	**STUDY** for UTT Chapter 03 Test	
30	In Class	**SUBMIT** UTT Chapter 03 Writing Assignment	55
	In Class	**TAKE** UTT Chapter 03 Test	
	At Home	**READ** UTT Chapter 04	

WEEK 7

DAY	5-Day	ASSIGNMENT	PG
31	In Class	**REVIEW** UTT Chapter 03 Test	
	In Class	**REVIEW** UTT Chapter 03 Assignment	
	In Class	**START** UTT Chapter 04 Writing Assignment (p. 71)	
	In Class	**VIEW** UTT Chapter 04 Objectives	57
	At Home	**READ** UTT Chapter 04	
32	In Class	**DISCUSS** UTT Chapter 04 Questions	58
	In Class	**EXPLORE** UTT Chapter 04 Activities	58
33	In Class	**DISCUSS** UTT Chapter 04 Questions	58
	In Class	**EXPLORE** UTT Chapter 04 Activities	58
34	In Class	**DISCUSS** UTT Chapter 04 Questions	58
	In Class	**EXPLORE** UTT Chapter 04 Activities	58
35	In Class	**DISCUSS** UTT Chapter 04 Questions	58
	In Class	**EXPLORE** UTT Chapter 04 Activities	58

WEEK 8

DAY	5-Day	ASSIGNMENT	PG
36	In Class	**DISCUSS** UTT Chapter 04 Questions	58
	In Class	**EXPLORE** UTT Chapter 04 Activities	58
	At Home	**READ** "Humanist Manifesto"	65
37	In Class	**TAKE** "Humanist Manifesto" Quiz	
	In Class	**DISCUSS** "Humanist Manifesto" Questions	66
	At Home	**WATCH** "The Secular Worldview"	67
38	In Class	**TAKE** "The Secular Worldview" Quiz	
	In Class	**DISCUSS** "The Secular Worldview" Questions	69
39	In Class	**STUDY** for UTT Chapter 04 Test	
40	In Class	**SUBMIT** UTT Chapter 04 Writing Assignment	71
	In Class	**TAKE** UTT Chapter 04 Test	
	At Home	**READ** UTT Chapter 05	

WEEK 9

DAY	5-Day	ASSIGNMENT	PG
41	In Class	**REVIEW** UTT Chapter 04 Test	
	In Class	**REVIEW** UTT Chapter 04 Assignment	
	In Class	**START** UTT Chapter 05 Writing Assignment (p. 93)	
	In Class	**VIEW** UTT Chapter 05 Objectives	73
	At Home	**READ** UTT Chapter 05	
42	In Class	**DISCUSS** UTT Chapter 05 Questions	74
	In Class	**EXPLORE** UTT Chapter 05 Activities	74
43	In Class	**DISCUSS** UTT Chapter 05 Questions	74
	In Class	**EXPLORE** UTT Chapter 05 Activities	74
44	In Class	**DISCUSS** UTT Chapter 05 Questions	74
	In Class	**EXPLORE** UTT Chapter 05 Activities	74
45	In Class	**DISCUSS** UTT Chapter 05 Questions	74
	In Class	**EXPLORE** UTT Chapter 05 Activities	74

WEEK 10

DAY	5-Day	ASSIGNMENT	PG
46	In Class	**DISCUSS** UTT Chapter 05 Questions	74
	In Class	**EXPLORE** UTT Chapter 05 Activities	74
	At Home	**READ** "The Communist Manifesto"	80
47	In Class	**TAKE** "The Communist Manefisto" Quiz	
	In Class	**DISCUSS** "The Communist Manifesto" Questions	88
	At Home	**WATCH** "The Marxist Worldview"	89
48	In Class	**TAKE** "The Marxist Worldview" Quiz	
	In Class	**DISCUSS** "The Marxist Worldview" Questions	91
49	In Class	**STUDY** for UTT Chapter 05 Test	
50	In Class	**SUBMIT** UTT Chapter 05 Writing Assignment	93
	In Class	**TAKE** UTT Chapter 05 Test	
	At Home	**READ** UTT Chapter 06	

WEEK 11

DAY	5-Day	ASSIGNMENT	PG
51	In Class	**REVIEW** UTT Chapter 05 Test	
	In Class	**REVIEW** UTT Chapter 05 Assignment	
	In Class	**START** UTT Chapter 06 Writing Assignment (p. 115)	
	In Class	**VIEW** UTT Chapter 06 Objectives	95
	At Home	**READ** UTT Chapter 06	
52	In Class	**DISCUSS** UTT Chapter 06 Questions	96
	In Class	**EXPLORE** UTT Chapter 06 Activities	96
53	In Class	**DISCUSS** UTT Chapter 06 Questions	96
	In Class	**EXPLORE** UTT Chapter 06 Activities	96
54	In Class	**DISCUSS** UTT Chapter 06 Questions	96
	In Class	**EXPLORE** UTT Chapter 06 Activities	96
55	In Class	**DISCUSS** UTT Chapter 06 Questions	96
	In Class	**EXPLORE** UTT Chapter 06 Activities	96

WEEK 12

DAY	5-Day	ASSIGNMENT	PG
56	In Class	**DISCUSS** UTT Chapter 06 Questions	96
	In Class	**EXPLORE** UTT Chapter 06 Activities	96
	At Home	**READ** "Bhagavad Gita" Ch. 6–9	102
57	In Class	**TAKE** "Bhagvad Gita" Ch. 6–9 Quiz	
	In Class	**DISCUSS** "Bhagvad Gita" Ch. 6–9 Questions	110
	At Home	**WATCH** "The New Spiritualist Worldview"	111
58	In Class	**TAKE** "The New Spiritualist Worldview" Quiz	
	In Class	**DISCUSS** "The New Spiritualist Worldview" Questions	113
59	In Class	**STUDY** for UTT Chapter 06 Test	
60	In Class	**SUBMIT** UTT Chapter 06 Writing Assignment	115
	In Class	**TAKE** UTT Chapter 06 Test	
	At Home	**READ** UTT Chapter 07	

WEEK 13

DAY	5-Day	ASSIGNMENT	PG
61	In Class	**REVIEW** UTT Chapter 06 Test	
	In Class	**REVIEW** UTT Chapter 06 Assignment	
	In Class	**START** UTT Chapter 07 Writing Assignment (p. 133)	
	In Class	**VIEW** UTT Chapter 07 Objectives	117
	At Home	**READ** UTT Chapter 07	
62	In Class	**DISCUSS** UTT Chapter 07 Questions	118
	In Class	**EXPLORE** UTT Chapter 07 Activities	118
63	In Class	**DISCUSS** UTT Chapter 07 Questions	118
	In Class	**EXPLORE** UTT Chapter 07 Activities	118
64	In Class	**DISCUSS** UTT Chapter 07 Questions	118
	In Class	**EXPLORE** UTT Chapter 07 Activities	118
65	In Class	**DISCUSS** UTT Chapter 07 Questions	118
	In Class	**EXPLORE** UTT Chapter 07 Activities	118

WEEK 14

DAY	5-Day	ASSIGNMENT	PG
66	In Class	**DISCUSS** UTT Chapter 07 Questions	118
	In Class	**EXPLORE** UTT Chapter 07 Activities	118
	At Home	**READ** "The Parable of the Mad Man"	124
67	In Class	**TAKE** "The Parable of the Mad Man" Quiz	
	In Class	**DISCUSS** "The Parable of the Mad Man" Questions	126
	At Home	**WATCH** "The Postmodern Worldview"	128
68	In Class	**TAKE** "The Postmodern Worldview" Quiz	
	In Class	**DISCUSS** "The Postmodern Worldview" Questions	131
69	In Class	**STUDY** for UTT Chapter 07 Test	
70	In Class	**SUBMIT** UTT Chapter 07 Writing Assignment	133
	In Class	**TAKE** UTT Chapter 07 Test	
	At Home	**READ** UTT Chapter 08	

WEEK 15

DAY	5-Day	ASSIGNMENT	PG
71	In Class	**REVIEW** UTT Chapter 07 Test	
	In Class	**REVIEW** UTT Chapter 07 Assignment	
	In Class	**START** UTT Chapter 08 Writing Assignment (p. 153)	
	In Class	**VIEW** UTT Chapter 08 Objectives	135
	At Home	**READ** UTT Chapter 08	
72	In Class	**DISCUSS** UTT Chapter 08 Questions	136
	In Class	**EXPLORE** UTT Chapter 08 Activities	136
73	In Class	**DISCUSS** UTT Chapter 08 Questions	136
	In Class	**EXPLORE** UTT Chapter 08 Activities	136
74	In Class	**DISCUSS** UTT Chapter 08 Questions	136
	In Class	**EXPLORE** UTT Chapter 08 Activities	136
75	In Class	**DISCUSS** UTT Chapter 08 Questions	136
	In Class	**EXPLORE** UTT Chapter 08 Activities	136

WEEK 16

DAY	5-Day	ASSIGNMENT	PG
76	In Class	**DISCUSS** UTT Chapter 08 Questions	136
	In Class	**EXPLORE** UTT Chapter 08 Activities	136
	At Home	**READ** "Why I am Not a Christian"	142
77	In Class	**TAKE** "Why I am Not a Christian" Quiz	
	In Class	**DISCUSS** "Why I am Not a Christian" Questions	147
	At Home	**WATCH** "Inside the Mind of the Skeptic"	148
78	In Class	**TAKE** "Inside the Mind of the Skeptic" Quiz	
	In Class	**DISCUSS** "Inside the Mind of the Skeptic" Questions	151
79	In Class	**STUDY** for UTT Chapter 08 Test	
80	In Class	**SUBMIT** UTT Chapter 08 Writing Assignment	153
	In Class	**TAKE** UTT Chapter 08 Test	
	At Home	**READ** UTT Chapter 09	

WEEK 17

DAY	5-Day	ASSIGNMENT	PG
81	In Class	**REVIEW** UTT Chapter 08 Test	
	In Class	**REVIEW** UTT Chapter 08 Assignment	
	In Class	**START** UTT Chapter 09 Writing Assignment (p. 177)	
	In Class	**VIEW** UTT Chapter 09 Objectives	155
	At Home	**READ** UTT Chapter 09	
82	In Class	**DISCUSS** UTT Chapter 09 Questions	156
	In Class	**EXPLORE** UTT Chapter 09 Activities	156
83	In Class	**DISCUSS** UTT Chapter 09 Questions	156
	In Class	**EXPLORE** UTT Chapter 09 Activities	156
84	In Class	**DISCUSS** UTT Chapter 09 Questions	156
	In Class	**EXPLORE** UTT Chapter 09 Activities	156
85	In Class	**DISCUSS** UTT Chapter 09 Questions	156
	In Class	**EXPLORE** UTT Chapter 09 Activities	156

WEEK 18

DAY	5-Day	ASSIGNMENT	PG
86	In Class	**DISCUSS** UTT Chapter 09 Questions	156
	In Class	**EXPLORE** UTT Chapter 09 Activities	156
	At Home	**READ** "Total Truth"	163
87	In Class	**TAKE** "Total Truth" Quiz	
	In Class	**DISCUSS** "Total Truth" Questions	171
	At Home	**WATCH** "Loving God with Your Mind"	172
88	In Class	**TAKE** "Loving God with Your Mind" Quiz	
	In Class	**DISCUSS** "Loving God with Your Mind" Questions	174
89	In Class	**STUDY** for UTT Chapter 09 Test	
90	In Class	**SUBMIT** UTT Chapter 09 Writing Assignment	177
	In Class	**TAKE** UTT Chapter 09 Test	
	At Home	**READ** UTT Chapter 10	

WEEK 19

DAY	5-Day	ASSIGNMENT	PG
91	In Class	**REVIEW** UTT Chapter 09 Test	
	In Class	**REVIEW** UTT Chapter 09 Assignment	
	In Class	**START** UTT Chapter 10 Writing Assignment (p. 193)	
	In Class	**VIEW** UTT Chapter 10 Objectives	179
	At Home	**READ** UTT Chapter 10	
92	In Class	**DISCUSS** UTT Chapter 10 Questions	180
	In Class	**EXPLORE** UTT Chapter 10 Activities	180
93	In Class	**DISCUSS** UTT Chapter 10 Questions	180
	In Class	**EXPLORE** UTT Chapter 10 Activities	180
94	In Class	**DISCUSS** UTT Chapter 10 Questions	180
	In Class	**EXPLORE** UTT Chapter 10 Activities	180
95	In Class	**DISCUSS** UTT Chapter 10 Questions	180
	In Class	**EXPLORE** UTT Chapter 10 Activities	180

WEEK 20

DAY	5-Day	ASSIGNMENT	PG
96	In Class	**DISCUSS** UTT Chapter 10 Questions	180
	In Class	**EXPLORE** UTT Chapter 10 Activities	180
	At Home	**WATCH** "Objective Morality" Debate	187
97	In Class	**TAKE** "Objective Morality" Quiz	
	In Class	**DISCUSS** "Objective Morality" Questions	188
	At Home	**WATCH** "Can We Be Moral without God"	189
98	In Class	**TAKE** "Can We Be Moral without God" Quiz	
	In Class	**DISCUSS** "Can We Be Moral without God" Questions	191
99	In Class	**STUDY** for UTT Chapter 10 Test	
100	In Class	**SUBMIT** UTT Chapter 10 Writing Assignment	193
	In Class	**TAKE** UTT Chapter 10 Test	
	At Home	**READ** UTT Chapter 11	

WEEK 21

DAY	5-Day	ASSIGNMENT	PG
101	In Class	**REVIEW** UTT Chapter 10 Test	
	In Class	**REVIEW** UTT Chapter 10 Assignment	
	In Class	**START** UTT Chapter 11 Writing Assignment (p. 217)	
	In Class	**VIEW** UTT Chapter 11 Objectives	195
	At Home	**READ** UTT Chapter 11	
102	In Class	**DISCUSS** UTT Chapter 11 Questions	196
	In Class	**EXPLORE** UTT Chapter 11 Activities	196
103	In Class	**DISCUSS** UTT Chapter 11 Questions	196
	In Class	**EXPLORE** UTT Chapter 11 Activities	196
104	In Class	**DISCUSS** UTT Chapter 11 Questions	196
	In Class	**EXPLORE** UTT Chapter 11 Activities	196
105	In Class	**DISCUSS** UTT Chapter 11 Questions	196
	In Class	**EXPLORE** UTT Chapter 11 Activities	196

WEEK 22

DAY	5-Day	ASSIGNMENT	PG
106	In Class	**DISCUSS** UTT Chapter 11 Questions	196
	In Class	**EXPLORE** UTT Chapter 11 Activities	196
	At Home	**READ** "On the Origin of Species"	202
107	In Class	**TAKE** "On the Origin of Species" Quiz	
	In Class	**DISCUSS** "On the Origin of Species" Questions	211
	At Home	**WATCH** "Myths of Evolution"	212
108	In Class	**TAKE** "Myths of Evolution" Quiz	
	In Class	**DISCUSS** "Myths of Evolution" Questions	215
109	In Class	**STUDY** for UTT Chapter 11 Test	
110	In Class	**SUBMIT** UTT Chapter 11 Writing Assignment	217
	In Class	**TAKE** UTT Chapter 11 Test	
	At Home	**READ** UTT Chapter 12	

WEEK 23

DAY	5-Day	ASSIGNMENT	PG
111	In Class	**REVIEW** UTT Chapter 11 Test	
	In Class	**REVIEW** UTT Chapter 11 Assignment	
	In Class	**START** UTT Chapter 12 Writing Assignment (p. 235)	
	In Class	**VIEW** UTT Chapter 12 Objectives	219
	At Home	**READ** UTT Chapter 12	
112	In Class	**DISCUSS** UTT Chapter 12 Questions	220
	In Class	**EXPLORE** UTT Chapter 12 Activities	220
113	In Class	**DISCUSS** UTT Chapter 12 Questions	220
	In Class	**EXPLORE** UTT Chapter 12 Activities	220
114	In Class	**DISCUSS** UTT Chapter 12 Questions	220
	In Class	**EXPLORE** UTT Chapter 12 Activities	220
115	In Class	**DISCUSS** UTT Chapter 12 Questions	220
	In Class	**EXPLORE** UTT Chapter 12 Activities	220

WEEK 24

DAY	5-Day	ASSIGNMENT	PG
116	In Class	**DISCUSS** UTT Chapter 12 Questions	220
	In Class	**EXPLORE** UTT Chapter 12 Activities	220
	At Home	**READ** "A Substantial Healing"	226
117	In Class	**TAKE** "A Substantial Healing" Quiz	
	In Class	**DISCUSS** "A Substantial Healing" Questions	229
	At Home	**WATCH** "Is Christianity Just a Crutch?"	230
118	In Class	**TAKE** "Is Christianity Just a Crutch?" Quiz	
	In Class	**DISCUSS** "Is Christianity Just a Crutch?" Questions	232
119	In Class	**STUDY** for UTT Chapter 12 Test	
120	In Class	**SUBMIT** UTT Chapter 12 Writing Assignment	235
	In Class	**TAKE** UTT Chapter 12 Test	
	At Home	**READ** UTT Chapter 13	

WEEK 25

DAY	5-Day	ASSIGNMENT	PG
121	In Class	**REVIEW** UTT Chapter 12 Test	
	In Class	**REVIEW** UTT Chapter 12 Assignment	
	In Class	**START** UTT Chapter 13 Writing Assignment (p. 261)	
	In Class	**VIEW** UTT Chapter 13 Objectives	237
	At Home	**READ** UTT Chapter 13	
122	In Class	**DISCUSS** UTT Chapter 13 Questions	238
	In Class	**EXPLORE** UTT Chapter 13 Activities	238
123	In Class	**DISCUSS** UTT Chapter 13 Questions	238
	In Class	**EXPLORE** UTT Chapter 13 Activities	238
124	In Class	**DISCUSS** UTT Chapter 13 Questions	238
	In Class	**EXPLORE** UTT Chapter 13 Activities	238
125	In Class	**DISCUSS** UTT Chapter 13 Questions	238
	In Class	**EXPLORE** UTT Chapter 13 Activities	238

WEEK 26

DAY	5-Day	ASSIGNMENT	PG
126	In Class	**DISCUSS** UTT Chapter 13 Questions	238
	In Class	**EXPLORE** UTT Chapter 13 Activities	238
	At Home	**READ** "Doing Life Together"	244
127	In Class	**TAKE** "Doing Life Together" Quiz	
	In Class	**DISCUSS** "Doing Life Together" Questions	255
	At Home	**WATCH** "Correct, Not Politically Correct"	256
128	In Class	**TAKE** "Correct, Not Politically Correct" Quiz	
	In Class	**DISCUSS** "Correct, Not Politically Correct" Questions	259
129	In Class	**STUDY** for UTT Chapter 13 Test	
130	In Class	**SUBMIT** UTT Chapter 13 Writing Assignment	261
	In Class	**TAKE** UTT Chapter 13 Test	
	At Home	**READ** UTT Chapter 14	

WEEK 27

DAY	5-Day	ASSIGNMENT	PG
131	In Class	**REVIEW** UTT Chapter 13 Test	
	In Class	**REVIEW** UTT Chapter 13 Assignment	
	In Class	**START** UTT Chapter 14 Writing Assignment (p. 283)	
	In Class	**VIEW** UTT Chapter 14 Objectives	263
	At Home	**READ** UTT Chapter 14	
132	In Class	**DISCUSS** UTT Chapter 14 Questions	264
	In Class	**EXPLORE** UTT Chapter 14 Activities	264
133	In Class	**DISCUSS** UTT Chapter 14 Questions	264
	In Class	**EXPLORE** UTT Chapter 14 Activities	264
134	In Class	**DISCUSS** UTT Chapter 14 Questions	264
	In Class	**EXPLORE** UTT Chapter 14 Activities	264
135	In Class	**DISCUSS** UTT Chapter 14 Questions	264
	In Class	**EXPLORE** UTT Chapter 14 Activities	264

WEEK 28

DAY	5-Day	ASSIGNMENT	PG
136	In Class	**DISCUSS** UTT Chapter 14 Questions	264
	In Class	**EXPLORE** UTT Chapter 14 Activities	264
	At Home	**READ** "The Law"	270
137	In Class	**TAKE** "The Law" Quiz	
	In Class	**DISCUSS** "The Law" Questions	278
	At Home	**WATCH** "The Philosophy of Law"	279
138	In Class	**TAKE** "The Philosophy of Law" Quiz	
	In Class	**DISCUSS** "The Philosophy of Law" Questions	281
139	In Class	**STUDY** for UTT Chapter 14 Test	
140	In Class	**SUBMIT** UTT Chapter 14 Writing Assignment	283
	In Class	**TAKE** UTT Chapter 14 Test	
	At Home	**READ** UTT Chapter 15	

WEEK 29

DAY	5-Day	ASSIGNMENT	PG
141	In Class	**REVIEW** UTT Chapter 14 Test	
	In Class	**REVIEW** UTT Chapter 14 Assignment	
	In Class	**START** UTT Chapter 15 Writing Assignment (p. 303)	
	In Class	**VIEW** UTT Chapter 15 Objectives	285
	At Home	**READ** UTT Chapter 15	
142	In Class	**DISCUSS** UTT Chapter 15 Questions	286
	In Class	**EXPLORE** UTT Chapter 15 Activities	286
143	In Class	**DISCUSS** UTT Chapter 15 Questions	286
	In Class	**EXPLORE** UTT Chapter 15 Activities	286
144	In Class	**DISCUSS** UTT Chapter 15 Questions	286
	In Class	**EXPLORE** UTT Chapter 15 Activities	286
145	In Class	**DISCUSS** UTT Chapter 15 Questions	286
	In Class	**EXPLORE** UTT Chapter 15 Activities	286

WEEK 30

DAY	5-Day	ASSIGNMENT	PG
146	In Class	**DISCUSS** UTT Chapter 15 Questions	286
	In Class	**EXPLORE** UTT Chapter 15 Activities	286
	At Home	**READ** "The Decleration of Independence"	292
147	In Class	**TAKE** "The Decleration of Independence" Quiz	
	In Class	**DISCUSS** "The Decleration of Independence" Questions	297
	At Home	**WATCH** "Your Constitutional Right to Be Offended"	298
148	In Class	**TAKE** "Your Constitutional Right..." Quiz	
	In Class	**DISCUSS** "Your Constitutional Right..." Questions	300
149	In Class	**STUDY** for UTT Chapter 15 Test	
150	In Class	**SUBMIT** UTT Chapter 15 Writing Assignment	303
	In Class	**TAKE** UTT Chapter 15 Test	
	At Home	**READ** UTT Chapter 16	

WEEK 31

DAY	5-Day	ASSIGNMENT	PG
151	In Class	**REVIEW** UTT Chapter 15 Test	
	In Class	**REVIEW** UTT Chapter 15 Assignment	
	In Class	**START** UTT Chapter 16 Writing Assignment (p. 329)	
	In Class	**VIEW** UTT Chapter 16 Objectives	305
	At Home	**READ** UTT Chapter 16	
152	In Class	**DISCUSS** UTT Chapter 16 Questions	306
	In Class	**EXPLORE** UTT Chapter 16 Activities	306
153	In Class	**DISCUSS** UTT Chapter 16 Questions	306
	In Class	**EXPLORE** UTT Chapter 16 Activities	306
154	In Class	**DISCUSS** UTT Chapter 16 Questions	306
	In Class	**EXPLORE** UTT Chapter 16 Activities	306
155	In Class	**DISCUSS** UTT Chapter 16 Questions	306
	In Class	**EXPLORE** UTT Chapter 16 Activities	306

WEEK 32

DAY	5-Day	ASSIGNMENT	PG
156	In Class	**DISCUSS** UTT Chapter 16 Questions	306
	In Class	**EXPLORE** UTT Chapter 16 Activities	306
	At Home	**READ** "Animal Farm"	312
157	In Class	**TAKE** "Animal Farm" Quiz	
	In Class	**DISCUSS** "Animal Farm" Questions	323
	At Home	**WATCH** "Pillars of Economic Wisdom"	324
158	In Class	**TAKE** "Pillars of Economic Wisdom" Quiz	
	In Class	**DISCUSS** "Pillars of Economic Wisdom" Questions	327
159	In Class	**STUDY** for UTT Chapter 16 Test	
160	In Class	**SUBMIT** UTT Chapter 16 Writing Assignment	329
	In Class	**TAKE** UTT Chapter 16 Test	
	At Home	**READ** UTT Chapter 17	

WEEK 33

DAY	5-Day	ASSIGNMENT	PG
161	In Class	**REVIEW** UTT Chapter 16 Test	
	In Class	**REVIEW** UTT Chapter 16 Assignment	
	In Class	**START** UTT Chapter 17 Writing Assignment (p. 353)	
	In Class	**VIEW** UTT Chapter 17 Objectives	331
	At Home	**READ** UTT Chapter 17	
162	In Class	**DISCUSS** UTT Chapter 17 Questions	332
	In Class	**EXPLORE** UTT Chapter 17 Activities	332
163	In Class	**DISCUSS** UTT Chapter 17 Questions	332
	In Class	**EXPLORE** UTT Chapter 17 Activities	332
164	In Class	**DISCUSS** UTT Chapter 17 Questions	332
	In Class	**EXPLORE** UTT Chapter 17 Activities	332
165	In Class	**DISCUSS** UTT Chapter 17 Questions	332
	In Class	**EXPLORE** UTT Chapter 17 Activities	332

WEEK 34

DAY	5-Day	ASSIGNMENT	PG
166	In Class	**DISCUSS** UTT Chapter 17 Questions	332
	In Class	**EXPLORE** UTT Chapter 17 Activities	332
	At Home	**READ** "Censoring the Past"	338
167	At Home	**TAKE** "Censoring the Past" Quiz	
	In Class	**DISCUSS** "Censoring the Past" Questions	347
	At Home	**WATCH** "Restoring All Things"	348
168	In Class	**TAKE** "Restoring All Things" Quiz	
	In Class	**DISCUSS** "Restoring All Things" Questions	350
169	In Class	**STUDY** for UTT Chapter 17 Test	
170	In Class	**SUBMIT** UTT Chapter 17 Writing Assignment	353
	In Class	**TAKE** UTT Chapter 17 Test	
	At Home	**READ** UTT Chapter 18	

WEEK 35

DAY	5-Day	ASSIGNMENT	PG
171	In Class	**REVIEW** UTT Chapter 17 Test	
	In Class	**REVIEW** UTT Chapter 17 Assignment	
	In Class	**VIEW** UTT Chapter 18 Objectives	355
	At Home	**READ** UTT Chapter 18	
172	In Class	**DISCUSS** UTT Chapter 18 Questions	356
173	In Class	**DISCUSS** UTT Chapter 18 Questions	356
174	In Class	**DISCUSS** UTT Chapter 18 Questions	356
175	In Class	**DISCUSS** UTT Chapter 18 Questions	356

WEEK 36

DAY	5-Day	ASSIGNMENT	PG
176	In Class	**DISCUSS** UTT Chapter 18 Questions	356
177	In Class	**STUDY** for UTT Chapter 18 Test	
178	In Class	**STUDY** for UTT Chapter 18 Test	
179	In Class	**STUDY** for UTT Chapter 18 Test	
180	In Class	**TAKE** UTT Chapter 18 Test	

UNIT

1

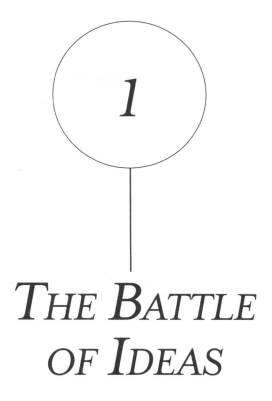

THE BATTLE OF IDEAS

CHAPTER 1 LEARNING OBJECTIVES

Students will be able to:

1. articulate why patterns are an important key to understanding the world. [1.1]

2. name two keys to successfully navigate through life. [1.2]

3. explain why David Noebel felt called to write this textbook. [1.3]

4. articulate why spotting patterns can sometimes be difficult. [1.4]

5. define a worldview. [1.5]

6. list reasons why it is important for Christians to study worldviews. [1.6]

7. explain why Christian worldviews come under attack. [1.7]

8. identify how worldviews spread and how to guard against adopting counterfeit worldviews. [1.8]

9. name and explain the six dominant worldviews of Western culture. [1.9]

10. explain how these disciplines guide how they look at the world. [1.10]

11. explain how Christianity addresses the ten academic disciplines. [1.11]

12. apply the four criteria for testing the truth of a worldview. [1.12]

13. respond to the parable of the elephant. [1.13]

14. state why every worldview cannot be correct. [1.14]

1. What can we learn from sports like tennis and games like chess about how the world works? [1.1–1.2]

2. Do the patterns we see around us every day suggest answers to some of life's bigger questions? What are some of those questions? [1.1–1.2]

3. You've never seen, touched or smelled an idea but you've had plenty of them. What are ideas and how do they influence us? [1.4]

4. Our ideas inform our beliefs and influence our behavior. Think of some bad ideas humans have had and what happened as a result. Now do the same with some good ideas.

5. Ideas flow together into complex patterns. Does the amount of information available to us today make it easier or harder to see and understand patterns? [1.4]

6. Where does the New Testament tell Christians to see the world differently from other people? Why is this shift in perspective so important? [1.5]

7. Everyone has a way of seeing the world—a worldview—even if he or she doesn't realize it. What is a "worldview" and how does it influence the way we live? [1.5]

8. Most of us rely on GPS programs. (When was the last time you looked at a paper map?) How many ways can you think of that a worldview and a GPS program are alike?

9. What are some of the fundamental questions a worldview seeks to answer? [1.5]

10. Do intangible ideas have tangible results? Do ideas have consequences? If so, in what ways? [1.6]

11. Can you give some examples from history where bad ideas had devastating consequences? [1.6]

12. What is the risk if you defend a Christian worldview and question the worldviews of others? [1.7]

13. Can you recall a time when you shared your Christian worldview or questioned the worldview of a teacher or other adult who disagreed with you? What was the response?

14. In what ways are ideas like viruses? [1.8]

15. How can we protect ourselves against bad ideas? [1.8]

16. Can you name the six dominant worldviews outlined in this chapter and summarize each in a few sentences? [1.9]

17. Of the six worldviews, which ones would be considered theistic and which ones would be called secular? [1.9]

18. An advanced education is comprised of basic disciplines or areas of study. This book explores how ten basic academic disciplines are understood in the six worldviews being studied. Can you name and define all ten? [1.10]

19. What does the text say is the Christian perspective on the ten disciplines that make up a worldview? [1.11]

20. It's not enough to say the Christian worldview is true and that it accurately represents reality. The book *Making Sense of Your World* suggests four tests for determining whether or not a worldview is true. Can you name and describe each in one sentence? [1.12]

21. In your opinion, how does the Christian worldview hold up when these tests are applied to it?

22. Retell the parable of the elephant in your own words. How does each blind man experience and describe the elephant? Are their descriptions true or false? [1.13]

23. The story of the blind men and the elephant is sometimes used to illustrate how different worldviews can all be true. When used like this, what's the moral of the story? [1.13]

24. What's the problem with this interpretation of the parable? [1.13]

25. Why can't all worldviews be true? [1.14]

26. Christians recognize that God has communicated through his creation as well as Scripture, so it's no surprise to find elements of truth in non-Christian worldviews. Can you give some examples? [1.14]

27. What's the major dividing line between Christian and non-Christian worldviews? [1.13–1.14]

"Plato's Cave" Reading

Plato (427–347 B.C.) was one of the most famous and influential philosophers of all time. Many of his writings are dialogues with his mentor, Socrates, as the speaker. *The Allegory of the Cave* found in Book VII of *The Republic* is a discussion between Socrates and Glaucon. It illustrates many of Plato's philosophical assumptions, including:

- The physical world isn't the real world but only a poor copy
- The real world can only be grasped intellectually
- The universe is ultimately good and beautiful
- Enlightened people have an obligation to enlighten others
- The good society is one in which the truly wise are the rulers

Plato's Cave
Except from Plato's *Republic*, Book VII

[**Socrates:**] Imagine human beings living in an underground, cavelike dwelling, with an entrance a long way up, which is both open to the light and as wide as the cave itself. They've been there since childhood, fixed in the same place, with their necks and legs fettered, able to see only in front of them, because their bonds prevent them from turning their heads around. Light is provided by a fire burning far above and behind them. Also behind them, but on higher ground, there is a path stretching between them and the fire. Imagine that along this path a low wall has been built, like the screen in front of puppeteers above which they show their puppets.

[**Gloucon:**] I'm imagining it.

[**Socrates:**] Then also imagine that there are people along the wall, carrying all kinds of artifacts that project above it—statues of people and other animals, made out of stone, wood, and every material. And, as you'd expect, some of the carriers are talking, and some are silent.

[**Gloucon:**] It's a strange image you're describing, and strange prisoners.

[**Socrates:**] They're like us. Do you suppose, first of all, that these prisoners see anything of themselves and one another besides the shadows that the fire casts on the wall in front of them? How could they, if they have to keep their heads motionless throughout life? What about the things being carried along the wall? Isn't the same true of them?

[**Gloucon:**] Of course.

[**Socrates:**] And if they could talk to one another, don't you think they'd suppose that the names they used applied to the things they see passing before them?'

[**Gloucon:**] They'd have to.

[**Socrates:**] And what if their prison also had an echo from the wall facing them? Don't you think they'd believe that the shadows passing in front of them were talking whenever one of the carriers passing along the wall was doing so?

[**Gloucon:**] I certainly do.

[**Socrates:**] Then the prisoners would in every way believe that the truth is nothing other than the shadows of those artifacts.

[**Gloucon:**] They must surely believe that.

[**Socrates:**] Consider, then, what being released from their bonds and cured of their ignorance would naturally be like if something like this came to pass. When one of them was freed and suddenly compelled to stand up, turn his head, walk, and look up toward the light, he'd be pained and dazzled and unable to see the things whose shadows he'd seen before. What do you think he'd say, if we told him that what he'd seen before was inconsequential, but that now—because he is a bit closer to the things that are and is turned towa r s d things that are more—he sees more correctly? Or, to put it another Way if we pointed to each of the things passing by, asked him what each of them and compelled him to answer, don't you think he'd be at a loss and that he'd believe that the things he saw earlier were truer than the ones he was now being shown?

[**Gloucon:**] Much truer.

[**Socrates:**] And if someone compelled him to look at the light itself, wouldn't his eyes hurt, and wouldn't he turn around and flee towards the things he's able to see, believing that they're really clearer than the ones he's being shown?

[**Gloucon:**] He would.

[**Socrates:**] And if someone dragged him away from there by force, up the rough, steep path, and didn't let him go until he had dragged him into the sunlight, wouldn't he be pained and irritated at being treated that way? And when he came into the light, with the sun filling his eyes, wouldn't he be unable to see a single one of the things now said to be true?

[**Gloucon:**] He would be unable to see them, at least at first.

[**Socrates:**] I suppose, then, that he'd need time to get adjusted before he could see things in the world above. At first, he'd see shadows most easily, then images of men and other things in water, then the things themselves. Of these, he'd be able to study the things in the sky and the sky itself more easily at night, looking at the light of the stars and the moon, than during the day, looking at the sun and the light of the sun.

[**Gloucon:**] Of course.

[**Socrates:**] Finally, I suppose, he'd be able to see the sun, not images of it in water or some alien place, but the sun itself, in its own place, and be able to study it.

[**Gloucon:**] Necessarily so.

[**Socrates:**] And at this point he would infer and conclude that the sun provides the seasons and the years, governs everything in the visible world, and is in some way the cause of all the things that he used to see.

[**Gloucon:**] It's clear that would be his next step.

[**Socrates:**] What about when he reminds himself of his first dwelling place, his fellow prisoners, and what passed for wisdom there? Don't you think that he'd count himself happy for the change and pity the others?

[**Gloucon:**] Certainly.

[**Socrates:**] And if there had been any honors, praises, or prizes among them for the one who was sharpest at identifying the shadows as they passed by and who best remembered which usually came earlier, which later, and which simultaneously, and who could thus best divine the future, do you think that our man would desire these rewards or envy those among the prisoners who were honored and held power? Instead, wouldn't he feel, with Homer, that he'd much prefer to "work the earth as a serf to another, one without possessions," and go through any sufferings, rather than share their opinions and live as they do?

[**Gloucon:**] I suppose he would rather suffer anything than live like that.

[**Socrates:**] Consider this too. If this man went down into the cave again and sat down in his same seat, wouldn't his eyes—coming suddenly out of the sun like that—be filled with darkness?
[**Gloucon:**] They certainly would.

[**Socrates:**] And before his eyes had recovered—and the adjustment would not be quick— while his vision was still dim, if he had to compete again with the perpetual prisoners in recognizing the shadows, wouldn't he invite ridicule? Wouldn't it be said of him that he'd returned from his upward journey with his eyesight ruined and that it isn't worthwhile even to try to travel upward? And, as for anyone who tried to free them and lead them upward, if they could somehow get their hands on him, wouldn't they kill him?

[**Gloucon:**] They certainly would.

[**Socrates:**] This whole image, Glaucon, must be fitted together with what we said before. The visible realm should be likened to the prison dwelling, and the light of the fire inside it to the power of the sun. And if you interpret the upward journey and the study of things above as the upward journey of the soul to the intelligible realm, you'll grasp what I hope to convey, since that is what you wanted to hear about. Whether it's true or not, only the god knows. But this is how I see it: In the knowable realm, the form of the good is the last thing to be seen, and it is reached only with difficulty. Once one has seen it, however, one must conclude that it is the cause of all that is correct and beautiful in anything, that it produces both light and its source in the visible realm, and that in the intelligible realm it controls and provides truth and understanding, so that anyone who is to act sensibly in private or public must see it.

Plato: Republic, translated by G.M.A. Grube, revised by C.D.C. Reeve, Copyright Hackett Publishing Company 1992. Reprinted with permission from the publisher.

1. Can you summarize Plato's parable of the cave in your own words?

2. Who do the prisoners represent? What do the shadows represent?

3. Why was the light painful for the newly freed man? What was Plato's point in this detail?

4. What does the sun represent?

5. Why did the freed prisoner not wish to go back to his former life?

6. Why would the prisoners try to kill anyone attempting to show them the light?

7. What is the point of Plato's parable of the cave?

8. What insights can we glean about worldviews from a parable written more than 2,000 years ago?

Eric Smith defines a worldview as "a pattern of ideas, beliefs, convictions, and habits that help us make sense of God, the world, and our relationship to God and the world." Worldviews answers life big questions: Why are we here? Does life have meaning and purpose? Is there right and wrong? Is there a God? Who am I?

In deciding which worldview is true, we can apply four tests of truth:

1. Test of reason: Is it reasonable? Is it consistent and not self-refuting?
2. Test of the outer world: Is there some external, self-corroborating evidence to support it?
3. Test of the inner world: Does it adequately match what we experience in our world?
4. Test of the real world: Are its consequences good or bad when applied in any given cultural context?

To access this video, go to www.summitu.com/utt and enter the passcode found in the back of your manual.

A _____ helps us make sense of the world we live in. We live in a world of ideas about what is right and wrong, how we should live, and so on. We don't have to memorize every grouping of ideas. We can look for patterns. Everything can be categorized into worldviews and we can see the world that way.

What is a worldview?

A _____ of ideas, beliefs, convictions, and habits that help us make sense of God, the world, and our relationship to God and the world.

What does a worldview do?

It answers life's big questions:

- Why are we here?
- Does _____ have meaning and purpose?
- Is there right and wrong?
- Is there a_____ ?
- Who am I?

Ideas can be collected into six different worldviews. These worldviews shape our ideas, habits, and identity. Habits, the things we do on a regular basis, shape and reinforce who we are. They reinforce the ideas we believe in.

Which worldview is true?

Four tests of truth:

1. Test of _____ : Is it reasonable? Can it be logically stated and defended? Is it consistent and not self-refuting?
2. Test of the _____ world: Is there some external, self-corroborating evidence to support it? Worldviews that claim to have roots in history, such as Christianity and Islam, must be corroborated by external evidence.
3. Test of the _____ world: Does it adequately match what we experience in our world? How does something line up with what we think and feel?
4. Test of the _____ world: Are its consequences good or bad when applied in any given cultural context? History is full of negative examples such as Marxism and Islam.

1. What is a worldview?

2. What does a worldview do?

3. Which worldview is true?

4. How does the "test of the outer world" apply to worldviews and religions?

5. How does the "test of the real world" apply to worldviews?

Chapter 1 Key Points

Key Questions:

1. What is a worldview?
2. Why is it important to study worldviews?

Key Verses:

1. Roman 12:2
2. 1 Peter 3:15

Key Terms:

1. Biology
2. Economics
3. Ethics
4. History
5. Law
6. Philosophy
7. Politics
8. Psychology
9. Religion
10. Sociology
11. Theology
12. Worldview*

Short answer or essay question on the exam

Hello!

Well, I'm finally settled into my dorm room. You wouldn't think that it would take so long to move into a room the size of a closet, but when you're sharing that space with a roommate, you have to be creative.

My roommate, Nathan, is really interesting. After noticing my Bible, he mentioned that he is taking a World Religions class this semester. It sounded like a fascinating class, so I signed up too! My course load this semester is fairly light since it is my first semester and all. In addition to World Religions, I am taking English Composition, Art History, Economics, and Basket Weaving. (Don't laugh!)

Yesterday was the first day of classes. I was really nervous, but I got through it. My World Religions professor is hilarious. He dresses like a hippie and even brought a ukulele to class. It will probably be my most fun course this term. When he began his lecture, he asked each of us to say what religion, if any, we believe in. Many of the students said they believed in Christianity, but a number of them held to Islam, Judaism, and even atheism. Nathan said he was "into spirituality," but I have no idea what he meant by that. I'll have to ask him sometime.

Anyway, back to the lecture. The professor gave a brief rundown of what he called the major "worldviews." Despite my confusion, everyone seemed to understand what that meant, so I didn't ask since I didn't want to look ignorant. He proceeded to say that by the end of the semester, most of the professed Christians would believe something different. Needless to say, I was shocked. After class, I asked the professor why he expected that to happen. We talked for a while before the professor asked me if I thought Christianity was the only way to God. I answered yes, since Christianity is the only religion that acknowledges Jesus as both God and Savior. The professor proposed a different view. He thought that all religions ultimately lead to God. He argued that ultimately religions are just different paths to the same destination. I stammered out a short reply, saying that not all religions believe in Jesus, but it didn't seem to satisfy him. He asked what I knew about other religions, and I admitted that I did not know much. The last thing he said has really had me thinking the last few days. He said, "If you don't know what other religions believe, then how do you know that other religions don't lead to God as well?" I didn't know what to say.

I'd like to be able to defend my faith to him, but the questions he asked made me wonder if I've thought through my beliefs carefully. My professor said he's open to talking about Christianity, but I don't think I know just how to explain it to him. Can you help me figure out what to say? **What is a worldview?** Can you also explain to me **why should we study worldviews?** I mean, I know I should since he pointed out how little I know, but I don't know if I could really say why. He's interested in learning about my beliefs, but **what does it mean to have a Christian worldview?**

Well, it's already past midnight, so I'd better get some sleep. I have a class at 8 a.m. tomorrow and can't skip breakfast if I want to have my brain awake that early!

One last thing … **do you know why you are a Christian?** I know I am, but after my conversation with the professor, I am not sure I know *why* I am. Just curious.

–Doug

UNIT

2

CHRISTIANITY

CHAPTER 2 LEARNING OBJECTIVES

Students will be able to:

1. explain Joad's book title *The Recovery of Faith*. [2.1]

2. state what two forms of revelation establish the Christian worldview. [2.2]

3. name the five claims of Christianity. [2.3]

4. define general and special revelation. [2.4]

5. explain how general revelation comes from nature. [2.5]

6. use Romans 1:19–20 to explain general revelation. [2.6]

7. explain why the Bible shows special revelation. [2.7]

8. identify how the Bible points out fallacies in other worldviews. [2.8]

9. use a scripture to examine. [2.9]

10. explain how a blind and dark world can see. [2.10]

1. Is Christianity a series of made-up stories or "the great myth that turned out to be true"? [2.2]

2. How do myths, stories, and fairy tales influence the way we think and live? [2.2]

3. What are the basics of the Christian worldview? [2.2]

4. According to Christianity, are we searching for God or does he take the initiative to find us? [2.2]

5. Can you briefly state the cosmological argument for God's existence? [2.3]

6. Can you give some examples of the fine-tuning of the universe? [2.3]

7. The Bible presents a "personal creator" as the "first cause" of everything. There is a person behind the plan, an *author* of the human story. What does it mean to say that God is personal? [2.3]

8. If God is a person, how can we get to know him? [2.3]

9. How would you answer a critic like Samuel Beckett who insists life is without meaning? [2.3]

10. What are some of the implications of being created by a personal God instead of just evolving through blind chance? [2.3]

11. What are some other things that retain their design or "image" even when they're broken? [2.3]

12. God's initial creation was "very good," but then something very bad happened—sin. How did sin affect creation? [2.3]

13. How does God respond to the fall? [2.3]

14. What's the difference between general revelation and special revelation? [2.4]

15. What are the two basic explanations of how the universe—and the life within it—came into being? [2.5]

16. Can general revelation lead people to God? [2.6]

17. Can a person who has never read the Bible or heard the gospel have a saving faith in God? [2.6]

18. What does special revelation add to general revelation? [2.7]

19. What does the doctrine of "divine inspiration" mean? [2.7]

20. How are we to understand the Bible? [2.7]

21. **What does the Bible say about humanity? [2.7]**

22. **What does the Bible say is wrong with us? [2.7]**

23. **What does the Bible say about how we should live? [2.7]**

24. **How does biblical Christianity compare to other worldviews? Upon what core truths do they agree or disagree? [2.8]**

25. Is Christianity a reasonable worldview or does it have to be taken by blind faith? [2.9]

26. If the evidence from general and special revelation is so compelling, why doesn't everyone become a Christian? [2.10]

Mark was probably the first gospel written, most likely by John Mark (Acts 12:12, 25; 15:37) and perhaps from Rome. The gospel is quoted extensively in Mathew and Luke. Mark emphasizes

- the cost of discipleship;
- the teachings of Jesus, often in parables;
- the miracles showing Jesus is the Son of God;
- the necessity of the cross.

Outline of Mark:

- The beginnings of Jesus's ministry, mostly in Galilee (1:1–6:29)
- Withdrawing from Galilee (6:30–9:50)
- Jesus's ministry in Judea and Perea (chapter 10)
- The passion of Jesus (chapters 11–15)
- The resurrection of Jesus (chapter 16)

The gospel reveals the worldview of Jesus in word and deed. He preaches the kingdom of God and explains it in parables. He also demonstrates its power in healings and exorcisms. He shows compassion to the needs of the people and calls out the religious leaders for their hypocrisy.

Chapters 11–15 are dedicated to the last week of Jesus's life, with chapter 16 dealing with his resurrection. These last words and actions of Jesus before his crucifixion reveal what was most important to him and what he wanted his disciples to pass on to future generations.

**Read chapters 1–3 and 11–16
in whichever Bible translation you prefer.**

1. Why do you think Jesus called a group of disciples to follow him and share his life in intimate detail (Mark 1:17–18)? What was he looking for in these original disciples? What were they looking for in him?

2. The parable was Jesus's favorite teaching tool. His short yet powerful stories are so memorable that even people who have never read the Bible know many of them. See how many of the main parables in Mark you can name. Which is your favorite? Why?

3. According to Jesus, what are the two greatest commandments (Mark 12:28–34)? What makes them so important?

4. Mark 11 records two instances where the meek and mild Jesus became angry or destructive: cursing the fig tree and cleansing the temple. Why did he do it, and why wasn't it sin?

5. According to Jesus, whWho was responsible for the death of Jesus?

6. According to Jesus, whWhat does it mean to *be* a disciple of Jesus? What does it mean to *make* disciples (Mark 16:15)?

Dr. Jeff Myers shows how the Christian worldview is shaped by the Bible, which is a true account of who God is and what he has done. The big story of the Bible has three parts: creation, fall, and redemption.

The world was created "very good" in every possible way; but humans chose to sin, which means to depart from a good way of life. God's response was to redeem the world by becoming human in Jesus Christ—the incarnation. Jesus is the way, the truth, and the life (John 14:6). To follow him has implications in every area of life, which Myers briefly outlines with a worldview chart showing what Christianity asserts in ten important areas.

To access this video, go to www.summitu.com/utt and enter the passcode found in the back of your manual.

All people are religious, not just Christians. _____ is a set of beliefs about the cause, nature, and purpose of the universe. To reject one belief is to accept another. Even an atheist has a set of beliefs. Even a person with no beliefs has a set of beliefs.

Everybody has a religion. Everybody has faith. But is their faith worthy? Is it based on truth?

Christianity draws on two sources of revelation: _____ **and the Bible.** The Bible is a true account of who God is and what he has done. From the Bible we can draw lessons about how we should live. The big story of the Bible has three parts:

1. _____: God created the world and humankind. A relational creator created human beings to do two things: to relate and create (Genesis 1:1; Colossians 1:16, 17). God made everything "very good" in every possible way (Genesis 1:31).

2. _____: Humans fell into sin. Sin is to depart from a good way of life or to miss the mark. The fall affects everyone (Jeremiah 17:9; Romans 3:10–23). We live in a world that is not as it ought to be.

3. _____: God is in the process of redeeming his people and all of creation (Genesis 3:15; Romans 16:20). Redemption means to restore to a healthy state. It makes it possible for us to crush Satan.

Incarnation is the key component of God's redemptive plan. God became flesh and lived among us. The incarnation is one reason Christianity has had such an influence on the world.

Jesus defines the _____ in John 14:6. He is the way, the truth, and the life. He is the answer to three important questions in life:

- What is good?
- What is true?
- What is beautiful?

The evidence for Jesus's claims can be seen in the many ways the world is better because of Christianity. Some examples include abolition of slavery, rights for women and children, hospitals, and higher education. Cultures that deny Christ don't fare well (e.g., Nazi Germany, Communist Russia, and China).

Christianity has a consistent and coherent _____ based on the Bible and the life and ministry of Jesus.

1. How would you prove the statement, "All people are religious, even atheists?"

2. What does it mean to be made in the image of God?

3. Why is the incarnation the key to redemption?

4. How does Jesus answer the three great philosophical questions of life: What is good? What is true? What is beautiful?

5. Here are the ten areas that comprise a worldview from the chart at the end of the lecture. Rank them in their order of importance, and be ready to justify your rankings.

Chapter 2 Key Points

Key Questions:

1. What are the tenets of the Christian worldview?

Key Work:

1. The Holy Bible

Key Terms:

1. Christianity*
2. General Revelation
3. Special Revelation

Key Verses:

1. Act 17:22–34
2. 2 Corinthians 10:3–5
3. Colossian 2:6–8
4. 1 Peter 3:13–17

*Short answer or essay question on the exam

Hey there!

Intramurals have started up here at the university, and I've joined one of the soccer teams! I met a girl named Sarah (she's on my team), and we've chatted a few times. The other day after practice, I asked Sarah how her weekend was, and she said she had a great time clubbing with some friends on Saturday night. I asked her what she did on Sunday, and she laughed at me. I guess she stayed out so late that she didn't wake up until one or two p.m. Well, I was up much earlier than that. I did play quite a bit of ultimate Frisbee with my roommate on Saturday, but I wasn't too tired for church on Sunday morning. I guess Sarah doesn't go to church. She doesn't even believe in God. As a biochem major, she said she doesn't believe in anything she can't investigate with her five senses. As she put it, "If God existed, why hasn't he made himself known?"

I knew she was wrong. So I told her that God *has* made himself known—through Jesus Christ. That's how I know him! She smiled wryly and asked, "Have you ever seen him? Have you touched him? Have you heard him?" I didn't quite know how to respond to her. Of course I haven't seen God, but I still know he's real.

I told her that the most convincing element of Christianity for me is the evidence of my changed life. Through Christ, God saved me from my sin and ultimately from myself. She asked defensively if I thought everyone needed saving from sin and from themselves. Of course, I told her yes. Everyone needs Jesus.

She replied that she, for one, was doing just fine on her own. She told me she didn't think there was anything wrong with her, so there's nothing for God to fix. And she wondered why I would believe all this "Jesus talk" without any evidence that he actually exists.

I told her that's exactly what faith is; it's believing something in spite of the evidence. If we knew everything, we wouldn't need to have faith, right? She just laughed at me, shaking her head condescendingly. She told me that "blind faith" might work for Christians, but she would only believe in something if there were good evidence for doing so.

As you can see, I got myself into a bit of a bind. I know I have good reasons for believing everything I told her, but I am having trouble articulating it. I wonder if you could help! I know God has revealed himself, but **in what ways has God made himself known?** I was also confused when I told her why I need Jesus. I know we all need Jesus. I know we all sin, but **what's wrong with humanity?** And **what is God's plan for redeeming humanity?** Lastly, her comments about "blind faith" unsettled me as well. I've always thought that faith was blind, but I wish that it wasn't. **Is biblical faith really blind?** I hope you can help me out!

Gotta go! Bye!
—Doug

UNIT 3

ISLAM

CHAPTER 3 LEARNING OBJECTIVES

Students will be able to:

1. contrast the difference between radical and moderate Islam. [3.2–3.3]

2. identify what characterized the early history of Islam and the differences between the three main factions of Islam. [3.4]

3. explain why Islam is a worldview. [3.5]

4. state what Islam teaches about the nature of God, the Bible, Jesus, salvation, and judgment. [3.6]

5. define what Islam teaches about general revelation. [3.7]

6. explain the sources of special revelation for Islam, what Islam says about humanity, what Islam says is wrong with us, and what Islam says about how we should live. [3.8]

7. discuss how Islam views other worldviews. [3.9]

1. In your opinion, the nineteen Muslims who used planes to brutally kill nearly three thousand innocent people were what?

2. What are some distinctions between moderate and radical Muslims? [3.2]

3. What makes a radical a radical? Are some religions more likely to produce radicals than others? [3.2]

4. Can the Islamic worldview coexist with other worldviews? [3.3]

5. Some experts make a distinction between Muslims and Islamists. These two groups believe the same book—the Quran—so what makes them different? [3.3]

6. How do you feel when you hear the word "jihad"? What is jihad and where does the idea come from? [3.3]

7. Islam means "submission" and a Muslim is "one who submits" to Allah. But what does this submission look like? [3.4]

8. How did Islam get started and how large has it grown? [3.4]

9. What are some key events in the life of Muhammad and early Muslim history? [3.4]

10. What are the three main divisions of Islam? [3.4]

11. Does Islam recognize a distinction between the spiritual and the secular? [3.5]

12. Why is conformity important and individualism dangerous to Islam? [3.5]

13. Is Christianity just as susceptible to groupthink and idolatry?

14. What are some beliefs the Islamic and Christian worldviews have in common? [3.6]

15. What does Islam teach about the nature of God? [3.6]

16. What does Islam teach about the Word of God? [3.6]

17. **What does Islam teach about Jesus? [3.6]**

18. **What does Islam teach about salvation? [3.6]**

19. **What does Islam teach about the final judgment? [3.6]**

20. **Islam and Christianity use a similar argument for the existence of God from general revelation; what is it? [3.7]**

21. On what sources of revelation does Islam draw? [3.8]

22. What does Islam say about humanity? [3.8]

23. What does Islam say is wrong with us? [3.8]

24. What does Islam say about how we should live? [3.8]

25. **What are the sources of Islamic law and practice? [3.8]**

26. **What is the principle of abrogation, and how does it create problems for modern Muslims? [3.8]**

27. **How does Islam relate to other worldviews? [3.9]**

28. **Do you know any Muslims or have any Muslim friends? If so, have you talked about your different worldviews? Do you care to share about those conversations?**

SURA 3 AND 4 READING

Sura 3:187–200 discusses how Allah gave purpose to the world when he created it. These verses also give support to jihad, teaching that those who are slain for Allah's sake will be saved from their sins. The section concludes with a charge to persevere in order to have success.

Sura 4:64–104 is often cited in support of jihad. Those who are slain for Allah's sake will be saved from their sins and those Muslims who do not fight in the name of Allah are questioned as to their faithfulness. Hell is mentioned as a warning for those who do not believe and heaven is promised to those who fear Allah.

As you read, consider what the Bible says on the subjects of heaven, hell, the day of resurrection and success, what it is and how do we achieve it.

To access this reading, go to www.summitu.com/utt and enter the passcode found in the back of your manual.

1. What does Allah promise to those who have fought and suffered in his name?

2. What does the Quran teach about the afterlife?

3. How will Jews and Christians be treated by Allah?

4. The media has a lot to say about "jihad," but what does the Quran actually teach about it?

5. According to the Quran, what is the source of good in the world? What is the source of evil?

"A Closer Look at Islam" Video

Alan Shlemon begins with 2 Corinthians 5:18–20, which says we are Christ's ambassadors and that our mission is to reconcile the world to Christ. He explains how we can do this with Muslims by having a better understanding of Islam. He explains the three sources of authority in Islam: The Quran, the Hadith and the Sunnah.

Next he briefly explains the Five Pillars of Islam, which are required *behavior* for Muslims: reciting the Creed, daily prayer, the fast of Ramadan, giving alms, and the pilgrimage to Mecca. Shlemon then expands on the Six Articles of Faith, which are required *beliefs* for Muslims: Belief in the unity of Allah, belief in Allah's angels, belief in Allah's prophets, belief in Allah's books, belief in the final judgment, and belief in divine destiny.

To access this video, go to www.summitu.com/utt and enter the passcode found in the back of your manual.

Three sources of authority in Islam:

1. _____: The highest authority, the literal words of Allah, dictated by the angel Gabriel word for word to Mohammed.

2. _____: written traditions of what Mohammed said or did, categorized by subject.

3. _____: The life example of Mohammed, who is the supreme embodiment of what it means to be a Muslim.

If something is found in these sources it's Islamic. If it isn't found here, it's not Islamic, no matter what Muslims say.

Is violent jihad a valid Islamic doctrine?

- According to the Quran, violent jihad is valid (it contains 164 verses about jihad).
- The Hadith has an entire section called "The Book of _____."
- The Sunnah has graphic details of Mohammed's violent actions against unbelievers.

Muslims respond to the reality of jihad in two ways:

1. "I'm not violent. Most Muslims don't practice violence." Therefore, they reason, Islam doesn't teach violence, but this is in spite of what Islam teaches, not because of it.

2. "Islam is a peaceful religion that's been hijacked by violent terrorists." The truth is that Islam is a violent religion that's been hijacked by peaceful people.

Five Pillars of Islam, which are required behavior:

1. Reciting the _____: "There is no God but Allah and Mohammed is his prophet."

2. Daily prayer: Five times a day facing Mecca

3. Fast of _____: Month-long fast from dawn to dusk

4. Giving alms: 2.5 percent of income given to poor and needy

5. Pilgrimage to _____ once in a lifetime: Greatest deed a Muslim can do

Six Articles of Faith, required beliefs:

1. Belief in the unity of _____
2. Belief in Allah's angels
3. Belief in Allah's prophets
4. Belief in Allah's books
5. Belief in the final _____
6. Belief in divine destiny

1. What are the three key sources of authority in Islam?

2. Is violent jihad a valid Islamic doctrine?

3. How do modern Muslims respond to violent jihad today?

4. What practices are required of all Muslims?

5. What beliefs are required of all Muslims?

Chapter 3 Key Points

Key Questions:

1. What are the tenets of the Islamic worldview?

Key Works:

1. The Hadith
2. The Quran

Key Terms:

1. *Dhimmitude*
2. *Dhimmi*
3. Hadith
4. *Hajj*
5. Islam*
6. Islamist
7. *Jihad*
8. Jihadi
9. *Jizyah*
10. *Salat*
11. *Sawm*
12. Shiite Islam
13. *Shahada*
14. Shariah Law
15. *Shirk*
16. Sufi Islam
17. *Sunnah*
18. Sunni Islam
19. *Ummah*
20. Quran
21. *Zakat*

Short answer or essay question on the exam

Hello again!

As the semester is moving forward, my homework is piling up and classes are getting a lot harder. I thought taking a Basket Weaving elective would be a piece-of-cake class, but I was definitely wrong. Don't laugh at me. It's been a lot of work!

As part of our freshman orientation, we had to attend a cultural event last weekend. It did interfere with intramural practices, but it was also very interesting. We went to a Middle Eastern gathering where they showcased the food, dress, and traditions of Islam. Most of the food was really good, and it was neat to see how another culture lives.

I sat next to Muhammad, a student I recognized from one of my classes. He told me he grew up a Muslim in the Middle East. When we started talking about Islam, I realized how little I really knew. All I knew was that the attacks of 9/11 were carried out by radical Muslim terrorists, so I guess my mindset towards the religion was initially jaded. I asked Muhammad if he agreed with the 9/11 bombings, and he shook his head emphatically and told me he wasn't "that kind" of Muslim. I didn't know there was more than one kind, so I asked him what kind of Muslim he was.

He told me that he was a normal Muslim who follows the five pillars of Islam, lives closely in line with the Quran, and obeys Allah so he can earn his eternal salvation. I nodded my head in feigned comprehension as I pretended not to be completely ignorant about Islam (which I was), knowing that I'd probably learn about everything from the guys leading this cultural event. But unfortunately for me, this was more of an event for the Muslim students on campus and not a chance to learn about religion. I learned a bit about clothing and food, but they didn't really "teach" me anything about Islam, per se. I'm still kind of confused about the whole thing. I wonder if could you help me?

First off, **what is a Muslim, and what are the five pillars of Islam?** I've heard of Allah, but I don't really know what the difference is between the Muslim god and the Christian God. **What does Islam teach about the nature of God and human beings?** Muhammad mentioned that he believes all the biblical prophets are considered prophets of Islam, including Jesus. Can that be right? **What does Islam really teach about the Bible and Jesus?** He said following the Quran would get you into paradise. **What does Islam teach about salvation?** I feel really ignorant about the subject.

Well, it's late, so I should go to bed. But thanks for your help! I hope you're doing well!

Bye!
—Doug

UNIT 4

SECULARISM

CHAPTER 4 LEARNING OBJECTIVES

Students will be able to:

1. give examples how Secularism rewrites the story of civilization. [4.1–4.2]

2. describe how materialism shapes the Secularist narrative. [4.3]

3. give a brief background of the history of Secularism in America. [4.4]

4. explain the importance of the *Humanist Manifesto* to the rise of Secularism. [4.5]

5. identify where Secularism is influential today. [4.6]

6. discuss why Secularism is a religious worldview. [4.7]

7. give examples of how Secularism views and understands nature, and the role evolution plays in the worldview of Secularism. [4.8]

8. state the key sources of revelation for Secularism; what Secularism says about humanity; what Secularism says is wrong with us; and what Secularism says about how we should live. [4.9]

9. identify how Secularism views other worldviews. [4.10]

10. describe the role faith plays in the Secularist worldview. [4.11}

1. Can you summarize the Secularist worldview in a few sentences? [4.1]

2. What is propaganda and how is it used in promoting worldviews? [4.2]

3. Can you give a few examples of Secularist propaganda in America and how it seeks to influence public opinion? [4.2]

4. In your own schooling, have you run into instances of Christianity being marginalized or portrayed as evil? [4.2]

5. Every worldview has its own version of the human story. What's the narrative of Secularism? [4.3]

6. What are the main tenants of Secularism? [4.3]

   ① Self-sufficiency

   ② materialism

   ③ here and now

   ④ Politically narrow

7. Do Secularists and Christians agree about anything in American culture? [4.3]

8. A few of America's Founding Fathers were deists. Who were they and what did they believe? [4.4]

9. **What is the *Humanist Manifesto* and what impact has it had on America? [4.5]**

10. **What percentage of Americans are Secularists? [4.6]**

11. **How much influence do Secularists have on college campuses? [4.6]**

12. **Given these findings, what can you expect as a Christian heading off to college? [4.6]**

13. **Why is it accurate to call Secularism a religious worldview? [4.7]**

14. **Can science and religion coexist in Secularism? [4.8]**

15. **Why does Secularism rule out creation and rely on evolution? [4.8]**

16. **To what sources do Secularists look for insight and inspiration? [4.9]**

17. What does Secularism say about humanity? [4.9]

18. What does Secularism say is wrong with us? [4.9]

19. What does Secularism say about how we should live? [4.9]

20. How does Secularism relate to New Spirituality? [4.10]

21. How does Secularism relate to Marxism? [4.10]

22. How does Secularism relate to Christianity and Islam? [4.10]

23. How does Secularism relate to Postmodernism? [4.10]

24. What role does faith play in Secularism? [4.11]

25. What are some realities for which Secularism has no good answers?

"Humanist Manifesto" Reading

In the 1930s, a group of atheist and agnostic professors wrote and signed a document called the *Humanist Manifesto* to give voice to a new movement that became known as Secular Humanism. Humanism sought to respect humanity and to make the world a better place by encouraging people to contribute to society. Two of their major premises are the denial of the supernatural and the rejection of religions as outdated and irrelevant.

As you read through the manifesto, compare its doctrines to those in the Bible. Think about how humans derive purpose from God in Christianity and contrast it to how humanists derive purpose from themselves.

To access this reading, go to www.summitu.com/utt and enter the passcode found in the back of your manual.

1. What factors prompted the writing of the *Humanist Manifesto*?

2. Was the *Humanist Manifesto* meant to be a religious statement or a nonreligious statement?

3. How do the major doctrines of Secular Humanism differ from the foundational doctrines of orthodox Christianity?

4. How does Secular Humanism view religion? Does it allow for divine revelation of any sort?

5. What type of society does the *Humanist Manifesto* promote?

The secular worldview asks, "Is God relevant to life?" It answers no, because to a secularist, if you can't see it, hear it, or feel it, it doesn't exist. In this lecture, Dr. Jeff Myers outlines the three foundational assumptions of secularism:

1. "God belief" is irrelevant.
2. Human beings are good by nature.
3. Society and its institutions are responsible for the evil we do.

Myers goes on to briefly explain ten key secular beliefs: atheism; naturalism; moral relativism; neo-Darwinian evolution; monism; nontraditional family, church, and state; positive law; political liberalism; economic interventionism; and historical evolution.

To access this video, go to www.summitu.com/utt and enter the passcode found in the back of your manual.

Is God relevant to the way we live? The secular worldview says no. The secular world-view focuses on the here and now and holds that belief in God is irrelevant at best and dangerous at worst.

The secular view of history holds that ___religion___ in general, and Christianity in particular, is responsible for most of the misery and exploitation humans have suffered. But this pessimistic view isn't supported by the facts; rather it shows a preexisting bias.

Key secular beliefs:

1. **"God belief" is** ___irrelevant___: Even if there is a deity, no deity will save us; we must save ourselves.
2. **Humans are** ___good___ **by nature:** We have no innate bent toward evil. We aren't inherently sinful; we are actually perfectible without any interference from the divine.
3. ___society___ **and its institutions are responsible for the evil we do:** If humans aren't evil, how can we create an evil society? Secularism teaches that when our interests run into the interests of others, we damage each other.

What Secularism asserts in the ten areas comprising a worldview:

1. **Theology**—Atheism
2. **Philosophy**—_nationalism_
3. **Ethics**—Moral Relativism
4. **Biology**—Neo-Darwinism
5. **Psychology**—_monism_
6. **Sociology**—Nontraditional Family and State
7. **Law**—Positive Law
8. **Politics**—Liberalism
9. **Economics**—_interventionism_
10. **History**—Historical Evolution

Video clip: The four-minute clip from the animated movie ___Up___ illustrates the depth of the human story that secularism doesn't address. There is so much more to us than can be explained by Secularism's materialistic worldview.

▶ "THE SECULAR WORLDVIEW" DISCUSSION QUESTIONS

1. Does a Secularist have to be an atheist?

2. How would you counter the Secularism's argument that people are good by nature and are "perfectible" apart from God?

3. What role do God and religion play in the secularist view of history?

4. Briefly define the positions held by the secular worldview—moral relativism, neo-Darwinism, and materialism—and state how they are different from the Christian worldview.

5. Why do you think Dr. Myers showed the clip from the movie *Up*? What did you get out of it?

Chapter 4 Key Points

Key Questions:

1. What are the tenets of the Secularist worldview?

Key Terms:

1. Materialism
2. Monism
3. Naturalism
4. Propaganda
5. Religion
6. Secular Humanism
7. Secularism*
8. Transhumanism

Short answer or essay question on the exam

Key Players:

1. John Dewey
2. Sigmund Freud
3. Julian Huxley
4. Paul Kurtz
5. Corliss Lamont
6. Thomas Paine
7. Bertrand Russell
8. Roy Wood Sellars

Key Works:

1. *Age of Reason,* Thomas Paine
2. *Democracy and Education,* John Dewey
3. *Civilization and Its Discontents,* Sigmund Freud
4. *Humanist Manifesto I,* Roy Woods Sellars
5. *Humanist Manifesto II,* Paul Kurtz
6. *Humanist Manifesto 2000,* Paul Kurtz
7. *On the Origin of Species,* Charles Darwin
8. *Why I Am Not a Christian,* Bertrand Russell

Hello again!

Intramurals are getting pretty intense. We have competitions every weekend now. In fact, we had three this past week! Plus homework is starting to really take its toll on me. I'm tired and sore, both physically and mentally. I wish the weekend would hurry up and get here.

You remember Sarah, right? I told you about her a few weeks ago. She's pretty nice, but ever since I told her I was a Christian, she finds opportunities to mock my beliefs. I know she's just joking, but sometimes it seems hurtful. The other day in practice, I made a really bad shot. We had a shot to take the lead, and I majorly blew it. Embarrassed, I joked, "Sorry guys! My fault. I'm a *terrible* human being!" She laughed a little sarcastically and said, "The Bible says so, right?" I didn't really appreciate her tone, but I also didn't want her to know that some of her comments bothered me.

After the game, I apologized for missing the shot. I told her that everyone makes mistakes. She agreed, but she took issue with the Christian notion of sin. I didn't exactly see what that had to do with intramurals, but she went there regardless. Before too long, she was addressing just about every "superstition" that Christianity holds dear. I don't remember everything she said, but she went on and on about the Dark Ages, the Crusades, and even the Salem witch trials. I think the gist of her point is that religion is evil. I have never heard anyone talk about Christianity like that before. Sure, I was told that I might meet some atheists in college, but this wasn't quite what I expected.

Sarah calls herself a "Secularist." I kind of know what it means to be "secular," but I don't think I fully understand where Sarah is coming from. It just seems like she *disbelieves* everything I say. I know there's gotta be more! Maybe you could help me out! You've been learning about different worldviews in school. Have you learned anything about this stuff yet?

First off, **what is a Secularist?** I know Sarah doesn't believe in the Christian view of original sin, so **what does Secularism say about humanity?** And **what does it say is wrong with us, if anything?** And if she doesn't go to church or tithe or read the Bible, what exactly does she do? **What does Secularism say about how we should live?** It makes my head hurt trying to figure all this stuff out. I can't believe you are learning about this kind of thing in high school. It would be great if you could help me!

I gotta go. My friends invited me to a pool tournament in the student center. I've been practicing, but I just learned how to play last month!

Wish me luck!
–Doug

MARXISM

CHAPTER 5 LEARNING OBJECTIVES

Students will be able to:

1. explain the history behind Marxism and its founder, Karl Marx and why it is important to study Marxism. [5.1]

2. cite examples of how Marxism is still active in the world today. [5.2]

3. name the two key ideas that Marxism teaches. [5.3]

4. describe why Marxism is a worldview. [5.4]

5. identify why evolution is integral to Marxism. [5.5]

6. detail how Marxism responds to the ultimate questions: what are the key sources for Marxism , what does Marxism say about humanity, what Marxism says is wrong with us, and what Marxism says about how we should live. [5.6]

7. give an example of how Marxism views each of the other worldviews. [5.7]

8. explain why Marxism entails violence. [5.8]

1. Can you summarize Marxism in a few sentences? [5.1]

2. How does Marxism understand communism, socialism, and capitalism? [5.1]

3. Both Christianity and Marxism are named after their founders. The life of Jesus was central to his message. How about Marx? Did he practice what he preached? [5.1]

4. What is the key document of communism? Does it advocate peaceful coexistence or violence? [5.1]

5. Is Marxism a political idea of the past or an ongoing threat today? [5.2]

6. One current version of communism is referred to as state capitalism. What is it and where can it be found today? [5.2]

7. Are you likely to run into Marxists on college campuses? [5.2]

8. Two central pillars of Marxism are dialectical materialism and economic determinism. Can you give a brief definition of each? [5.3]

9. Could you be a good Marxist and believe in God? [5.3]

10. Where does socialism begin and where does it lead? [5.3]

11. According to Marxism, history can be understood and explained by the drive to eliminate what? [5.4]

12. What role does evolution play in Marxist ideology? [5.5]

13. On what sources does Marxism draw for ideas and inspiration? [5.6]

14. What does Marxism believe about humanity? [5.6]

15. Why did many communist countries allow for freedom of worship in their constitutions? [5.6]

16. What does Marxism say is wrong with us? [5.6]

17. **What does Marxism say about how we should live?** [5.6]

18. **How does Marxism relate to Christianity?** [5.7]

19. **How does Marxism relate to Secularism?** [5.7]

20. **How does Marxism relate to New Spirituality?** [5.7]

21. **How does Marxism relate to Islam?** [5.7]

22. **How does Marxism relate to Postmodernism?** [5.7]

23. **Is it possible for Marxism to achieve its goals without violence?** [5.8]

24. **Can you make a case for socialism from the Bible? Doesn't God command us to care for the poor, to sell our property for the sake of those in need, to work hard and not rely on society to care for us?**

No, christians should be able to give and care for others outside of their government telling them to.

"THE COMMUNIST MANIFESTO" READING

Today's reading is from *The Communist Manifesto*, the most famous Marxist document ever written. It discusses the basic reasons for the development of the Communist Party and describes the communist philosophy of history. The problems of the world are reduced to the class struggle of the bourgeois (upper class), versus the proletariat (lower class).

The second part of *The Communist Manifesto* (see below) is more radical than the first. It advocates the abolition of private property, the abolition of inheritances, the abolition of religion, the confiscation of the property of all emigrants, and implementation of a heavy tax. All these propositions are aimed at destroying the bourgeois class and making all classes equal. Perhaps the most radical intention is to destroy the family as it exists in capitalist countries.

As you read the list of principles essential to communism at the end of the section, think about the liberties it seeks to take away and compare what the Christian worldview says about these liberties.

A SELECTION FROM *THE COMMUNIST MANIFESTO*
by Karl Marx and Frederick Engels

II. Proletarians and Communists

In what relation do the Communists stand to the proletarians as a whole?

The Communists do not form a separate party opposed to the other working-class parties.

They have no interests separate and apart from those of the proletariat as a whole.

They do not set up any sectarian principles of their own, by which to shape and mould the proletarian movement.

The Communists are distinguished from the other working-class parties by this only:

1. In the national struggles of the proletarians of the different countries, they point out and bring to the front the common interests of the entire proletariat, independently of all nationality.
2. In the various stages of development which the struggle of the working class against the bourgeoisie has to pass through, they always and everywhere represent the interests of the movement as a whole.

The Communists, therefore, are on the one hand, practically, the most advanced and resolute section of the working-class parties of every country, that section which pushes forward all others; on the other hand, theoretically, they have over the great mass of the proletariat the advantage of clearly understanding the line of march, the conditions, and the ultimate general results of the proletarian movement.

The immediate aim of the Communists is the same as that of all other proletarian parties: formation of the proletariat into a class, overthrow of the bourgeois supremacy, conquest of political power by the proletariat.

The theoretical conclusions of the Communists are in no way based on ideas or principles that have been invented, or discovered, by this or that would-be universal reformer.

They merely express, in general terms, actual relations springing from an existing class struggle, from a historical movement going on under our very eyes. The abolition of existing property relations is not at all a distinctive feature of communism.

All property relations in the past have continually been subject to historical change consequent upon the change in historical conditions.

The French Revolution, for example, abolished feudal property in favour of bourgeois property.

The distinguishing feature of Communism is not the abolition of property generally, but the abolition of bourgeois property. But modern bourgeois private property is the final and most complete expression of the system of producing and appropriating products, that is based on class antagonisms, on the exploitation of the many by the few.

In this sense, the theory of the Communists may be summed up in the single sentence: Abolition of private property.

We Communists have been reproached with the desire of abolishing the right of personally acquiring property as the fruit of a man's own labour, which property is alleged to be the groundwork of all personal freedom, activity and independence.

Hard-won, self-acquired, self-earned property! Do you mean the property of petty artisan and of the small peasant, a form of property that preceded the bourgeois form? There is no need to abolish that; the development of industry has to a great extent already destroyed it, and is still destroying it daily.

Or do you mean the modern bourgeois private property?

But does wage-labour create any property for the labourer? Not a bit. It creates capital, *i.e.*, that kind of property which exploits wage-labour, and which cannot increase except upon condition of begetting a new supply of wage-labour for fresh exploitation. Property, in its present form, is based on the antagonism of capital and wage labour. Let us examine both sides of this antagonism.

To be a capitalist, is to have not only a purely personal, but a social *status* in production. Capital is a collective product, and only by the united action of many members, nay, in the last resort, only by the united action of all members of society, can it be set in motion.

Capital is therefore not only personal; it is a social power.

When, therefore, capital is converted into common property, into the property of all members of society, personal property is not thereby transformed into social property. It is only the social character of the property that is changed. It loses its class character.

Let us now take wage-labour.

The average price of wage-labour is the minimum wage, *i.e.*, that quantum of the means of subsistence which is absolutely requisite to keep the labourer in bare existence as a labourer. What, therefore, the wage-labourer appropriates by means of his labour, merely suffices to prolong and reproduce a bare existence. We by no means intend to abolish this personal appropriation of the products of labour, an appropriation that is made for the maintenance and reproduction of human life, and that leaves no surplus wherewith to command the labour of others. All that we want to do away with is the miserable character of this appropriation, under which the labourer lives merely to increase capital, and is allowed to live only in so far as the interest of the ruling class requires it.

In bourgeois society, living labour is but a means to increase accumulated labour. In Communist society, accumulated labour is but a means to widen, to enrich, to promote the existence of the labourer.

In bourgeois society, therefore, the past dominates the present; in Communist society, the present dominates the past. In bourgeois society capital is independent and has individuality, while the living person is dependent and has no individuality.

And the abolition of this state of things is called by the bourgeois, abolition of individuality and freedom! And rightly so. The abolition of bourgeois individuality, bourgeois independence, and bourgeois freedom is undoubtedly aimed at.

By freedom is meant, under the present bourgeois conditions of production, free trade, free selling and buying.

But if selling and buying disappears, free selling and buying disappears also. This talk about free selling and buying, and all the other "brave words" of our bourgeois about freedom in general, have a meaning, if any, only in contrast with restricted selling and buying, with the fettered traders of the Middle Ages, but have no meaning when opposed to the Communistic abolition of buying and selling, of the bourgeois conditions of production, and of the bourgeoisie itself.

You are horrified at our intending to do away with private property. But in your existing society, private property is already done away with for nine-tenths of the population; its existence for the few is solely due to its non-existence in the hands of those nine-tenths. You reproach us, therefore, with intending to do away with a form of property, the necessary condition for whose existence is the non-existence of any property for the immense majority of society.

In one word, you reproach us with intending to do away with your property. Precisely so; that is just what we intend.

From the moment when labour can no longer be converted into capital, money, or rent, into a social power capable of being monopolised, *i.e.*, from the moment when individual property can no longer be transformed into bourgeois property, into capital, from that moment, you say, individuality vanishes.

You must, therefore, confess that by "individual" you mean no other person than the bourgeois, than the middle-class owner of property. This person must, indeed, be swept out of the way, and made impossible.

Communism deprives no man of the power to appropriate the products of society; all that it does is to deprive him of the power to subjugate the labour of others by means of such appropriations.

It has been objected that upon the abolition of private property, all work will cease, and universal laziness will overtake us.

According to this, bourgeois society ought long ago to have gone to the dogs through sheer idleness; for those of its members who work, acquire nothing, and those who acquire anything do not work. The whole of this objection is but another expression of the tautology: that there can no longer be any wage-labour when there is no longer any capital.

All objections urged against the Communistic mode of producing and appropriating material products, have, in the same way, been urged against the Communistic mode of producing and appropriating intellectual products. Just as, to the bourgeois, the disappearance of class property is the disappearance of production itself, so the disappearance of class culture is to him identical with the disappearance of all culture.

That culture, the loss of which he laments, is, for the enormous majority, a mere training to act as a machine.

But don't wrangle with us so long as you apply, to our intended abolition of bourgeois property, the standard of your bourgeois notions of freedom, culture, law, &c. Your very ideas are but the outgrowth of the conditions of your bourgeois production and bourgeois property, just as your jurisprudence is but the will of your class made into a law for all, a will whose essential character and direction are determined by the economical conditions of existence of your class.

The selfish misconception that induces you to transform into eternal laws of nature and of reason, the social forms springing from your present mode of production and form of property—historical relations that rise and disappear in the progress of production – this misconception you share with every ruling class that has preceded you. What you see clearly in the case of ancient property, what you admit in the case of feudal property, you are of course forbidden to admit in the case of your own bourgeois form of property.

Abolition [*Aufhebung*] of the family! Even the most radical flare up at this infamous proposal of the Communists.

On what foundation is the present family, the bourgeois family, based? On capital, on private gain. In its completely developed form, this family exists only among the bourgeoisie. But this state of things finds its complement in the practical absence of the family among the proletarians, and in public prostitution.

The bourgeois family will vanish as a matter of course when its complement vanishes, and both will vanish with the vanishing of capital.

Do you charge us with wanting to stop the exploitation of children by their parents? To this crime we plead guilty.

But, you say, we destroy the most hallowed of relations, when we replace home education by social.

And your education! Is not that also social, and determined by the social conditions under which you educate, by the intervention direct or indirect, of society, by means of schools, etc? The Communists have not invented the intervention of society in education; they do but seek to alter the character of that intervention, and to rescue education from the influence of the ruling class.

The bourgeois clap-trap about the family and education, about the hallowed co-relation of parents and child, becomes all the more disgusting, the more, by the action of Modern Industry, all the family ties among the proletarians are torn asunder, and their children transformed into simple articles of commerce and instruments of labour.

But you Communists would introduce community of women, screams the bourgeoisie in chorus.

The bourgeois sees his wife a mere instrument of production. He hears that the instruments of production are to be exploited in common, and, naturally, can come to no other conclusion that the lot of being common to all will likewise fall to the women.

He has not even a suspicion that the real point aimed at is to do away with the status of women as mere instruments of production.

For the rest, nothing is more ridiculous than the virtuous indignation of our bourgeois at the community of women which, they pretend, is to be openly and officially established by the Communists. The Communists have no need to introduce community of women; it has existed almost from time immemorial.

Our bourgeois, not content with having wives and daughters of their proletarians at their disposal, not to speak of common prostitutes, take the greatest pleasure in seducing each other's wives.

Bourgeois marriage is, in reality, a system of wives in common and thus, at the most, what the Communists might possibly be reproached with is that they desire to introduce, in substitution for a hypocritically concealed, an openly legalised community of women. For the rest, it is self-evident that the abolition of the present system of production must bring with it the abolition of the community of women springing from that system, i.e., of prostitution both public and private.

The Communists are further reproached with desiring to abolish countries and nationality.

The working men have no country. We cannot take from them what they have not got. Since the proletariat must first of all acquire political supremacy, must rise to be the leading class of the nation, must constitute itself *the* nation, it is so far, itself national, though not in the bourgeois sense of the word.

National differences and antagonism between peoples are daily more and more vanishing, owing to the development of the bourgeoisie, to freedom of commerce, to the world market, to uniformity in the mode of production and in the conditions of life corresponding thereto.

The supremacy of the proletariat will cause them to vanish still faster. United action, of the leading civilised countries at least, is one of the first conditions for the emancipation of the proletariat.

In proportion as the exploitation of one individual by another will also be put an end to, the exploitation of one nation by another will also be put an end to. In proportion as the antagonism between classes within the nation vanishes, the hostility of one nation to another will come to an end.

The charges against Communism made from a religious, a philosophical and, generally, from an ideological standpoint, are not deserving of serious examination.

Does it require deep intuition to comprehend that man's ideas, views, and conception, in one word, man's consciousness, changes with every change in the conditions of his material existence, in his social relations and in his social life?

What else does the history of ideas prove, than that intellectual production changes its character in proportion as material production is changed? The ruling ideas of each age have ever been the ideas of its ruling class.

When people speak of the ideas that revolutionise society, they do but express that fact that within the old society the elements of a new one have been created, and that the dissolution of the old ideas keeps even pace with the dissolution of the old conditions of existence.

When the ancient world was in its last throes, the ancient religions were overcome by Christianity. When Christian ideas succumbed in the 18th century to rationalist ideas, feudal society fought its death battle with the then revolutionary bourgeoisie. The ideas of religious liberty and freedom of conscience merely gave expression to the sway of free competition within the domain of knowledge.

"Undoubtedly," it will be said, "religious, moral, philosophical, and juridical ideas have been modified in the course of historical development. But religion, morality, philosophy, political science, and law, constantly survived this change."

"There are, besides, eternal truths, such as Freedom, Justice, etc., that are common to all states of society. But Communism abolishes eternal truths, it abolishes all religion, and all morality, instead of constituting them on a new basis; it therefore acts in contradiction to all past historical experience."

What does this accusation reduce itself to? The history of all past society has consisted in the development of class antagonisms, antagonisms that assumed different forms at different epochs.

But whatever form they may have taken, one fact is common to all past ages, *viz.*, the exploitation of one part of society by the other. No wonder, then, that the social consciousness of past ages, despite all the multiplicity and variety it displays, moves within certain common forms, or general ideas, which cannot completely vanish except with the total disappearance of class antagonisms.

The Communist revolution is the most radical rupture with traditional property relations; no wonder that its development involved the most radical rupture with traditional ideas.

But let us have done with the bourgeois objections to Communism.

We have seen above, that the first step in the revolution by the working class is to raise the proletariat to the position of ruling class to win the battle of democracy.

The proletariat will use its political supremacy to wrest, by degree, all capital from the bourgeoisie, to centralise all instruments of production in the hands of the State, *i.e.*, of the proletariat organised as the ruling class; and to increase the total productive forces as rapidly as possible.

Of course, in the beginning, this cannot be effected except by means of despotic inroads on the rights of property, and on the conditions of bourgeois production; by means of measures, therefore, which appear economically insufficient and untenable, but which, in the course of the movement, outstrip themselves, necessitate further inroads upon the old social order, and are unavoidable as a means of entirely revolutionising the mode of production.

These measures will, of course, be different in different countries.

Nevertheless, in most advanced countries, the following will be pretty generally applicable.

1. Abolition of property in land and application of all rents of land to public purposes.
2. A heavy progressive or graduated income tax.
3. Abolition of all rights of inheritance.
4. Confiscation of the property of all emigrants and rebels.
5. Centralisation of credit in the hands of the state, by means of a national bank with State capital and an exclusive monopoly.
6. Centralisation of the means of communication and transport in the hands of the State.

7. Extension of factories and instruments of production owned by the State; the bringing into cultivation of waste-lands, and the improvement of the soil generally in accordance with a common plan.
8. Equal liability of all to work. Establishment of industrial armies, especially for agriculture.
9. Combination of agriculture with manufacturing industries; gradual abolition of all the distinction between town and country by a more equable distribution of the populace over the country.
10. Free education for all children in public schools. Abolition of children's factory labour in its present form. Combination of education with industrial production, etc, etc.

When, in the course of development, class distinctions have disappeared, and all production has been concentrated in the hands of a vast association of the whole nation, the public power will lose its political character. Political power, properly so called, is merely the organised power of one class for oppressing another. If the proletariat during its contest with the bourgeoisie is compelled, by the force of circumstances, to organise itself as a class, if, by means of a revolution, it makes itself the ruling class, and, as such, sweeps away by force the old conditions of production, then it will, along with these conditions, have swept away the conditions for the existence of class antagonisms and of classes generally, and will thereby have abolished its own supremacy as a class.

In place of the old bourgeois society, with its classes and class antagonisms, we shall have an association, in which the free development of each is the condition for the free development of all.

....

The Communist Manifesto by Karl Marx and Frederic Engels. Published in 1848, this work meets the criteria for fair use.

1. Why does *The Communist Manifesto* insist on the abolition of private property?

2. Why does *The Communist Manifesto* insist on the abolition of the family?

3. Why does *The Communist Manifesto* insist on the abolition of marriage?

4. Why does *The Communist Manifesto* insist on the abolition of nations?

5. Why does *The Communist Manifesto* insist on the abolition of religion?

▶ "THE MARXIST WORLDVIEW" VIDEO

Jeff Myers defines the Marxist worldview as "secularism weaponized." The goal of Marxists is to bring about through revolution the overthrow of the structures of society. Today, more than half the world has to deal with Marxist doctrines or policies. Jeff explains how *Marxism* is the body of ideas traveling on the road of *socialism* to the destination of *communism*.

Dr. Myers outlines the two key concepts on which Marxism is based: *dialectical materialism* and *economic determinism*. He points out the four key institutions of society Marxists need to overthrow: *economy, government, religion,* and *family*. He closes with the three keys to a biblical view of economics: *private property and individual responsibility, rule of law,* and *the image of God*, which lead to innovation and the use of information.

To access this video, go to www.summitu.com/utt and enter the passcode found in the back of your manual.

Marxism is Secularism _____. The goal of Marxism is to bring about through revolution the overthrow of the structures of society. Today one of five people on the planet live in communist countries. There are many other countries where Marxists are part of the government. More than half the world has to deal with Marxist doctrines or policies.

Marxism is the body of ideas traveling on the road of _____ to the destination of _____.

Two key concepts on which Marxism is based:

1. _____: Thesis—antitheses—synthesis. Marx took this philosophical process and applied it to history. He saw communism as the ultimate synthesis of historical struggle.

2. _____: Struggle between the bourgeoisie and the proletariat. Bourgeoisie are the rich who control the means of production, capital, resources, and labor. Proletariat are the workers, who are purified from evil intent through their poverty. When put in charge they will do what is right.

Four key institutions of society Marxists intend to overthrow:

1. Economy
2. _____
3. Religion
4. _____

Wealth in America: In the United States, the rich are getting richer, but the poor are also getting richer, just not as fast as the rich are getting richer. Percentage-wise, the poorer classes have grown more rich than the wealthy. The most valuable things today are based on information. Wealth increases through innovation and invention.

The greatest challenge for the next generation is the national debt. Average debt per person:

- 1917 — $617
- 1975 — $8,767
- 2011 — $47,093

1. What are the three main aspects of the Marxist worldview?

2. What are the two key concepts on which Marxism is based?

3. What are the four key institutions of society that Marxists intend to overthrow?

4. Are Bernie Sanders and other Democratic Socialists right about fixing America's economy by redistributing wealth from the rich to the poor?

5. What is the greatest challenge facing the next generation in America?

Chapter 5 Key Points

Key Questions:

1. What are the tenets of the Marxist worldview?

Key Terms:

1. Bourgeoisie
2. Capitalism
3. Class Consciousness
4. Communism
5. Dialectical Materialism
6. Economic Determinism
7. Marxism*
8. Progressivism
9. Proletariat
10. Proletariat Morality
11. State capitalism
12. Socialism

Key Players:

1. Fidel Castro
2. Friedrich Engels
3. Che Guevara
4. Michael Hardt
5. V.I. Lenin
6. Mao Tse-Tung (Mao Zedong)
7. Karl Marx
8. Antonio Negri
9. Joseph Stalin
10. Leon Trotsky

Key Works:

1. *Commonwealth* by Michael Hardt and Antonio Negri
2. *The Communist Manifesto* by Karl Marx and Friedrich Engels
3. *Das Kapital* by Karl Marx
4. *Empire* by Michael Hardt and Antonio Negri
5. *The Motorcycle Dairies* by Che Guevara
6. *Multitude* by Michael Hardt and Antonio Negri

*Short answer or essay question on the exam

Hey friend!

My life has been pretty crazy over the last few weeks! Midterms are intense around here, even though I'm only a freshman. For some reason, the teachers think it's okay if they assign a bunch of homework on top of all the studying we have to do for their midterms! I think one of my most difficult classes is gonna be economics. We have to know quite a few of the major economists in addition to what their contributions were. I have trouble keeping their names and dates straight. We also have to know a bunch of equations and graphs. It will be rough.

My last Econ class was really interesting though. We talked about the effects of price ceilings and floors on supply and demand. Apparently, if the government places a ceiling, or a maximum legal price for a good, in a market where the actual value of that product is more than the ceiling, it creates all kinds of problems. The demand will exceed the supply, and a shortage will occur. Sometimes black markets even result. Then with price floors, such as minimum wage, lots of people lose their jobs because companies can't afford to hire as many people since their skills are not worth the price set by the floor. If that whole discussion confuses you, you're not alone. I think I have a grasp on the general idea, but the specifics can get kind of confusing for me.

We did have an interesting discussion about all that in class though, which is why I told you about it. There's a guy in my class named Mark, and he disagreed with most of what the professor has said so far. During this last discussion, he kept piping up and saying things like, "If we just made it to where everyone earned the same amount of money, we wouldn't have problems with price floors and minimum wage." And "I don't see the problem with ceilings. If the government mandated that all producers had to set their prices the same, we'd get rid of all these supply and demand complications, and capitalists wouldn't take everyone's money because of unfair pricing!"

He keeps talking about this guy named Lenin. I totally embarrassed myself by saying, "Wait, I didn't know John Lennon was an economist!" Everyone laughed at me. Apparently it's a different Lenin . . . shows how much I know. He also quotes someone named "Marx" who apparently formulated a whole worldview called "Marxism." I'm assuming you've heard of this guy. **What does Marxism teach?** I'm guessing there is more to it than just economics. **What does Marxism say about humanity?** And **what does Marxism say is wrong with us?** Finally, **what does Marxism say about how we should live?**

Thanks so much for helping me with my questions . . . again! I feel like I can speak more intelligently with my friends after I get your letters back. I look forward to your answers on this one!

Gotta go! Bye!
—Doug

UNIT

6

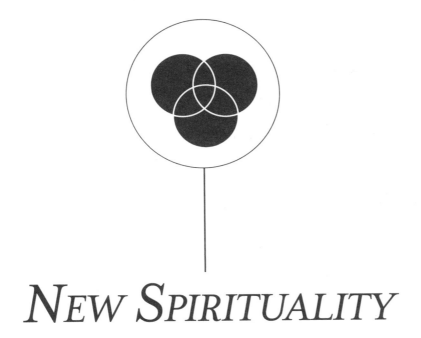

NEW SPIRITUALITY

CHAPTER 6 LEARNING OBJECTIVES

Students will be able to:

1. describe the ancient foundations behind New Spirituality. [6.2]

2. explain how New Spirituality views the world. [6.3]

3. analyze the modern foundations behind New Spirituality and why it is important to study New Spirituality. [6.4]

4. define terms that New Spirituality uses to teach about consciousness and existence. [6.5]

5. give examples that show why New Spirituality is a worldview. [6.6]

6. list and define how New Spirituality views nature and science. [6.7]

7. discuss what New Spirituality says about humanity, what is wrong with us, and how we should live. [6.8]

8. detail how New Spirituality views other worldviews. [6.9]

1. What do the Bhagavad Gita and New Spirituality share in common? [6.2]

2. Is there anything "new" in the worldview known as New Spirituality? [6.2]

3. Can you name three truths upon which New Spirituality and Christianity agree? [6.3]

4. Who are some of the most popular teachers and evangelists of the New Age Movement? How do they promote their message? [6.3]

5. What is transcendentalism and what role does it play in New Spirituality? [6.4]

6. How do New Spirituality and organized religion get along? [6.4]

7. What are the four basic teachings of New Spirituality? [6.5]

8. In contrast to New Spirituality, what does the Bible teach about the nature of God? [6.5]

9. What role does reincarnation play in New Spirituality? [6.5]

10. New Spirituality is a worldview, and as such it has core beliefs in the key disciplines we have been studying. Can you summarize what it teaches about theology, philosophy, ethics, biology, and psychology in one sentence each? [6.6]

11. How does New Spirituality understand the universe and our place in it? [6.7]

12. What is the Gaia hypothesis? [6.7]

13. **On what sources of revelation does New Spirituality draw? [6.8]**

14. **What does New Spirituality say about humanity? [6.8]**

15. **What does New Spirituality say is wrong with us? [6.8]**

16. **What does New Spirituality say about how we should live? [6.8]**

17. Many popular books and movies are based on the "hero's journey" popularized by Joseph Campbell. What is the hero's journey and how does this relate to New Spirituality? [6.9]

18. How does New Spirituality relate to Christianity? [6.9]

19. How does New Spirituality relate to Secularism? [6.9]

20. How does New Spirituality relate to Marxism? [6.9]

21. How does New Spirituality relate to Islam? [6.9]

"BHAGAVAD GITA" READING

Today's reading is from the conclusion of the Bhagavad Gita. Chapter six deals with meditation and introduces yoga as the way to discipline oneself to consistently remain detached from the physical world. Chapter seven revisits the way of knowledge in a deeper sense. A strong sense of pantheism is present here.

Chapter eight deals more with the way to salvation. Krishna explains how a person may release himself or herself from the cycles of life through complete meditation in Krishna alone at the point of death. Chapter nine discusses the nature of the pursuit of Brahman, including the concept that all people are truly worshiping Brahman, even if they do not know it.

Consider the concepts of worship found in these chapters and compare them to the idea of worship as presented in the Bible.

A SELECTION FROM THE BHAGAVAD GITA

Chapter Six: The Yoga of Meditation

[1] **The blessed Lord said:** If you do your duties without desiring the fruits for yourself, you are a true renunciate (*sannyasi*) and a true yogi, unlike those who live without sacrifice and devotion. [2] Renunciation is the essence of Yoga, Arjuna; you don't become a true yogi until you renounce personal desire.

[3] Karma Yoga, selfless service, is the way of the wise in order to attain the state of Yoga. Serenity is the nature of those who have reached that state. [4] You experience the true yogic state when you let go [of] attachment to sense objects and the desire for the fruits of your efforts. [5] You can rise up through the efforts of your own mind; or in the same manner, draw yourself down, for you are your own friend or enemy.

[6] As you gain control of your mind, with the help of your higher Self; then your mind and ego become your allies. But the uncontrolled mind behaves as an enemy.

[7] With a self-disciplined mind, you experience a state of constant serenity, correctly identifying with your highest Self (*Atman*) who remains unaffected in heat or cold, pleasure or pain, praise or blame.

[8] A true and steady yogi is utterly content with the wisdom of real knowing, is not disturbed by anything, has controlled and calmed his or her senses and looks with equal vision on a dirt clod, a stone or a nugget of gold. [9] A person stands supreme who has equal regard for friends, companions, enemies, neutral arbiters, hateful people, relatives, saints and sinners.

¹⁰ Yoga practitioners should continue to concentrate their minds until they master their minds and bodies, and thus experience a state of solitude wherever they may be; then desires and possessiveness drop away.

¹¹ To practice meditation, fix up a clean meditation place with your seat neither too high nor too low. Insulate the seat with a grass mat, then a deer skin, and over those, a clean cloth. ¹² Then sit and calm the mind and senses by concentrating on one thing; thus you practice Yoga (meditation) for self-purification. ¹³ Keep the body, head and neck erect without looking about; gaze instead toward the tip of your nose. ¹⁴ Sit thus in Yoga meditation, serene and fearless. Finn in the vow of *brahmacharya* and with the mind calm, think of me and only me. ¹⁵ By steadily and continuously practicing Yoga in this way, the yogi wins over his or her mind and realizes the peace that is my nature. This in turn naturally leads to *nirvana*.

¹⁶ It is impossible to practice Yoga effectively if you eat or sleep either too much or too little. ¹⁷ But if you are moderate in eating, playing, sleeping, staying awake and avoiding extremes in everything you do, you will see that these Yoga practices eliminate all your pain and suffering. ¹⁸ When you have your mind well-trained so it rests solely in *Atman*, without wanting anything, then you are established in Yoga (union with God).

¹⁹ The well-trained mind of a yogi, concentrating on the Self, is as steady as a flame in a windless place. ²⁰ Disciplined by Yoga practices, the mind becomes calm and tranquil. Then the individual self (*jiva*) beholds the true Self and is completely satisfied. ²¹ Once your intelligence actually experiences this greatest joy—which surpasses all pleasures of the senses—you become consciously established in absolute reality, and never slip from that again. ²² Once you are established in this (reality), there's absolutely nothing else to achieve, nor will anything ever shake you again—not even the worst possible affliction.

²³ Yoga is a means to disconnect your identification with that which experiences pain. Therefore, be determined to steadily practice Yoga with a one-pointed mind. ²⁴ Completely let go of all personal desires and expectations. Then with your own mind, you can withdraw the senses from all sides. ²⁵ Little by little your mind becomes one-pointed and still, and you can focus on the Self without thinking of anything else.

²⁶ However your mind may wander away, continue to draw it back again to rest in the true Self. ²⁷ Yogis who learn to calm their minds and quell their passions unquestionably experience the greatest joy, become one with *Brahman* (infinite consciousness) and are free of sin.

²⁸ All sins fall away from yogis who continually direct their minds this way; they naturally ascend to experience the infinite bliss of *Brahman*. ²⁹ As your mind becomes harmonized through Yoga practices, you begin to see the *Atman* in all beings and all beings in your Self; you see the same Self everywhere and in everything.

³⁰ Those who see me wherever they look and recognize everything as my manifestation, never again feel separate from me, nor I from them. ³¹ Whoever becomes established in the all-pervading oneness [of Brahman] and worships me abiding in all beings—however he or she may be living, that yogi lives in me.

[32] The yogi who perceives the essential oneness everywhere naturally feels the pleasure or pain of others as his or her own.

[33] Then **Arjuna** spoke: Krishna, you say that equanimity of mind is Yoga. But I do not see how that is possible, because the mind by nature is constantly changing. [34] Not only is it restless, Krishna, the mind is often turbulent and powerfully obstinate. Trying to control the mind is like trying to control the wind.

[35] Then **Sri Krishna** said: O mighty Arjuna, undoubtedly the mind is restless and very difficult to control. But with steady practice (*abhyasa*) and non-attachment (*vairagya*), it can be controlled. [36] Success in Yoga (Self-realization) is extremely difficult if you cannot control your mind. But if you persist [and] control your mind, and earnestly strive for realization using the right methods, you will certainly be successful.

[37] **Arjuna** asked: Krishna, what happens to those who have sincere belief, but cannot yet control the mind, or those who fall away from these practices before achieving perfection through Yoga? [38] Have they fallen both from this world and the world to come? O great Krishna, do they perish like clouds dissolved by the wind? Do they find themselves without support and deluded on their quests for God? [39] Please, my Lord. No one but you can completely destroy my doubts.

[40] Then **the blessed Lord** said: Do not worry, Arjuna. There is no destruction—either in this world or in the next—for anyone who has embarked on the yogic path. O my son, know for certain that anyone who does good never comes to a bad end.

[41] Those who embark on the yogic path—and leave their bodies before reaching their highest goal—attain heavenly states of the virtuous. They stay there a very long time and then take birth again in this world in a home of the pure and prosperous in order to continue their quest. [42] Or they are reborn into families of wise yogis. Such births in this world are rare indeed. [43] In this environment, Arjuna, they soon recall the knowledge gained in former births, and strive for realization even more earnestly than before. [44] In spite of one's lapses, the Yoga practitioner is led onward by the strength of his or her former practices. Even a person who simply wants to know how to practice Yoga sees more clearly than those merely going through the prescribed motions of religious life.

[45] By earnest and persistent effort—even over many lifetimes—a yogi becomes completely purified of all selfish desire and reaches the supreme goal of life.

[46] That [purified] yogi rises beyond the ascetics, those with psychic knowledge, and even those who do meritorious works. Therefore, Arunja, be that yogi! [47] Of all the yogis [however], the very best is the one who continually worships me with sincere belief and becomes one with me.

Chapter Seven: The Yoga of Knowledge and Realization

[1] **The blessed Lord** said: Listen, Arjuna, focus your mind on me; take refuge in me; and practice Yoga. Then you will surely unite with me and know me fully.

[2] I will teach you wisdom which will lead you to directly experience the supreme truth. After that there is nothing else to know.

³ There's scarcely one person in a thousand who truly strives for perfection. And even among those who succeed, rarely does one know me fully. ⁴ The eight aspects of my *prakriti* are: earth, water, fire, air, *akasha*, mind, intellect and ego. ⁵ Even these eight (including the more subtle manifestations) are gross, Arjuna, when compared to my higher *prakriti* which gives life to all the universe.

⁶ Everything originates out of these two aspects of my *prakriti*. I create and dissolve the entire cosmos. ⁷ Apart from me, there is nothing whatsoever. The entire creation is strung on me like a necklace of precious gems.

⁸ Arjuna, I am the taste in pure water, the radiance in the sun and moon; in all scriptures, the sacred word Om; the sound in the silence; and the virility in men. ⁹ I am the fragrance of the earth, the brilliance in fire, the life in all beings and the purifying force in austerity.

¹⁰ Know me, Arjuna, forever present as the origin of all beings. I am intelligence in those who are wise, and splendor in all that is beautiful. ¹¹ I am the power in strength, that is untainted by passion or personal desire. In fact, I am the desire in all beings, Arjuna, when desire is in accord with *dharma*.

¹² The qualities of nature (the *gunas*) come out of me; they are my manifestations. Yet I am not contained in them. ¹³ Most people fail to look beyond the three qualities of my *prakriti*. People see only these changing qualities, and don't see me, the transcendent One. In the midst of all that changes, I am what doesn't change. ¹⁴ No doubt it is hard to see through this, my divine illusion (*maya*) comprised of the *gunas*, but those who take refuge in me absolutely pass over this illusion. ¹⁵ Others, still deluded by *maya*, lose their discrimination (*viveka*) and sink to their lower nature. Thus, they do evil things, feel no devotion to me and don't seek refuge in me.

¹⁶ Good people worship me, Arjuna, for four basic reasons: to be relieved of suffering, to understand life, to rise from poverty to wealth and just because they are wise already. ¹⁷ Of these [four], the wise excel. Because their devotion is steady, they love me more than anything else, and they are my beloved. ¹⁸ All sincere spiritual seekers are certainly blessed with noble souls. Among them, however, those who know the truth and, with a steady mind, set me as their highest goal, soon identify with me; and I regard them as my very Self.

¹⁹ After many lifetimes, a person grows wise and takes refuge in me and nothing else. Then he or she realizes that I am all that is. Such a great soul is rare indeed. ²⁰ Others still allow personal desires to lead astray their good judgment. [Thus] they follow their lower nature and worship lesser gods for their blessings.

²¹ Devotees may select any name or form as the object of their worship. But if they have sincere belief (*shraddha*), I make their faith strong and steady. ²² Then when they worship with steady faith the form they have chosen, they get what they want. But actually, I am the one fulfilling their desires. ²³ However, those of limited understanding obtain limited satisfaction. Those who worship the gods (*devas*) go to the gods; my devotees come to me.

²⁴ Because their understanding is still shallow, many still believe that I, the unmanifested one, am limited to one particular manifestation. They have not yet seen my true nature which is unchanging and supreme. ²⁵ Not everyone can see me as I truly am, because I veil myself in *maya*. Thus deluded, the world does not recognize me as the one who was never born and never changes. ²⁶ Arjuna, I know all about every creature in the past, present and even the future. Yet no one knows all about me.

²⁷ People are deluded by attraction and aversion, which spawn all the pairs of opposites. These dualities, Arjuna, subject all to *maya* at birth. ²⁸ But people who do good free themselves from doing bad (sin), and thus rise above [the delusion] of these dualities. In this way their worship of me becomes very steady.

²⁹ Whoever takes refuge in me—even as they are striving to escape the conditions of old age and death —will know *Brahman*, *Atman* and karma. ³⁰ Those who see me pervading all the elements of nature; who realize me as the object of all worship, and who understand that I am the essence of self-sacrifice, will be conscious of my presence continually, even at the time of bodily death.

Chapter Eight: The Yoga of the Absolute Truth

¹ **Arjuna** asked: What is *Brahman*, the Absolute? What is the supreme Self (*adhyatman*)? What is karma, Sri Krishna? What is this earthly realm (*adhibhuta*)? And what is the kingdom of Light (*adhidaiva*)? ² What is the essence of self-sacrifice (*adhiyajna*)? How does one make such an offering? And how is it possible to control the mind during physical death in order to stay conscious of your presence, my Lord?

³ **The blessed Lord** said: My highest nature is the imperishable *Brahman* that gives life to all beings, and dwells in individuals as the supreme Self (*adhyatman*). My offering that causes all beings to come forth is karma. ⁴ The perishable earthly realm (*adhibhuta*) is the physical body. And *Purusha* is the realm of light and object of all worship. I alone am the essence of sacrifice (*adhiyajna*) present in your very body, noble Arjuna.

⁵ If you are thinking of me at the time of physical death, you will leave your body and come directly to me; there is no doubt about it. ⁶ You go to whatever you are thinking of at the time of physical death, Arjuna, because your mind established that direction. ⁷ Therefore, think of me constantly and fight [for what's right]! If your heart and mind are given to me, then you will surely come directly to me. ⁸ If your mind is not wandering or seeking anything else, Arjuna, because you made it steady and one-pointed through regular Yoga practice, then when you meditate on the supreme resplendent *Purusha* (the absolute Self), you experience that.

⁹ Think continuously of the Knower, the origin of all, the highest one, who is more subtle than antimatter, and yet upholds everything; whose form is beyond thought and who is beyond darkness and is self-effulgent like the sun. ¹⁰ Who thus meditates on this resplendent and supreme Self (*Purusha*) with devotion and a mind grown steady through Yoga, during the time of physical death will be able to direct all vital energy (*prana*) to the brow *chakra* and realize God.

[11] Without many words, I will tell you about reality. This is corroborated by those who know the essence of holy scriptures. The eternal truth can be experienced by those who learn to control their minds, renounce all personal attachments and thirst only for Brahman.

[12] This is the effective Yoga technique: At the time of leaving the body, mentally withdraw attention from the gates of the body into the heart area, and from there direct the *prana* into the head. [13] Then say aloud or think of the sacred word, *Om*, which is the manifestation of *Brahman*; and you will leave the body and achieve the supreme goal.

[14] It is easy to reach me, Arjuna, for the Yoga practitioner, steady in practice, who thinks of me constantly and has no greater attachments. [15] Those who come to me are great souls. They have so perfected themselves that it is unnecessary for them to be reborn again at this painful level of mortality. [16] Every creature in the universe returns to nothing, Arjuna, even Brahma, the creative function of myself. Only those who realize me transcend life and death.

[17] Whoever understands the day of Brahma and the night of Brahma—each of which lasts literally for thousands of ages (*yugas*)—that person truly knows day and night. [18] As the cosmic day [of Brahma] dawns, all creation rises to manifestation out of the unmanifested state. And at the coming of night, all again merge into the oneness of the unmanifested. [19] Creation in all its infinite variety repeatedly arises, Arjuna, and naturally merges into oneness at the approach of night, then re-manifests as separate forms again at the dawn of another day. [20] Beyond these manifested and un-manifested states, there is yet another unmanifested, eternal reality which continues forever when all else appears to perish. [21] This unmanifested reality, which is infinite and indestructible, is my very nature; it is the supreme goal. The one who realizes this has come home, abides with me and need never again return to separateness.

[22] You can experience this highest of states, Arjuna, with steady, one-pointed devotion to the Supreme One, in whom all creation exists and who pervades all beings. [23] Noble Arjuna, now I will tell you of the two paths of the soul at the time of physical death—one leads to rebirth, the other to liberation.

[24] If yogis who know reality leave their bodies during the six months of the northern passage of the sun, which is the path of light, fire, day and the bright two weeks of the moon, they go directly to *Brahman* (absolute oneness). [25] If yogis leave the body during the six months of the southern passage of the sun, which is the path of haze, night and the dark two weeks of the moon, their souls pass through the light of the moon to physical rebirth.

[26] These two paths of light and dark continue forever in this world. One leads to liberation; the other to rebirth. [27] Anyone who understands these two paths will never again be deluded. If you persevere in your study and practice of Yoga, Arjuna, you will attain this understanding. [28] Certainly there are many benefits from scriptural study, selfless service, accepting austerity and charitable giving. But if you practice Yoga and understand the light and the dark, you rise beyond all merit and attain the supreme and original abode.

Chapter Nine: Yoga of the Regal Science and the Royal Secret

[1] **The blessed Lord** said: Because your faith is not undermined by flaw-seeking, I will now reveal to you the most profound and secret knowledge. When you combine this knowledge with personal realization, you will be completely free of even the worst wrong-doing.

[2] This is the royal secret, the kingly science, the supreme purifier. Righteous and imperishable, it can be directly realized. [3] Those without sincere belief (*shraddha*) in this *dharma* will not realize who I am, Arjuna, and must therefore return to the mortal world of death after death,

[4] Unmanifest, I pervade the entire universe. All creatures exist in me, yet I am not contained in all of them. [5] Now behold the mystery of my divine Yoga: All creatures in truth do not exist in me. Though I bring forth and support all that exists, I, myself, am not contained in them. [6] All the creation moving about abides in me, even as the great winds going here and there are actually resting in space (*akasha*).

[7] At the end of a *kalpa* (cycle of eons), all creatures return to my *prakriti*. I generate them all again, Arjuna, at the beginning of the next *kalpa*. [8] By animating my *prakriti*, I repeatedly create the infinite varieties of all beings which are subject to the rule of my nature. [9] I myself am not affected by these actions [of my *prakriti*] because I witness it all with pure detachment,

[10] Through my presence, the elements of nature generate all that is stationary and all that moves. And thus, Arjuna, the world revolves.

[11] Foolish people don't look beyond physical appearance. Thus they overlook my true nature which is the Lord of everything. [12] Thus deluded by self-preoccupation (ego), their knowledge is superficial; their lives are disastrously full of wrong-doing; and their works and hopes are all in vain.

[13] But the great souls (*mahatmas*) have seen my true nature and take refuge therein. They realize I am the source of everything, and worship me with one-pointed devotion. [14] Because they strive for the highest with unflagging perseverance, their resolve is firm. They stick by their vows and humbly prostrate before me. Filled with devotion, they continuously sing my glory. [15] Others, on the path of *jnana* (wisdom), worship me by offering up the fruits of their knowledge. Thus they behold me both as the One and the many; wherever they look, they see my face.

[16] In religious acts, I am the ritual itself, the sacrifice and the offering. I am the most potent herb and the sacred sound (mantra). I am also the pure offering, the fire into which it is offered, and he who receives it.

[17] I am the father and mother of the whole universe, and also its most ancient grand-father. I am the one who gives you the results of your actions (karma). I am what is to be known. I am the purifier, the *Om* sound and I am the most sacred scriptures.

[18] I am the goal. I uphold everything; I am the Lord, the witness, the abode, the refuge, the friend, the beginning and the end. I am the foundation, the infinite treasure house and the indestructible see [of Creation].

[19] I am the heat. I am the one who holds back or sends rain. I am both immortality and death. I am also what is and what is not.

[20] Those who sincerely perform religious rituals, continually sacrifice for me and take *soma* (a plant whose juice is used in Vedic sacrifices), in time will see their hearts purified and their lives free of the last taint of wrongdoing. They naturally rise to the high realms of the gods where they enjoy the pleasures of heaven. [21] After they spend their merits to fully experience the joys of heaven, they must return to this world again. Though they may

[22] However, I provide everything for those who want me above everything else, and constantly think of me. I add to what they already have and comfort them with absolute security.

[23] Even those devotees who are endowed with *shraddha*, true faith, using methods not prescribed in scripture, nevertheless are worshipping me, Arjuna. [24] In truth, I am the object of all worship and the one who enjoys sacrifice and ritual. But until the worshipper sees me as I am, he must continually take rebirth, [25] Those who worship the *devas* go to the *devas*. Those who most revere their ancestors will become united with them. Those most fascinated with spirits will go to that level. But my devotees come to me.

[26] Whatever is offered to me with true devotion—if only a leaf, a flower, a fruit or a sip of water—I accept it because it is given with love. [27] Whatever you do, Arjuna, make that an offering. Whether it's eating, sacrificing yourself, giving help or even your suffering (*tapas*), offer it to me. [28] In this way you free yourself from the bondage of karma and its good or bad results. Through this Yoga, you thus achieve true renunciation (*sannyas*) [of personal desires] and come to me in a state of liberation.

[29] I am the same toward all beings. Before me, no one is hateful and no one is more or less cherished. However, those who lovingly worship me will realize that they are actually part of me and I live in them.

[30] Even if the worst sinners devote their lives to me with firm resolve, they will be transformed into saints. [31] For soon, he or she becomes a person of *dharma* (righteousness) and discovers lasting peace. This is certain, Arjuna: my devotee cannot be harmed.

[32] No matter your birth, race, gender or caste—even if you are scorned by others—if you take refuge in me, then certainly you will attain the Supreme Goal. 33 Even the saintly kings and holy sages through devotion seek this very goal. Therefore, if you find yourself in this transient world of suffering, just turn to me. 34 Think of me constantly; devote your life to me; offer all your actions to me, and bow down and surrender before me. Thus you become steady on your path to the supreme goal, and come unto me.

Reprinted from *The Living Gita* by Swami Satchidananda, with permission of Integral Yoga® Publications, www.integralyoga.org.

1. According to the Bhagavad Gita, what is yoga and what does it accomplish?

2. Can yoga be practiced by Christians as a spiritual discipline?

3. How does the concept of God in the Bhagavad Gita differ from the God of the Bible?

4. Why is reincarnation important to the followers of Krishna? How would you refute reincarnation from the Bible?

5. What role does karma play in the salvation of the soul according to the Bhagavad Gita? How would you refute the concept of karma from the Bible?

▶ "THE NEW SPIRITUALIST WORLDVIEW" VIDEO

The basic question the New Spiritualist worldview asks and answers is, "Why can't we all just get along?" Dr. Jeff Myers shares four underlying assumptions of this worldview and gives examples of each in modern media: (1) everything is spiritual, (2) God is within everything, (3) life is about the search for higher consciousness, and (4) higher consciousness brings the unity that solves the world's problems. Myers goes on to unpack ten beliefs of this particular worldview: pantheism, non-naturalism, moral relativism, cosmic evolution, higher consciousness, nontraditional family, self-law, self-government, universal enlightened production, and evolutionary godhood.

To access this video, go to www.summitu.com/utt and enter the passcode found in the back of your manual.

The key question asked and answered by the New Spiritualist worldview is, "Why can't we all just _____?" New Spirituality says everyone can get along once we attain higher consciousness and realize our own godhood. The problem is _____ of our divinity and the solution is the human race evolving toward godhood and cosmic oneness.

Basic assumptions of New Spirituality:

1. **Everything is _____**: As opposed to materialists, New Spiritualists believe only the spiritual exists. Physical existence is illusory and spiritual enlightenment is realizing this is so.
2. **God is within _____**: We are all God, and God comprises all of us.
3. **Life is about the search for higher _____**: This higher consciousness is becoming aware of our own existence, our godhood, and the oneness of all things.
4. **Higher consciousness brings the unity that solves the world's problems:** The universe wants us to be successful; and when we accept this, it becomes so. If we all believe and assert this together, it will change the world.

What New Spirituality asserts in the ten areas comprising a worldview:

1. **Theology**—_____
2. **Philosophy**—Non-naturalism
3. **Ethics**—Moral Relativism; The Law of _____
4. **Biology**—Cosmic Evolution
5. **Psychology**—Higher Consciousness
6. **Sociology**—Nontraditional Family and State
7. **Law**—_____
8. **Politics**—Self-Government
9. **Economics**—Universal Enlightened Production
10. **History**—Evolutionary Godhood

Most worldviews have identified some truths, but they don't account for all of reality. The Christian worldview does the best job of explaining the world and life as we experience it.

1. What does the New Spiritualist mean by the word *God*?

2. How do movie franchises like *The Matrix* and *Star Wars* promote New Spirituality?

3. How is the higher consciousness of New Spirituality different from the spiritual maturity Christians are trying to attain?

4. What are some things the New Spiritualist and Christian worldviews have in common? Where do they differ?

5. What is the Law of Karma? What is the Christian response to this concept?

Chapter 6 Key Points

Key Questions:

1. What are the tenets of the New Spirituality worldview?

Key Terms:

1. Channeling
2. Consciousness
3. Deep Ecology
4. Ecofeminism
5. Gaia Hypothesis
6. Karma
7. Meditation
8. Monomyth
9. New Spirituality*
10. Nirvana
11. Pantheism
12. Reincarnation
13. Transcendentalism

Key Players:

1. Rhonda Byrne
2. Joseph Campbell
3. Deepak Chopra
4. Marilyn Ferguson
5. The Dalai Lama
6. James Lovelock
7. Shirley MacLaine
8. Robert Muller
9. James Redfield
10. David Spangler
11. Eckhart Tolle
12. Neale Donald Walsch
13. Ken Wilber

Key Works:

1. *The Aquarian Conspiracy* by Marilyn Ferguson
2. The Bhagavad Gita
3. *The Celestine Prophecy* by James Redfield
4. Conversations with God series by Neale Donald Walsch
5. *Emergence* by David Spangler
6. *Gaia* by James Lovelock
7. *The Hero with a Thousand* Faces by Joseph Campbell

Short answer or essay question on the exam

Hello again!

I finally have enough time to write you! Midterms were just as rough as I thought they would be. I mean, tests in high school were hard too, but these were just brutal. Anyway, intramurals are pretty much over for a little while, which is half-sad and half-relieving. Even though it was fun, it took a lot of time.

I had a funny experience today at the cafeteria! Apparently, there's a tradition at our school that everyone in the cafeteria claps when someone drops a dish. Unfortunately, today was my turn for a standing ovation. I didn't just drop a fork or spill a little soda either. I made a scene! I slipped on a wet spot and went right down onto the floor with every item from my lunch tray following. When I looked down, I was wearing my lunch. I stood up and took a bow and everyone clapped. It was pretty funny even though it was little embarrassing as well.

When I got back to my room to change, Nathan was talking on the phone with a friend of his. From what I gathered, he was giving his friend advice about some crisis he was going through. At first I thought Nathan was talking about God, but then I heard him tell his friend to spend some time meditating and "emptying his mind." I didn't catch everything Nathan said (or maybe I just didn't understand what he was saying), but I clearly heard him say "life is suffering" and that the solution to our suffering could be found within us. Nathan told his friend to practice "empting himself" and to "reconnect with the divine consciousness." None of that seemed very comforting to me, but it made me curious.

Later I asked my friend Sarah about it. She said Nathan is into to "New Spirituality" and that he reads too much Eastern religious literature. She said it is all a bunch of . . . well, it doesn't rhyme with baloney, but it basically means the same thing!

I bet you know about Nathan's beliefs! I know it has something to do with God, but I have no idea what Nathan was saying about consciousness. **What does New Spirituality teach about God and consciousness?** It doesn't sound Christian, but then again, I'm not sure what it sounds like. **What does New Spirituality say about humanity?** And **what does New Spirituality say is wrong with us?** It sounded like meditation and "becoming one with the universe" is some kind of cure-all for problems. **What does New Spirituality say about how we should live?**

You're basically my worldview dictionary. It's pretty awesome. I hope you don't mind! I'll talk to you later. I'm meeting up with everyone in the Commons for a Ping-Pong tournament.

Bye!
–Doug

UNIT **7**

POSTMODERNISM

CHAPTER 7 LEARNING OBJECTIVES

Students will be able to:

1. explain the seven assumptions on which Postmodernism rests. [7.2]

2. describe the history behind Postmodernism. [7.3]

3. define the key characteristics of Postmodernism. [7.4]

4. give examples of why Postmodernism is a worldview. [7.5]

5. paraphrase how Postmodernism views scientific reliability. [7.6]

6. explain key sources of revelation for Postmodernism, what Postmodernism says about humanity, what Postmodernism says is wrong with us, and what Postmodernism says about how we should live. [7.7]

7. identify how Postmodernism views other worldviews. [7.8]

8. discuss the flaws embedded in Postmodern thought. [7.9]

CHAPTER 7 DISCUSSION QUESTIONS

1. **Can you summarize the postmodern worldview in a few words?** [7.1]

ultimate Knowledge is inaccesible true is a collection of feelings more than objective reality.

2. **If "Postmodernism" means "after modernism," what is modernism?** [7.2]

3. **How does Postmodernism define truth?** [7.2]

4. **What do Postmodernists have to say about the Abrahamic faiths?** [7.2]

5. **What are the seven assumptions on which Postmodernism rests? [7.2]**

1. postmodernest reject used universable truth as knowable, only personal experience matters

2. reject "reason" applics everywhere at all times.

3. reject that we can be objective in our knowledge

4. the worlds too complex to say one worldview explains everything

5. reject the idea of "god". 6. reject that institutions can make desisitions

7. reject the idea that any person can be neutral

6. **The history of Postmodernism can be traced through the lives and teachings of several philosophers including Gorgias, Nietzsche, and Foucault. What did Gorgias contribute to what became Postmodernism? [7.3]**

7. **What did Friedrich Nietzsche contribute to Postmodernism? [7.3]**

we have moved past the need for God

ubermench

8. **What did Michel Foucault contribute to Postmodernism? [7.3]**

9. How does Postmodernism use language to discredit other worldviews? [7.4]

10. What are structuralism and poststructuralism? What role do they play in Postmodernism? [7.4]

an intelletual movement that believes human knowledge is not based on an accurate understanding of reality is the product of language developed over time.

11. Why is deconstruction central to postmodern thinking? [7.4]

12. What do Postmodernists mean by the term anti-realism? [7.4]

13. Is it accurate to call Postmodernism a worldview since it's more of a critique of other worldviews than a positive pattern of ideas, beliefs, convictions, and habits of its own? [7.5]

14. Does Postmodernism accept scientific explanations of reality? [7.6]

15. Can Postmodernists actually live as though facts aren't real or objective truth can't be known? How can they be shown to be hypocrites? [7.6]

16. On what sources of revelation and inspiration does Postmodernism draw? [7.7]

17. What does Postmodernism say about humanity? [7.7]

18. What does Postmodernism say is wrong with us? [7.7]

19. What does Postmodernism say about how we should live? [7.7]

20. How does Postmodernism view Christianity? [7.8]

21. How does Postmodernism view Islam? [7.8]

22. How does Postmodernism view New Spirituality? [7.8]

23. How does Postmodernism view Secularism? [7.8]

24. How does Postmodernism view Marxism? [7.8]

25. Can you briefly summarize some of the flaws in Postmodernism? [7.9]

"THE PARABLE OF THE MADMAN" READING

"The Parable of the Madman" is by Friedrich Nietzsche, one of the most interesting thinkers of the nineteenth century. It provides a scathing critique of the modern philosophy of his time, which he declares has killed God. The madman is chosen to tell the truth about God's death and he chooses to do so in the marketplace. Ultimately, he is dismissed so he goes to the church to share his news and is kicked out. Upon his removal, he declares that the church has become the tomb of God.

Think about Nietzsche's assumptions and compare them to what you have learned about Postmodernism, determining whether or not you believe Nietzsche's predictions have come true.

▶ "THE POSTMODERN WORLDVIEW" VIDEO OUTLINE

The Postmodern worldview:

Every worldview has a different idea of what's wrong with the world. The key problem postmodernists see is that people believe they know the and they proclaim it in a way the makes others uncomfortable.

Postmodernists believe we can't know anything about _____ and anyone who says we can know is part of the problem. The search for truth is the problem because we can't know what's real.

The roots of Postmodernism:

Postmodernism goes back to Greeks like _____, a sophist who taught that:

- Nothing exists.
- Even if something exists, nothing can be known about it.
- Even if something can be known about it, knowledge about it can't be communicated to others.
- Even if it can be communicated, it cannot be _____.

These ideas resurfaced in the 1800s. One philosopher who championed them was _____, who influenced many philosophers and still influences many today, especially college professors.

Promise of progressivism didn't come true in the twentieth century, which saw more deaths at the hands of governments than all previous centuries combined. Postmodernists say this is where religion and science got us. They want to get beyond religion and science.

Three key principles of Postmodernism:

1. _____: We cannot know the world directly; we can only know it as we interpret it.

2. _____: The origin of the text is not the important thing, rather it is the destination—the reader.

3. _____: Broad explanations deserve suspicion because people's experiences are so varied. Their experiences are what we should pay attention to.

Responses to Postmodernism:

- Postmodernism highlights important concerns but takes them _____.
- Postmodernism is blind to the true power struggle language brings about.
- Postmodernists _____ themselves.
- Postmodernism's view of personhood is unsettling.
- Postmodernism, when applied, can lead to grotesque results.

1. What problem does Postmodernism see with the world?

2. How did we get from premodern to modern to postmodern?

3. What are the three key principles of postmodernism?

4. What are some appropriate responses to postmodernism?

5. What does Postmodernism think of the soul?

Chapter 7 Key Points

Key Questions:

1. What are the tenets of the Postmodern worldview?

Key Terms:

1. Anti-realism
2. Christian Postmodernism
3. Correspondence Theory of Truth
4. Deconstruction
5. Metanarrative
6. Nihilism
7. Postmodernism*
8. Poststructuralism
9. Pragmatism
10. Sophism
11. Structuralism

Key Players:

1. Walter Truett Anderson
2. J.L. Austin
3. Roland Barthes
4. Jean Baudrillard
5. Jacques Derrida
6. Stanley Fish
7. Michel Foucault
8. Martin Heidegger
9. Jacques Lacan
10. Jean-François Lyotard
11. Friedrich Nietzsche
12. Richard Rorty
13. Ludwig Wittgenstein

Key Works:

1. *Beyond Good and Evil* by Friedrich Nietzsche
2. "The Death of the Author" by Roland Barthes
3. *The History of Sexuality* (three volumes) by Michel Foucault
4. *Madness and Civilization* by Michel Foucault
5. *Of Grammatology* by Jacques Derrida
6. *Phenomenology* by Jean-François Lyotard
7. *Philosophy and the Mirror of Nature* by Richard Rorty
8. *Philosophy and Social* Hope by Richard Rorty
9. *The Postmodern Condition* by Jean-François Lyotard
10. *Reality Isn't What It Used To Be* by Walter Truett Anderson
11. *Thus Spoke Zarathustra* by Friedrich Nietzsche
12. *The Truth about Truth* by Walter Truett Anderson

Short answer or essay question on the exam

Hi there!

It's only eight p.m. here, but I'm so tired already! Some of the guys in my dorm decided it would be a fun prank to pull the fire alarm every night at two a.m. Not fun. Everyone has to leave the building even during false alarms, and it usually takes around half an hour for the firemen to check everything. I'm. So. Tired! They somehow haven't caught the perpetrators; it seems like they pull the alarm on different floors every night. I hope it stops soon.

Anyway, it's been a good week other than that. Nothing too eventful has happened, and I haven't had much homework, which is always nice. I had to write a big paper for my art class this week, which was fun since I wrote about the impressionists. I've always enjoyed their art. We're moving through the romantic period all the way up to the present. This week we studied postmodern art. I'm not sure how I feel about it. At first I wasn't impressed, but I think I'm warming up to some of the works. Postmodern art is basically a reaction to modern art, which was all about structure and getting down to the foundations of art itself—stripping away everything that distracts from the main message of the piece. Postmodern art challenges the very definition of art itself. A lot of artists just put junk on a pedestal and call it art. One guy even took a urinal, signed it, and called it "Fountain." Seems kind of disgusting to me, but it's displayed in a museum somewhere. I guess if it gets people talking, then that's something.

Paige, a friend of mine from class, is really into postmodern art. She says that labels and definitions for things that are "art" and things that are "junk" are just that—labels. Everything is sacred, and nothing is sacred. She believes that since reality is fragmented and chaotic, art should display the same attitude. Since there's no definition of what makes us human, or what makes a thing a "thing," art should reflect this. My head is spinning just trying to make sense of everything!

I guess Postmodernism isn't just about art. After class, Paige told me a little bit about Postmodernism. I guess it's a worldview, or at least she made it seem that way. I was able to follow a little of what she said, but I must admit, I was mostly lost. **What is Postmodernism?** She apparently doesn't believe in human nature, but I'm not sure how to even make sense of that. **What does Postmodernism say about humanity?** I'm guessing that Postmodernism doesn't believe in the fall, so **what does Postmodernism say is wrong with us?** Sadly, we didn't get a chance to talk about ethics at all. **What does Postmodernism say about how we should live?** From the way Paige was talking, I wouldn't be surprised if you couldn't answer these questions in a way that makes sense. It doesn't seem like anything she said was coherent!

Once again, thanks for your help! You're the best worldview dictionary a friend can have.

Talk to you later!
–Doug

UNIT

8

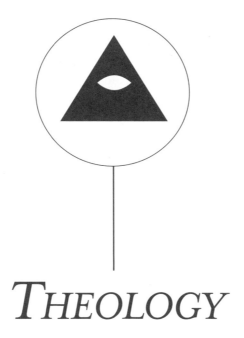

THEOLOGY

CHAPTER 8 LEARNING OBJECTIVES

Students will be able to:

1. articulate what theology is and why it is important. [8.1]

2. explain Secularism's approach to theology. [8.2]

3. explain Marxism's approach to theology. [8.3]

4. explain Postmodernism's approach to theology. [8.4]

5. explain New Spirituality's approach to theology. [8.5]

6. explain Islam's approach to theology. [8.6]

7. explain Christianity's approach to theology. [8.7]

8. identify four reasons to believe that God exists. [8.8]

9. name five characteristics of the Christian God. [8.9]

10. discuss how the Christian view of God compares with other views of God. [8.10]

1. When it comes to the study of God (theology), what are the three basic options? [8.1]

2. Can you summarize the theology of Secularism? [8.2]

3. Can you name a few other New Atheists who have large media platforms and wide influence? [8.2]

4. Who was the most influential atheist of the twentieth century and what made him so? [8.2]

5.   **What is the Marxist view of theology? [8.3]**

6.   **Why is the war against capitalism also a war against religion to Marxists? [8.3]**

7.   **What is liberation theology and how is it related to Marxism? [8.3]**

8.   **What is Postmodernism's view of theology? [8.4]**

9. What is wrong with the Postmodernist assertion that truth can't be objectively known? [8.4]

10. What are the two forms of religious pluralism, and which version does Postmodernism favor? [8.4]

11. What is New Spirituality's view of theology? [8.5]

12. How does New Spirituality attempt to use modern science to support its pantheistic views? [8.5]

13. If our bodies are just "meat suits" and our spiritual energy is what's important, why do New Spiritualists believe in reincarnation? [8.5]

14. What is Islam's view of theology? [8.6]

15. Do Muslims, Christians, and Jews all worship the same God? [8.6]

16. What is Christianity's view of theology? [8.7]

17. How does general revelation support the Christian case for theism? [8.8]

18. What are four scientific discoveries that point to the existence of God? [8.8]

19. How does special revelation support the Christian case for theism? [8.9]

20. What are five central truths about God's character revealed in the Bible? [8.9]

21. We can identify with God's character because we are made in his image and have the same traits, although in very flawed and weakened form. What are some of his attributes that we don't share? [8.9]

22. What aspects of God's love are expressed in John 3:16? [8.10]

23. If the Christian worldview is true, what can be said about the other worldviews? [8.10]

In the excerpt from the essay, "Why I Am Not a Christian," Bertrand Russell, a staunch atheist, explains why the ethics of Christianity repelled him. Though he acknowledges that much of Christ's teaching is moral, he accuses Christ of failing morally as well. For example, Russell does not think someone who is truly ethical can preach the doctrine of hell.

Russell, a prominent philosopher of the early twentieth century, blatantly spoke out against Christianity and religion in general. As you read through this essay, consider Russell's arguments and how you would respond to them if you were presented with them today.

A SELECTION FROM "WHY I AM NOT A CHRISTIAN"
by Bertrand Russell

The Moral Arguments for Deity

Now we reach one stage further in what I shall call the intellectual descent that the Theists have made in their argumentations, and we come to what are called the moral arguments for the existence of God. You all know, of course, that there used to be in the old days three intellectual arguments for the existence of God, all of which were disposed of by Immanuel Kant in the Critique of Pure Reason; but no sooner had he disposed of those arguments than he invented a new one, a moral argument, and that quite convinced him. He was like many people: in intellectual matters he was skeptical, but in moral matters he believed implicitly in the maxims that he had imbibed at his mother's knee. That illustrates what the psychoanalysts so much emphasize—the immensely stronger hold upon us that our very early associations have than those of later times.

Kant, as I say, invented a new moral argument for the existence of God, and that in varying forms was extremely popular during the nineteenth century. It has all sorts of forms. One form is to say that there would be no right and wrong unless God existed. I am not for the moment concerned with whether there is a difference between right and wrong, or whether there is not: that is another question. The point I am concerned with is that, if you are quite sure there is a difference between right and wrong, then you are then in this situation: is that difference due to God's fiat or is it not? If it is due to God's fiat, then for God himself there is no difference between right and wrong, and it is no longer a significant statement to say that God is good. If you are going to say, as theologians do, that God is good, you must then say that right and wrong have some meaning which is independent of God's fiat, because God's fiats are good and not bad independently of the mere fact that he made them. If you are going to say that, you will then have to say that it is not only through God that right and wrong came into being, but that they are in their essence logically anterior to God. You could, of course, if you liked, say that there was a superior deity who gave orders to the God who made this world, or could take up the line that some of the agnostics ["Gnostics"] took up—a line which I often thought was a very plausible one—that as a matter of fact this world that we know was made by the Devil at a moment when God was not looking. There is a good deal to be said for that, and I am not concerned to refute it.

The Argument for the Remedying of Injustice

Then there is another very curious form of moral argument, which is this: they say that the existence of God is required in order to bring justice into the world. In the part of the universe that we know there is a great injustice, and often the good suffer, and often the wicked prosper, and one hardly knows which of those is the more annoying; but if you are going to have justice in the universe as a whole you have to suppose a future life to redress the balance of life here on earth, and so they say that there must be a God, and that there must be Heaven and Hell in order that in the long run there may be justice. That is a very curious argument. If you looked at the matter from a scientific point of view, you would say, "After all, I only know this world. I do not know about the rest of the universe, but so far as one can argue at all on probabilities one would say that probably this world is a fair sample, and if there is injustice here then the odds are that there is injustice elsewhere also." Supposing you got a crate of oranges that you opened, and you found all the top layer of oranges bad, you would not argue: "The underneath ones must be good, so as to redress the balance." You would say: "Probably the whole lot is a bad consignment"; and that is really what a scientific person would argue about the universe. He would say: "Here we find in this world a great deal of injustice, and so far as that goes that is a reason for supposing that justice does not rule in the world; and therefore so far as it goes it affords a moral argument against deity and not in favor of one." Of course I know that the sort of intellectual arguments that I have been talking to you about is not really what moves people. What really moves people to believe in God is not any intellectual argument at all. Most people believe in God because they have been taught from early infancy to do it, and that is the main reason.

Then I think that the next most powerful reason is the wish for safety, a sort of feeling that there is a big brother who will look after you. That plays a very profound part in influencing people's desire for a belief in God.

The Character of Christ

I now want to say a few words upon a topic which I often think is not quite sufficiently dealt with by Rationalists, and that is the question whether Christ was the best and the wisest of men. It is generally taken for granted that we should all agree that that was so. I do not myself. I think that there are a good many points upon which I agree with Christ a great deal more than the professing Christians do. I do not know that I could go with Him all the way, but I could go with Him much further than most professing Christians can. You will remember that He said: "Resist not evil, but whosoever shall smite thee on thy right cheek, turn to him the other also." That is not a new precept or a new principle. It was used by Lao-Tse and Buddha some 500 or 600 years before Christ, but it is not a principle which as a matter of fact Christians accept. I have no doubt that the present Prime Minister, for instance, is a most sincere Christian, but I should not advise any of you to go and smite him on one cheek. I think you might find that he thought this text was intended in a figurative sense.

Then there is another point which I consider excellent. You will remember that Christ said, "Judge not lest ye be judged." That principle I do not think you would find was popular in the law courts of Christian countries. I have known in my time quite a number of judges who were very earnest Christians, and they none of them felt that they were acting contrary to Christian principles in what they did. Then Christ says, "Give to him that asketh of thee, and from him that would borrow of thee turn thou not away." This is a very good principle. Your chairman has reminded you that we are not here to talk politics, but I cannot help observing that the last general election was fought on the question of how desirable it was to turn away from him that would borrow of thee, so that one must assume that the liberals and conservatives of this country are composed of people who do not agree with the teaching of Christ, because they certainly did very emphatically turn away on that occasion.

Then there is one other maxim of Christ which I think has a great deal in it, but I do not find that it is very popular among some of our Christian friends. He says, "If thou wilt be perfect, go and sell that which thou hast, and give to the poor." That is a very excellent maxim, but, as I say, it is not much practiced. All these, I think, are good maxims, although they are a little difficult to live up to. I do not profess to live up to them myself; but then, after all, I am not by way of doing so, and it is not quite the same thing as for a Christian.

Defects in Christ's Teaching

Having granted the excellence of these maxims, I come to certain points in which I do not believe that one can grant either the superlative wisdom or the superlative goodness of Christ as depicted in the Gospels; and here I may say that one is not concerned with the historical question. Historically, it is quite doubtful whether Christ ever existed at all, and if He did we do not know anything about Him, so that I am not concerned with the historical question, which is a very difficult one. I am concerned with Christ as He appears in the Gospels, taking the Gospel narrative as it stands, and there one does find some things that do not seem to be very wise. For one thing, he certainly thought his second coming would occur in clouds of glory before the death of all the people who were living at that time. There are a great many texts that prove that. He says, for instance: "Ye shall not have gone over the cities of Israel till the Son of Man be come." Then He says: "There are some standing here which shall not taste death till the Son of Man comes into His kingdom"; and there are a lot of places where it is quite clear that He believed His second coming would happen during the lifetime of many then living. That was the belief of his earlier followers, and it was the basis of a good deal of His moral teaching. When He said, "Take no thought for the morrow," and things of that sort, it was very largely because He thought the second coming was going to be very soon, and that all ordinary mundane affairs did not count. I have, as a matter of fact, known some Christians who did believe the second coming was imminent. I knew a parson who frightened his congregation terribly by telling them that the second coming was very imminent indeed, but they were much consoled when they found that he was planting trees in his garden. The early Christians really did believe it, and they did abstain from such things as planting trees in their gardens, because they did accept from Christ the belief that the second coming was imminent. In this respect clearly He was not so wise as some other people have been, and he certainly was not superlatively wise.

The Moral Problem

Then you come to moral questions. There is one very serious defect to my mind in Christ's moral character, and that is that He believed in hell. I do not myself feel that any person that is really profoundly humane can believe in everlasting punishment. Christ certainly as depicted in the Gospels did believe in everlasting punishment, and one does find repeatedly a vindictive fury against those people who would not listen to His preaching—an attitude which is not uncommon with preachers, but which does somewhat detract from superlative excellence. You do not, for instance, find that attitude in Socrates. You find him quite bland and urbane toward the people who would not listen to him; and it is, to my mind, far more worthy of a sage to take that line than to take the line of indignation. You probably all remember the sorts of things that Socrates was saying when he was dying, and the sort of things that he generally did say to people who did not agree with him.

You will find that in the Gospels Christ said: "Ye serpents, ye generation of vipers, how can ye escape the damnation of hell." That was said to people who did not like His preaching. It is not really to my mind quite the best tone, and there are a great many of these things about hell. There is, of course, the familiar text about the sin against the Holy Ghost: "Whosoever speaketh against the Holy Ghost it shall not be forgiven him neither in this world nor in the world to come." That text has caused an unspeakable amount of misery in the world, for all sorts of people have imagined that they have committed the sin against the Holy Ghost, and thought that it would not be forgiven them either in this world or in the world to come. I really do not think that a person with a proper degree of kindliness in his nature would have put fears and terrors of this sort into the world.

Then Christ says, "The Son of Man shall send forth His angels, and they shall gather out of His kingdom all things that offend, and them which do iniquity, and shall cast them into a furnace of fire; there shall be wailing and gnashing of teeth"; and He goes on about the wailing and gnashing of teeth. It comes in one verse after another, and it is quite manifest to the reader that there is a certain pleasure in contemplating wailing and gnashing of teeth, or else it would not occur so often. Then you all, of course, remember about the sheep and the goats; how at the second coming He is going to divide the sheep from the goats, and He is going to say to the goats: "Depart from me, ye cursed, into everlasting fire." He continues: "And these shall go away into everlasting fire." Then He says again, "If thy hand offend thee, cut it off; it is better for thee to enter into life maimed, than having two hands to go into hell, into the fire that never shall be quenched, where the worm dieth not and the fire is not quenched." He repeats that again and again also. I must say that I think all this doctrine, that hell-fire is a punishment for sin, is a doctrine of cruelty. It is a doctrine that put cruelty into the world, and gave the world generations of cruel torture; and the Christ of the Gospels, if you could take Him as his chroniclers represent Him, would certainly have to be considered partly responsible for that.

There are other things of less importance. There is the instance of the Gadarene swine, where it certainly was not very kind to the pigs to put the devils into them and make them rush down the hill into the sea. You must remember that He was omnipotent, and He could have made the devils simply go away; but He chose to send them into the pigs. Then there is the curious story of the fig-tree, which always rather puzzled me. You remember what happened about the fig-tree. "He was hungry; and seeing a fig-tree afar off having leaves, He came if haply He might find anything thereon; and when he came to it He found nothing but leaves, for the time of figs was not yet. And Jesus answered and said unto it: 'No man eat fruit of thee hereafter for ever.' ... and Peter ... saith unto Him: 'Master, behold the fig-tree which thou cursedst is withered away.'" This is a very curious story, because it was not the right time of year for figs, and you really could not blame the tree. I cannot myself feel that either in the matter of wisdom or in the matter of virtue Christ stands quite as high as some other people known to History. I think I should put Buddha and Socrates above Him in those respects.

From *Why I am Not a Christian* by Bertrand Russell. Published in 1927, this work meets the criteria for fair use.

1. What was the moral argument for God expounded by Immanuel Kant and why did Russell reject it?

2. What was the remedying injustice argument for God and how did Russell refute it?

3. According to Russell, why do most people believe in God?

4. Did Russell have a high regard for Jesus and his teachings?

5. What was the most serious moral defect Russell saw in the character and teaching of Jesus?

Alex McFarland, a well-known author, speaker, and defender of the Christian faith defines apologetics as "content and methodologies that may be used by the Holy Spirit to contribute toward the discipleship of believers and the evangelism of non-believers." He gives the Five Big Questions apologetics addresses and the four lines of witness God has provided to point to his existence: creation, conscience, Scripture, and the Savior.

McFarland also touches on why God allows pain and suffering and explains the difference between a "convert" and a "disciple." He concludes with the admonition that the best apologetic for the faith is a living witness for Christ.

To access this video, go to www.summitu.com/utt and enter the passcode found in the back of your manual.

What is apologetics?

Apologetics is defined as "content and methodologies that may be used by the Holy Spirit to contribute toward the discipleship and mobilization of believers and the evangelism of non-believers."

_____ involves presenting, explaining, and defending the faith. It is a reasoned defense of what we believe and why. The primary motive for apologetics is not the conversion of people but the glory of God.

The Five Big Questions: What are the most important questions apologetics addresses?

1. Does _____ exist?
2. Is God real?
3. Is the _____ trustworthy?
4. Was Jesus authentic?
5. Why is there pain and suffering?

Four Lines of Witness: There are four lines of witness pointing to the existence of God: creation, conscience, Scripture, and the Savior.

- Creation and conscience answer the question, "Does _____ exist?"
- Scripture and the Savior answer the question, "What kind of God is he?"

The witness of creation and conscience are known as _____ revelation and are available to all mankind. The witness of Scripture and the Savior are known as _____ revelation.

Why does God allow pain and suffering?

Some people reject God because they don't understand how a good and all-powerful being can allow such pain and suffering. God's answer is not to remove pain but to deal with its source—sin—and to provide redemption and restoration through a _____.

What's the difference between a "convert" and a "disciple"?

A convert is someone who has acquired _____, but a disciple is someone who is committed to a lifestyle of following Jesus. A disciple is someone who dies to self and lives for Christ.

The best apologetic for the faith is a living _____ for Christ.

1. What is "apologetics"?

2. How do 1 Peter 3:15 and 1 Peter 2:15 relate to apologetics?

3. What are the Five Big Questions people ask? In what order would you prioritize them in terms of their importance to you?

4. How do these four lines of witness point to the existence of God: creation, conscience, Scripture, and the Savior?

5. Does being a Christian mean being exempt from pain and suffering? Do we get a special pass through this vale of tears as God's children?

Chapter 8 Key Points

Key Questions:

1. What is theology?
2. How do the six dominant Western worldviews approach theology?

Key Terms:

1. Anthropic Principle
2. Atheism
3. Descriptive Religious Pluralism
4. Genetic Information Theory
5. Liberation Theology
6. Monotheism*
7. New Atheism
8. Panspermia
9. Pantheism*
10. Polytheism
11. Prescriptive Religious Pluralism
12. Reincarnation
13. Religious Pluralism
14. Second Law of Thermodynamics
15. Spontaneous Generation
16. Theism
17. Theological Suspicion*
18. Theology*
19. Trinitarian Monotheism*

Key Verses:

1. Exodus 3:14
2. Psalm 19:1
3. Isaiah 44:6

Key Players:

1. Richard Dawkins
2. Daniel Dennett
3. John Dewey
4. Ludwig Feuerbach
5. Sam Harris
6. Christopher Hitchens
7. Bertrand Russell

Key Works:

1. *The End of Faith* by Sam Harris
2. *The Essence of Religion* by Ludwig Feuerbach
3. *The God Delusion* by Richard Dawkins
4. *God Is Not Great* by Christopher Hitchens
5. *Why I Am Not a Christian* by Bertrand Russell

Short answer or essay question on the exam

Hello there!

I learned a valuable lesson today while I was biking to class; never leave home without an umbrella. As I am sure you can guess, I was caught in a torrential downpour. After the first few minutes, I embraced the flood and attempted to enjoy the remaining ten minutes of my bike ride. By the time I walked into class though, I looked like I had jumped into a lake. I bet it was a pretty funny sight. My Art History professor enjoyed teasing me about tracking water into her class. I have absolutely learned my lesson.

On a positive, and much drier, note, Sarah and Nathan had a really cool idea to start a book club at a local coffee shop near campus. Mark, Paige, and Muhammad joined our discussion too! Today was the first day, and we were supposed to pick out a book. We couldn't really settle on a genre, so the conversation basically turned into a discussion on what each person wanted to read. Sarah wanted to read about the rise of the feminist movement, but Nathan suggested a book on meditation and self-healing. To be honest, I am still a bit confused by what he was saying. I could understand more of it than I did before I read your letter. Thanks again!

Somehow, our conversation shifted towards everyone's belief in the supernatural. Muhammad and I agreed in the existence of God, but Sarah and Mark kept saying it was an irrational conclusion since we can't experience him with our five senses. Nathan was on a completely different planet when he was trying to explain that we are all gods. Paige was pretty quiet, but she did mention something about not conforming to the metanarratives set forth by mainstream religions. I bet this has something to do with her thoughts on Postmodernism.

After about two hours of listening to them—mainly Sarah and Mark versus Nathan—we decided to meet up next week with some specific books in mind. I am not sure what book I will suggest. It is still strange to me that some people don't believe in God or believe we are all god. I know Muhammad and I at least agree that there is only one God, but we seem to part ways after that. He said Christianity believes in three gods. I tried to explain that the Trinity isn't three gods but one. However, I didn't do a very job. Muhammad remains unconvinced.

After I left, I began to think about all they said. Mark calls himself a Marxist, but Sarah says she is a Secularist. It seems like they agree about their theology, but it's hard to wrap my head around how anyone could deny that God exists. **Why do Secularists deny God's existence?** And **why do Marxists deny God's existence?** Also, Paige didn't really speak up too much this time. **How does Postmodernism view God?** Nathan, on the other hand, was calling all of us gods, saying we need to discover the inner divine in all of us. **What is the New Spiritualist view of God?** I'm hoping you can help me figure out how to explain Christian theology to Muhammad. I feel I need to know more about our differences. **What is the difference between the Islamic view of God and the Christian view of God?**

I really appreciate you taking the time to explain all this worldview stuff. It can be quite confusing when all your friends have different beliefs about God.

You are the BEST!
–Doug

UNIT

9

PHILOSOPHY

CHAPTER 9 LEARNING OBJECTIVES

Students will be able to:

1. define what philosophy is and why it is important. [9.1]

2. explain Secularism's approach to philosophy. [9.2]

3. explain Marxism's approach to philosophy. [9.3]

4. explain Postmodernism's approach to philosophy. [9.4]

5. explain New Spirituality's approach to philosophy. [9.5]

6. explain Islam's approach to philosophy. [9.6]

7. explain Christianity's approach to philosophy. [9.7]

1. Why should Christians be concerned about philosophy? [9.1]

2. What are the three Big Questions philosophy seeks to answer? [9.1]

    – what is ultimaltey real?
       ↳ meta physics – there is something
                           beyond the physical

    – what does it mean to know?

3. What is the mind/body problem? [9.1]

4. Can you think of some analogies to illustrate the relationship of the mind to the brain? [9.1]

5. The basic foundation for all forms of Secularist philosophy is what? [9.2]

6. Can you summarize the metaphysics of secular philosophy? [9.2]

7. Can you summarize the epistemology of secular philosophy? [9.2]

8. Can you summarize how Secularists handle the mind/body problem? [9.2]

9. Why is scientific empiricism key to Secularist philosophy? [9.2]

10. Can you summarize the epistemology of Marxist philosophy? [9.3]

11. Can you summarize the metaphysics of Marxist philosophy? [9.3]

12. Can you summarize how Marxists handle the mind/body problem? [9.3]

13. Can you summarize the epistemology of Postmodernist philosophy? [9.4]

14. What does Postmodernism substitute for capital "T" truth as a means for understanding reality? [9.4]

15. Can you summarize the metaphysics of Postmodernist philosophy? [9.4]

16. Can you summarize the metaphysics of New Spirituality? [9.5]

17. **Can you summarize the epistemology of New Spirituality? [9.5]**

18. **Can you summarize how New Spirituality handles the mind/body problem? [9.5]**

19. **Can you summarize the metaphysics of Islamic philosophy? [9.6]**

20. **Can you summarize the epistemology of Islamic philosophy? [9.6]**

21. Can you summarize how Islam handles the mind/body problem? [9.6]

22. Every worldview begins with basic assumptions about reality that can't be absolutely proven. Faith is required. Upon what is atheism grounded? Upon what is Christianity grounded? [9.7]

23. Can you summarize the epistemology of Christian philosophy? [9.7]

24. Can you summarize the metaphysics of Christian philosophy? [9.7]

25. Can you summarize how Christianity handles the mind/body problem? [9.7]

26. If the Christian worldview is capital "T" True—consistent with the nature of reality and reflecting what actually exists—then what is false about other worldviews? [9.7]

Just a generation or two ago, Christianity was accepted as the dominant worldview in the Western world. Now many see it as an outdated worldview competing for acceptance in the public sphere among so many other worldviews. This excerpt from *Total Truth* by Nancy Pearcey explains exactly what is at stake in our culture if Christians fail to form a solid and accurate worldview. She explains how society has been divided into public and private spheres and how religion has been relegated to the private sphere.

As you read this, think about your own worldview. Consider your own faith and ask if it is an emotional faith or a faith rooted in knowledge and reason.

TOTAL TRUTH

by Nancy Pearcey

Introduction

"Your earlier book says Christians are called to redeem entire cultures, not just individuals," a schoolteacher commented, joining me for lunch at a conference where I had just spoken. Then he added thoughtfully, "I'd never heard that before."

The teacher was talking about *How Now Shall We Live?*[1] and at his words I looked up from my plate in surprise. Was he really saying he'd never even heard the idea of being a redemptive force in every area of culture? He shook his head: "No, I've always thought of salvation strictly in terms of individual souls."

That conversation helped confirm my decision to write a follow-up book dealing with the worldview themes in *How Now Shall We Live?* Just a few years ago, when I began my work on that earlier volume, using the term worldview was not on anyone's list of good conversation openers. To tell people that you were writing a book on worldview was to risk glazed stares and a quick change in subject. But today as I travel around the country, I sense an eagerness among evangelicals to move beyond a purely privatized faith, applying biblical principles to areas like work, business, and politics. Flip open any number of Christian publications and you're likely to find half a dozen advertisements for worldview conferences, worldview institutes, and worldview programs. Clearly the term itself has strong marketing cachet these days, which signals a deep hunger among Christians for an overarching framework to bring unity to their lives.

This book addresses that hunger and offers new direction for advancing the worldview movement. It will help you identify the secular/sacred divide that keeps your faith locked into the private sphere of "religious truth." It will walk you through practical, workable steps for crafting a Christian worldview in your own life and work. And it will teach you how to apply a worldview grid to cut through the bewildering maze of ideas and ideologies we encounter in a postmodern world. The purpose of world-view studies is nothing less than to liberate Christianity from its cultural captivity, unleashing its power to transform the world.

"The gospel is like a caged lion," said the great Baptist preacher Charles Spurgeon. "It does not need to be defended, it just needs to be let out of its cage." Today the cage is our accommodation to the secular/sacred split that reduces Christianity to a matter of private personal belief. To unlock the cage, we need to become utterly convinced that, as Francis Schaeffer said, Christianity is not merely religious truth, it is total truth—truth about the whole of reality.

Politics Is Not Enough

The reason a worldview message is so compelling today is that we are still emerg-ing from the fundamentalist era of the early twentieth century. Up until that time, evangelicals had enjoyed a position of cultural dominance in America. But after the Scopes trial and the rise of theological modernism, religious conservatives turned in on themselves: They circled the wagons, developed a fortress mentality, and cham-pioned "separatism" as a positive strategy. Then, in the 1940s and 50s, a movement began that aimed at breaking out of the fortress. Calling themselves neo-evangelicals, this group argued that we are called not to escape the surrounding culture but to engage it. They sought to construct a redemptive vision that would embrace not only individuals but also social structures and institutions.

Yet many evangelicals lacked the conceptual tools needed for the task, which has seriously limited their success. For example, in recent decades many Christians have responded to the moral and social decline in American society by embracing political activism. Believers are running for office in growing numbers; churches are organizing voter registration; public policy groups are proliferating; scores of Christian publications and radio programs offer commentary on public affairs. This heightened activism has yielded good results in many areas of public life, yet the impact remains far less than most had hoped. Why? Because evangelicals often put all their eggs in one basket: They leaped into political activism as the quickest, surest way to make a difference in the public arena—failing to realize that politics tends to reflect culture, not the other way around.

Nothing illustrates evangelicals' infatuation with politics more clearly than a story related by a Christian lawyer. Considering whether to take a job in the nation's capital, he consulted with the leader of a Washington-area ministry, who told him, "You can either stay where you are and keep practicing law, or you can come to Washington and change the culture." The implication was that the only way to effect cultural change was through national politics. Today, battle-weary political warriors have grown more realistic about the limits of that strategy. We have learned that "politics is downstream from culture, not the other way around," says Bill Wichter-man, policy advisor to Senate Majority Leader Bill Frist. "Real change has to start with the culture. All we can do on Capitol Hill is try to find ways government can nurture healthy cultural trends."[2]

On a similar note, a member of Congress once told me, "I got involved in politics after the 1973 abortion decision because I thought that was the fastest route to moral reform. Well, we've won some legislative victories, but we've lost the culture." The most effective work, he had come to realize, is done by ordinary Christians fulfilling God's calling to reform culture within their local spheres of influence—their families, churches, schools, neighborhoods, workplaces, professional organizations, and civic institutions. In order to effect lasting change, the congressman concluded, "we need to develop a Christian worldview."

Losing Our Children

Not only have we "lost the culture," but we continue losing even our own children. It's a familiar but tragic story that devout young people, raised in Christian homes, head off to college and abandon their faith. Why is this pattern so common? Largely because young believers have not been taught how to develop a biblical worldview. Instead, Christianity has been restricted to a specialized area of religious belief and personal devotion.

I recently read a striking example. At a Christian high school, a theology teacher strode to the front of the classroom, where he drew a heart on one side of the blackboard and a brain on the other. The two are as divided as the two sides of the blackboard, he told the class: The heart is what we use for religion, while the brain is what we use for science.

An apocryphal story? A caricature of Christian anti-intellectualism? No, the story was told by a young woman who was in the class that day. Worse, out of some two hundred students, she was the only one who objected. The rest apparently found nothing unusual about restricting religion to the domain of the "heart."[3]

As Christian parents, pastors, teachers, and youth group leaders, we constantly see young people pulled down by the undertow of powerful cultural trends. If all we give them is a "heart" religion, it will not be strong enough to counter the lure of attractive but dangerous ideas. Young believers also need a "brain" religion—training in worldview and apologetics—to equip them to analyze and critique the competing worldviews they will encounter when they leave home. If forewarned and forearmed, young people at least have a fighting chance when they find themselves a minority of one among their classmates or work colleagues. Training young people to develop a Christian mind is no longer an option; it is part of their necessary survival equipment.

Heart versus Brain

The first step in forming a Christian worldview is to overcome this sharp divide between "heart" and "brain." We have to reject the division of life into a sacred realm, limited to things like worship and personal morality, over against a secular realm that includes science, politics, economics, and the rest of the public arena.

This dichotomy in our own minds is the greatest barrier to liberating the power of the gospel across the whole of culture today.

Moreover, it is reinforced by a much broader division rending the entire fabric of modern society—what sociologists call the public/private split. "Modernization brings about a novel dichotomization of social life," writes Peter Berger. "The dichotomy is between the huge and immensely powerful institutions of the public sphere[by this he means the state, academia, large corporations] . . . and the private sphere"—the realm of family, church, and personal relationships.

The large public institutions claim to be "scientific" and "value-free," which means that values are relegated to the private sphere of personal choice. As Berger explains: "The individual is left to his own devices in a wide range of activities that are crucial to the formation of a meaningful identity, from expressing his religious preference to settling on a sexual life style."[4] We might diagram the dichotomy like this:

Modern societies are sharply divided:

PRIVATE SPHERE
Personal Preferences

PUBLIC SPHERE
Scientific Knowledge

In short, the private sphere is awash in moral relativism. Notice Berger's telling phrase "religious preference." Religion is not considered an objective truth to which we submit, but only a matter of personal taste which we choose. Because of this, the dichotomy is sometimes called the fact/value split.

Values have been reduced to arbitrary, existential decisions:

VALUES
Individual Choice

FACTS
Binding on Everyone

As Schaeffer explains, the concept of truth itself has been divided—a process he illustrates with the imagery of a two-story building: In the lower story are science and reason, which are considered public truth, binding on everyone. Over against it is an upper story of noncognitive experience, which is the locus of personal meaning. This is the realm of private truth, where we hear people say, "That may be true for you but it's not true for me."[5]

The two-realm theory of truth:

UPPER STORY
Nonrational, Noncognitive

LOWER STORY
Rational, Verifiable

When Schaeffer was writing, the term postmodernism had not yet been coined, but clearly that is what he was talking about. Today we might say that in the lower story is modernism, which still claims to have universal, objective truth—while in the upper story is postmodernism.

Today's two-story truth:

POSTMODERNISM
Subjective, Relative to Particular Groups

MODERNISM
Objective, Universally Valid

The reason it's so important for us to learn how to recognize this division is that it is the single most potent weapon for delegitimizing the biblical perspective in the public square today. Here's how it works: Most secularists are too politically savvy to attack religion directly or to debunk it as false. So what do they do? They consign religion to the value sphere—which takes it out of the realm of true and false altogether. Secularists can then assure us that of course they "respect" religion, while at the same time denying that it has any relevance to the public realm.

As Phillip Johnson puts it, the fact/value split "allows the metaphysical naturalists to mollify the potentially troublesome religious people by assuring them that science does not rule out 'religious belief' (so long as it does not pretend to be knowledge)."[6] In other words, so long as everyone understands that it is merely a matter of private feelings. The two-story grid functions as a gatekeeper that defines what is to be taken seriously as genuine knowledge, and what can be dismissed as mere wish-fulfillment.

Just a Power Grab?

This same division also explains why Christians have such difficulty communicating in the public arena. It's crucial for us to realize that nonbelievers are constantly filtering what we say through a mental fact/value grid. For example, when we state a position on an issue like abortion or bioethics or homosexuality, we intend to assert an objective moral truth important to the health of society—but they think we're merely expressing our subjective bias. When we say there's scientific evidence for design in the universe, we intend to stake out a testable truth claim—but they say, "Uh oh, the Religious Right is making a political power grab." The fact/value grid instantly dissolves away the objective content of anything we say, and we will not be successful in introducing the content of our belief into the public discussion unless we first find ways to get past this gatekeeper.

That's why Lesslie Newbigin warned that the divided concept of truth is the primary factor in "the cultural captivity of the gospel." It traps Christianity in the upper story of privatized values, and prevents it from having any effect on public culture.[7] Having worked as a missionary in India for forty years, Newbigin was able to discern what is distinctive about Western thought more clearly than most of us, who have been immersed in it all our lives. On his return to the West, Newbigin was struck by the way Christian truth has been marginalized. He saw that any position labeled religion is placed in the upper story of values, where it is no longer regarded as objective knowledge.

To give just one recent example, in the debate over embryonic stem cell research, actor Christopher Reeve told a student group at Yale University, "When matters of public policy are debated, no religions should have a seat at the table."[8]

To recover a place at the table of public debate, then, Christians must find a way to overcome the dichotomy between public and private, fact and value, secular and sacred. We need to liberate the gospel from its cultural captivity, restoring it to the status of public truth. "The barred cage that forms the prison for the gospel in contemporary western culture is[the church's] accommodation . . . to the fact-value dichotomy," says Michael Goheen, a professor of worldview studies.[9] Only by recovering a holistic view of total truth can we set the gospel free to become a redemptive force across all of life.

Mental Maps

To say that Christianity is the truth about total reality means that it is a full-orbed worldview. The term means literally a view of the world, a biblically informed perspective on all reality. A worldview is like a mental map that tells us how to navigate the world effectively. It is the imprint of God's objective truth on our inner life.

We might say that each of us carries a model of the universe inside our heads that tells us what the world is like and how we should live in it. A classic book on worldviews is titled The Universe Next Door, suggesting that we all have a mental or conceptual universe in which we "live"—a network of principles that answer the fundamental questions of life: Who are we? Where did we come from? What is the purpose of life? The author of the book, James Sire, invites readers to examine a variety of worldviews in order to understand the mental universe held by other people—those living "next door."

A worldview is not the same thing as a formal philosophy; otherwise, it would be only for professional philosophers. Even ordinary people have a set of convictions about how reality functions and how they should live. Because we are made in God's image, we all seek to make sense of life. Some convictions are conscious, while others are unconscious, but together they form a more or less consistent picture of reality. Human beings "are incapable of holding purely arbitrary opinions or making entirely unprincipled decisions," writes Al Wolters in a book on worldview. Because we are by nature rational and responsible beings, we sense that "we need some creed to live by, some map by which to chart our course."[10]

The notion that we need such a "map" in the first place grows out of the biblical view of human nature. The Marxist may claim that human behavior is ultimately shaped by economic circumstances; the Freudian attributes everything to repressed sexual instincts; and the behavioral psychologist regards humans as stimulus-response mechanisms. But the Bible teaches that the overriding factor in the choices we make is our ultimate belief or religious commitment. Our lives are shaped by the "god" we worship—whether the God of the Bible or some substitute deity.

The term worldview is a translation of the German word Weltanschauung, which means a way of looking at the world (Welt = world; schauen = to look). German Romanticism developed the idea that cultures are complex wholes, where a certain outlook on life, or spirit of the age, is expressed across the board—in art, literature, and social institutions as well as in formal philosophy. The best way to understand the products of any culture, then, is to grasp the underlying worldview being expressed. But, of course, cultures change over the course of history, and thus the original use of the term worldview conveyed relativism.

The word was later introduced into Christian circles through Dutch neo-Calvinist thinkers such as Abraham Kuyper and Herman Dooyeweerd. They argued that Christians cannot counter the spirit of the age in which they live unless they develop an equally comprehensive biblical worldview—an outlook on life that gives rise to distinctively Christian forms of culture—with the important qualification that it is not merely the relativistic belief of a particular culture but is based on the very Word of God, true for all times and places.

Not Just Academic

As the concept of worldview becomes common currency, it can all too easily be misunderstood. Some treat it as merely another academic subject to master—a mental exercise or "how to" strategy. Others handle worldview as if it were a weapon in the culture war, a tool for more effective activism. Still others, alas, treat it as little more than a new buzzword or marketing gimmick to dazzle the public and attract donors.

Genuine worldview thinking is far more than a mental strategy or a new spin on current events. At the core, it is a deepening of our spiritual character and the character of our lives. It begins with the submission of our minds to the Lord of the universe—a willingness to be taught by Him. The driving force in worldview studies should be a commitment to "love the Lord your God with all your heart, soul, strength, and mind" (see Luke 10:27).

That's why the crucial condition for intellectual growth is spiritual growth, asking God for the grace to "take every thought captive to obey Christ" (2 Cor. 10:5). God is not just the Savior of souls, He is also the Lord of creation. One way we acknowledge His Lordship is by interpreting every aspect of creation in the light of His truth. God's Word becomes a set of glasses offering a new perspective on all our thoughts and actions.

As with every aspect of sanctification, the renewal of the mind may be painful and difficult. It requires hard work and discipline, inspired by a sacrificial love for Christ and a burning desire to build up His Body, the Church. In order to have the mind of Christ, we must be willing to be crucified with Christ, following wherever He might lead—whatever the cost. "Through many tribulations we must enter the kingdom of

God" (Acts 14:22). As we undergo refining in the fires of suffering, our desires are purified and we find ourselves wanting nothing more than to bend every fiber of our being, including our mental powers, to fulfill the Lord's Prayer: "Thy Kingdom come." We yearn to lay all our talents and gifts at His feet in order to advance His purposes in the world. Developing a Christian worldview means submitting our entire self to God, in an act of devotion and service to Him.

....

This essay originally appeared as a chapter in Nancy Pearcey, *Total Truth: Liberating Christianity from Its Cultural Captivity* (Wheaton, IL: Crossway, 2004), 17–25. It is reproduced here with the permission of the publisher, Crossway Books (http://crossway.org).

[1] *How Now Shall We Live?* was coauthored by Charles Colson and published by Tyndale (Wheaton, Ill., 1991), and hereafter cited as *How Now?* I would also like to recognize the contribution of Harold Fickett, an outstanding writer and storyteller, who wrote the chapter in *How Now?* consisting of extended stories. In offering the current book in part as an advance on themes developed in *How Now?* I'd like to clarify that all citations of that earlier volume refer solely to chapters that I authored.

[2] Bill Wichterman, in discussion with the author. Wichterman develops his thesis in greater detail in "The Culture: Upstream from Politics," in *Building a Healthy Culture: Strategies for an American Renaissance,* ed. Don Eberly (Grand Rapids, Mich.: Eerdmans, 2001), 76–101. "While cultural conservatives bemoan judicial activism that reinterprets the plain meaning of the written Constitution, they forget that the courts are only finishing on parchment a job already begun in the hearts of the American people . . . Politics is largely an expression of culture."

[3] Cited in Mary Passantino, "The Little Engine That Can," a review of Phillip Johnson's The Right Questions (foreword by Nancy Pearcey), in Christian Research Journal, April 2003.

[4] Peter Berger, *Facing Up to Modernity: Excursions in Society, Politics, and Religion* (New York: Basic Books, 1977), 133.

[5] Francis Schaeffer deals with the divided concept of truth in *Escape from Reason* and *The God Who Is There* (in The Complete Works of Francis Schaeffer[Wheaton, IL.: Crossway, 1982]).

[6] Phillip E. Johnson, The Wedge of Truth: Splitting the Foundations of Naturalism (Downers Grove, IL.: InterVarsity Press, 2000), 148, emphasis added. See also my review of the book: "A New Foundation for Positive Cultural Change: Science and God in the Public Square," Human Events (September 15, 2000).

[7] Lesslie Newbigin, *A Word in Season: Perspectives on Christian World Missions* (Grand Rapids, MI.: Eerdmans, 1994), see especially the chapter titled, "The Cultural Captivity of Western Christianity as a Challenge to a Missionary Church."

[8] "Reeve: Keep Religious Groups Out of Public Policy," The Associated Press, April 3, 2003, emphasis added.

[9] Michael Goheen, "As the Father Has Sent Me, I Am Sending You": J.E. Lesslie Newbigin's Missionary Ecclesiology (Zoetermeer: Uitgeverij Boekencentrum, 2000), 377.

[10] Albert M. Wolters, *Creation Regained: Biblical Basics for a Reformational Worldview* (Grand Rapids, MI.: Eerdmans, 1985), 4.

1. What is a worldview and how does it help us live in a postmodern world?

2. What was the Christian approach to politics in the twentieth century?

3. Does politics tend to change culture or to reflect culture?

4. How would you respond to the statement, "The heart is what we use for religion, while the brain is what we use for science"?

5. What is the two-realm theory of truth and how does it neutralize the Christian worldview?

We should love God with all of our strength, all of our hearts, and all of our minds. J. P. Moreland outlines just how important the mind is for loving God. He contrasts the Christian worldview with other dominant worldviews and shows how it is a reliable source of truth *and* knowledge. He explains the correspondence theory of truth, which has held sway for most of history, and describes three kinds of knowledge and how they relate to reason and belief.

To access this video, go to www.summitu.com/utt and enter the passcode found in the back of your manual.

Worldviews affect our whole orientation toward life. The three dominant worldviews today are Postmodernism, Christianity, and scientific _____. Postmodernism and scientific naturalism assert there is no such thing as non-scientific knowledge of reality. Christianity disagrees.

Christianity has always claimed to be a source of truth *and* _____.

There are three kinds of knowledge:

1. **Knowledge by** _____: This can be by direct experience through our five senses or non-sensory through awareness of our own consciousness (thinking).

2. _____**knowledge:** This is true belief based on adequate reasons. Propositional knowledge does not require certainty. You can know something without being certain you're right. This kind of knowledge is based on three things:

   - **Truth:** Truth is when things are the way one thinks them to be. It is a matching of thought and reality. If you think there's a clock in the room, and there is one, that's truth. This is called the _____ theory of truth and it has been the classic view of truth until quite recently.

   - **Belief:** A belief is a thought you take to be true with somewhere between 51 and 100 percent certainty. Fifty-one percent certainty would be a weak belief, while 90 percent certainty would be a strong belief.

   - **Adequate reasons:** Adequate reasons do not have to be totally certain or conclusive. One can have _____ or questions but still feel there is adequate reason for belief.

3. **Know-how or** _____: The ability to do something well. The Bible is an incredible source of instructions and examples of skill at life.

Christianity provides these three kinds of knowledge. You can be directly aware of God through the senses and non-sensory acquaintance. You can believe in God with certainty based on adequate reasons, even though you may have doubts and questions. And Christianity provides know-how on living skillfully.

▶ "LOVING GOD WITH YOUR MIND" DISCUSSION QUESTIONS

1. What's a good way to marginalize Christians in society?

2. What is truth?

3. Propositional knowledge is based on what three things?

4. Do you need absolute certainty to believe something is true?

5. Another type of knowledge is "know-how" or "skill," the ability to do something well. How can you demonstrate the Bible is an incredible source of know-how for living?

Chapter 9 Key Points

Key Questions:

1. What is philosophy?
2. How do the six dominant Western worldviews approach philosophy?

Key Verses:

1. Luke 10:27
2. John 1:1–4

Key Players:

1. Jean Baudrillard
2. Joseph Campbell
3. Michel Foucault
4. Al-Ghazali
5. Ken Wilber

Key Works:

1. *A Brief History of Everything* by Ken Wilber
2. "The Gulf War Did Not Take Place" by Jean Baudrillard
3. *The Power of Myth* by Joseph Campbell
4. "This Is Not a Pipe" by Michel Foucault

Key Terms:

1. Anti-realism*
2. Constructivism
3. Correspondence Theory of Truth
4. Dialectical Materialism*
5. Dualism*
6. Empiricism
7. Epistemological Humility
8. Epistemology
9. Foundationalism
10. Knowledge
11. Materialism*
12. Metaphysics
13. Mind/Body Dualism
14. Mind/Body Monism
15. Mind/Body Problem
16. Monism
17. Naturalism*
18. Philosophy*
19. Pragmatism
20. Realism
21. Scientific Empiricism
22. Spiritual Monism*

Short answer or essay question on the exam

Hello!

Finals are quickly approaching, so I am spending most of my time in the library. Nothing has changed too much since I last wrote except for my coffee consumption. Let's just say if I were to bleed, I'm pretty sure I would bleed espresso. Honestly though, I'm not too worried about most of my finals, but Art History has a really long paper due in a few days. Paige and I are going to meet up tomorrow so she can help me put together a decent paper. She is the one really interested in postmodern art.

In other news, I went back home this weekend to visit my family. It was awesome eating homemade food instead of the dining hall chow I am usually subject to. Nothing beats Mom's homemade lemon meringue pie. It also gave me a chance to catch up on sleep. I hadn't realized how tired I was. Now I am all rested, armed with several dozen chocolate chip cookies, ready to take on finals next week.

While at home, I registered for a philosophy class with Sarah and Mark for next semester. We checked out some of the required texts, and it looks like I have a lot of difficult reading ahead of me! At book club yesterday, we already started discussing some of the concepts we will cover in class. Have you ever heard of some of these terms: *metaphysics, epistemology, ontology*, and *epiphenomenalism*? I had no idea that philosophy would be so complicated.

I also didn't realize that philosophy could be so divisive. My friends at book club all had different opinions over the subject. Sarah said the only way to know anything is by the scientific method. She argued that nothing about the immaterial or supernatural could be known since it was outside the realm of scientific inquiry. Mark seemed to agree until Sarah said there is no inherent purpose in the world. Mark responded that history does have a purpose, and the world is gradually progressing toward economic equality. Nathan piped up saying we there is purpose, but took issue with the idea that matter is all there is. Paige declared the whole conversation pointless since we are all constrained by our own experiences. All the while, I am sitting there just trying to follow what everyone was saying.

After a while, though, I had to go study. I left more confused than when I arrived. Maybe you can help me! Sarah and Mark appear to agree on a lot, but they obviously have some different thoughts on philosophy. **How do Marxism and Secularism differ in their views on philosophy?** Paige didn't really talk about what she thought. **What is the philosophical position of Postmodernism?** As usual, Mark has some strange things to say. **What are the philosophical views of New Spirituality?** After these conversations, I am confused about what I am supposed to think as a Christian about philosophy. **What does Christianity have to say about philosophy?**

I really appreciate your help! You *rock*!

Later!
–Doug

UNIT

10

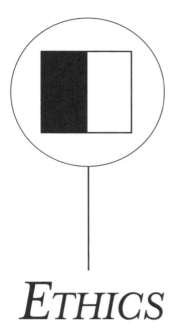

ETHICS

CHAPTER 10 LEARNING OBJECTIVES

Students will be able to:

1. define what ethics is and why it is important. [10.1]

2. identify the difference between ethics and morality and the two overarching ethical theories. [10.2]

3. explain Secularism's approach to ethics. [10.3]

4. explain Marxism's approach to ethics. [10.4]

5. explain Postmodernism's approach to ethics. [10.5]

6. explain New Spirituality's approach to ethics. [10.6]

7. explain Islam's approach to ethics. [10.7]

8. explain Christianity's approach to ethics and Christianity's response to ethical relativism. [10.8]

1. What is ethics? What are the two big questions it seeks to answer? [10.1]

2. What is the underlying basis for Christian ethics? [10.1]

3. Can you explain the difference between morality and ethics? [10.2]

4. Into what main categories can theories of ethics be divided? [10.2]

5.   To which ethical categories do the major systems of philosophy belong? [10.2]

6.   What are some problems with teleological ethical theories? [10.2]

7.   What is the main problem with deontological ethical theories? [10.2]

8.   Is it ever right to do wrong? [10.2]

9. What is the ethics of Secularism based on? [10.3]

10. If there's no God or fixed moral code, where does morality come from according to Secularists? [10.3]

11. Who are some of the philosophers who led the shift away from a God-based morality to a humanistic moral relativism? [10.3]

12. What is situation ethics and where does it lead? [10.3]

13. What is scientism and where does it lead? [10.3]

14. How are Secularists being inconsistent when they accept the Golden Rule as good for humanity? [10.3]

15. What is at the core of Marxist ethics? [10.4]

16. Why is hatred a good thing in Marxism when other ethical codes see it as evil? [10.4]

17. What does "the good life" consist of according to New Spirituality? [10.5]

18. Not all New Spiritualists are absolute individualists. How do Buddhists and Hindus differ in their approach to ethics? [10.5]

19. If everyone does what he or she wants, is there any accountability in New Spiritualty? [10.5]

20. What is unique about the Postmodernist approach to ethics? [10.6]

21. What role does pragmatism play in Postmodernist ethics? [10.6]

22. What is the source of morality and ethics in Islam? [10.7]

23. What are the basic beliefs and behaviors required by Islamic ethics? [10.7]

24. What is the source of morality and ethics in Christianity? [10.8]

25. According to Christianity, where do moral absolutes come from? [10.8]

26. See how many of the eight Beatitudes from the Sermon on the Mount (Matt 5–7) you can recite from memory. Try ranking them in order of importance.

In a *Cross Examination* debate with Michael Shermer, Sean McDowell asks, "Can there be goodness if God doesn't exist?" Shermer believes goodness exists whether God does or not. He uses marriage to illustrate his claim, insisting we know infidelity is wrong, even if there is no God. It's part of our social contract.

The two agree there are objective moral standards but disagree as to what they are based upon. Shermer makes the case for their development as part of the evolutionary process. McDowell maintains morality requires a standard outside of evolution: a mind that created the universe and gives life a purpose.

In part two of the debate, Michael Shermer says moral behavior evolved naturally because we are a social primate species; we learn there are consequences for our behavior; and we have to work together and get along to survive, as individuals and as groups.

McDowell maintains that morality requires something beyond evolution and subjective feelings. Even when Christians did not live up to the principles of Scripture in regard to practices like slavery and discrimination, we know those behaviors are wrong, not because they violate a social contract but because they violate the character of God.

To access this video, go to www.summitu.com/utt and enter the passcode found in the back of your manual.

1. Can there be objective moral laws without God?

2. Do people have moral value in and of themselves?

3. Why do some people reject divine revelation as the source of belief in God and objective truth?

4. What is reciprocity and what role does it play in Shermer's understanding of morality?

5. If God and the Bible are the source of morality, how do we explain the things God commanded or allowed in the Old Testament that we consider immoral today?

"CAN WE BE MORAL WITHOUT GOD?" VIDEO

Can we be moral without God? Where does the moral law come from in the first place? Can people who don't believe in it be good? Do we have the right to judge others? Frank Beckwith takes on these questions and the issues of modern morality in this enlightening lecture. He describes the four characteristics of moral law and deals with the three theories of where it comes from.

To access this video, go to www.summitu.com/utt and enter the passcode found in the back of your manual.

awareness of moral law. Which worldview makes the most sense of this? Not materialism or naturalism, because they don't believe there is anything outside the physical universe that has an impact on reality. Christianity insists there is a moral law and it comes from a moral lawgiver—God.

Moral _____ doubt the existence of moral law, but they turn around and appeal to it when their rights are violated. The New Atheists attack Christianity by judging it against an objective moral law. But how can Christianity be evil if there's no objective standard of good from which it deviates?

There are four characteristics of natural moral law:

1. Moral law is _____. It consists of concepts (like ideas) that lack physical substance.
2. Moral law is a form of _____. It has intellectual content.
3. Moral law has _____. This is a sense that we have a moral call to do or not do something. It is sometimes called conscience.
4. Moral law, when violated, creates a deep sense of discomfort known as _____.

If moral law exists, how did it come to be? Here are three possibilities:

1. *It is an* _____: Natural selection tricked us into believing in moral law. These rules help us survive as we evolve, but they aren't objectively real.
2. *It is based on* _____: If moral law is a product of chance, there's no reason to obey it. If there's no mind behind it, then there's no intellectual content, so why obey it?
3. *It is the product of an* _____ *mind:* What sort of intelligence does it have to be? A mind that can be the ground for natural moral law. This mind would have to be self-existent, perfectly good, and have authority to issue judgment. This being couldn't be finite or contingent on anything else for existence. The only being who meets these criteria is God.

1. What is the natural moral law?

2. How are moral relativists and atheists inconsistent in their denial of moral law?

3. What are the four characteristics of moral law?

4. If moral law exists, how did it come to be?

5. How would you answer the argument that the moral law is a product of naturalistic evolution?

Chapter 10 Key Points

Key Questions:

1. What is ethics?
2. How do the six dominant Western worldviews approach ethics?

Key Terms:

1. Agape*
2. Cultural Relativism*
3. Deontological Ethics
4. Divine Command Theory*
5. Ethical Egoism
6. Ethics*
7. Hedonism
8. Karma*
9. Morality
10. Moral Relativism*
11. Proletariat Morality*
12. Scientism
13. Situation Ethics
14. Teleological Ethics
15. Utilitarianism*

Key Verses:

1. Matthew 5–7
2. Luke 10:27
3. Romans 12:9

Key Players:

1. Joseph Fletcher
2. Thomas Hobbes
3. Immanuel Kant
4. John Stuart Mill
5. Friedrich Nietzsche

Key Works:

1. *Groundwork of the Metaphysics of Morals* by Immanuel Kant
2. *Leviathan* by Thomas Hobbes
3. *On the Genealogy of Morals* by Friedrich Nietzsche
4. *Situation Ethics* by Joseph Fletcher
5. *Utilitarianism* by John Stuart Mill

Short answer or essay question on the exam

Hey there!

I am so happy it is Christmas break. Finally I can have a few weeks to relax before the next semester starts. Finals went well thanks to all those hours in the library. I can't believe how much I studied this semester! I don't think I have ever studied so much in my life. Paige was a lifesaver on that Art History paper. Anyway, I am going to spend this holiday sleeping (a lot!) and of course hanging out with you and the rest of my old friends. I think I might also try to pick up a few games of soccer with my little brother. He just joined the middle school team. It will be fun to show him the ropes while I am at home. Hopefully I haven't lost my game since intramurals!

I had an interesting conversation with Muhammad and Nathan before school ended. While we were working out at the gym, a news special on academic dishonesty was playing on the televisions. Apparently a group of seniors at some university up north were expelled due to a huge cheating scandal. That, of course, started us talking about cheating and dishonesty, which eventually led us to the topic of ethics. Nathan shook his head and muttered something about karma. Naturally, I had heard of karma before, but I wasn't quite sure what he meant. He went on to say that the consequences of what we do for good or bad will eventually be returned back to us. This sounds very similar to Christianity, since I think I remember the Bible saying something about how your sins will eventually find you out. Of course, I doubt it is that simple.

This started me thinking about what Sarah and Mark might say. I know they don't believe in God or the Bible, so what do they base their ethical views on? Also, are they different? **What is the Secularist's basis for ethics?** And what is the Marxist's basis for ethics? I can imagine Paige, as a Postmodernist, would say that all truth is constructed and that we make our own truth, but what does that mean for ethics? **What do Postmodernists think about ethics?** To some degree, I understand Nathan's position, but **what is the basis of ethics for New Spiritualists?** Muhammad spoke up and said that it isn't karma that ultimately judges our actions. It is Allah. If we continually break Allah's law and act contrary to the example set by the prophet, then we will be eternally punished. I know that Islam calls God "Allah," but I am not sure what the prophet Muhammad had to do with right and wrong. And Christians believe that God gave us laws to obey. **What is the difference between the Islamic and Christian understanding of ethics?**

Thanks a lot for helping me out with all my questions! Good thing I have such an intelligent friend like you!

Talk to you later,
–Doug

UNIT

11

BIOLOGY

CHAPTER 11 LEARNING OBJECTIVES

Students will be able to:

1. discuss the history behind the battle between faith and science. [11.1]

2. identify how biology can provide a way of knowing about life. [11.2]

3. explain Secularism's approach to biology. [11.3]

4. explain Marxism's approach to biology. [11.4]

5. explain Postmodernism's approach to biology. [11.5]

6. explain New Spirituality's approach to biology. [11.6]

7. explain Islam's approach to biology. [11.7]

8. explain Christianity's approach to biology. [11.8]

9. state five reasons for concluding that the universe was designed. [11.8]

10. describe why intelligence best accounts for the existence and complexity of life. [11.9]

1. What is the central question biology seeks to answer? [11.2]

2. What is the next logical question to ask after "What is life?" [11.2]

3. How does Secularism view evolution? [11.3]

4. Why is it important to distinguish between microevolution and macroevolution? [11.3]

5. **What are the mechanisms believed to underlie macroevolution? [11.3]**

6. **What is neo-Darwinism? [11.3]**

7. **Is there a way to test Secularist evolutionary assumptions? [11.3]**

8. **Why is Darwinian evolution so important to Marxists? [11.4]**

9. Does Darwinian evolution actually support the Marxist idea of dialectical materialism? [11.4]

10. How does Postmodernism view evolution? [11.5]

11. What role does anti-essentialism play in Postmodernism? [11.5]

12. How does New Spirituality view evolution? [11.6]

13. What does New Spirituality see as the ultimate outcome of evolution? [11.6]

14. How does Islam view evolution? [11.7]

15. What aspects of creation are Muslims divided over? [11.7]

16. How does Christianity view evolution? [11.8]

17. How does the argument "Life only comes from pre-existing life" support the case for intelligent design? [11.8]

18. How does the argument "Random processes don't produce intelligible information" support the case for intelligent design? [11.8]

19. How does the argument "Living organisms give the appearance of design" support the case for intelligent design? [11.8]

20. Do most scientists today believe in Darwinian or neo-Darwinian evolution? [11.8]

21. We've looked at several arguments supporting intelligent design. What are some of the arguments against it? [11.9]

Today's reading is from Charles Darwin's seminal book *On the Origin of Species*, first published in 1859. This work is what launched evolution into worldwide fame and the theory became a household topic. Charles Darwin, whether intentionally or not, changed the course of science forever and, as a result, science and Christianity seemed to be at odds. It gave more and more scientists what they saw as a valid reason for rejecting God.

However, Darwin had some doubts about his theory and was mostly honest about them. For example, the concept of irreducible complexity was something he alluded to as being able to destroy his theory. Darwin did not believe he had discovered such a thing; thus he held that his theory was correct.

Darwin admitted ignorance of what actually causes the slight variations in natural selection. Still, he explains natural selection in a positive way, claiming that any change that results from it will always be beneficial. For this and other reasons, he confidently asserted his faith in this worldview.

A SELECTION FROM *ON THE ORIGIN OF SPECIES*
by Charles Darwin

Organs of Extreme Perfection and Complication

To suppose that the eye, with all its inimitable contrivances for adjusting the focus to different distances, for admitting different amounts of light, and for the correction of spherical and chromatic aberration, could have been formed by natural selection, seems, I freely confess, absurd in the highest possible degree. Yet reason tells me, that if numerous gradations from a perfect and complex eye to one very imperfect and simple, each grade being useful to its possessor, can be shown to exist; if further, the eye does vary ever so slightly, and the variations be inherited, which is certainly the case; and if any variation or modification in the organ be ever useful to an animal under changing conditions of life, then the difficulty of believing that a perfect and complex eye could be formed by natural selection, though insuperable by our imagination, can hardly be considered real. How a nerve comes to be sensitive to light, hardly concerns us more than how life itself first originated; but I may remark that several facts make me suspect that any sensitive nerve may be rendered sensitive to light, and likewise to those coarser vibrations of the air which produce sound.

In looking for the gradations by which an organ in any species has been perfected, we ought to look exclusively to its lineal ancestors; but this is scarcely ever possible, and we are forced in each case to look to species of the same group, that is to the collateral descendants from the same original parent-form, in order to see what gradations are possible, and for the chance of some gradations having been transmitted from the earlier stages of descent, in an unaltered or little altered condition. Amongst existing Vertebrata, we find but a small amount of gradation in the structure of the eye, and from fossil species we can learn nothing on this head. In this great class we should probably have to descend far beneath the lowest known fossiliferous stratum to discover the earlier stages, by which the eye has been perfected.

In the Articulata we can commence a series with an optic nerve merely coated with pigment, and without any other mechanism; and from this low stage, numerous gradations of structure, branching off in two fundamentally different lines, can be shown to exist, until we reach a moderately high stage of perfection. In certain crustaceans, for instance, there is a double cornea, the inner one divided into facets, within each of which there is a lens-shaped swelling. In other crustaceans the transparent cones which are coated by pigment, and which properly act only by excluding lateral pencils of light, are convex at their upper ends and must act by convergence; and at their lower ends there seems to be an imperfect vitreous substance. With these facts, here far too briefly and imperfectly given, which show that there is much graduated diversity in the eyes of living crustaceans, and bearing in mind how small the number of living animals is in proportion to those which have become extinct, I can see no very great difficulty (not more than in the case of many other structures) in believing that natural selection has converted the simple apparatus of an optic nerve merely coated with pigment and invested by transparent membrane, into an optical instrument as perfect as is possessed by any member of the great Articulate class.

He who will go thus far, if he find on finishing this treatise that large bodies of facts, otherwise inexplicable, can be explained by the theory of descent, ought not to hesitate to go further, and to admit that a structure even as perfect as the eye of an eagle might be formed by natural selection, although in this case he does not know any of the transitional grades. His reason ought to conquer his imagination; though I have felt the difficulty far too keenly to be surprised at any degree of hesitation in extending the principle of natural selection to such startling lengths.

It is scarcely possible to avoid comparing the eye to a telescope. We know that this instrument has been perfected by the long-continued efforts of the highest human intellects; and we naturally infer that the eye has been formed by a somewhat analogous process. But may not this inference be presumptuous? Have we any right to assume that the Creator works by intellectual powers like those of man? If we must compare the eye to an optical instrument, we ought in imagination to take a thick layer of transparent tissue, with a nerve sensitive to light beneath, and then suppose every part of this layer to be continually changing slowly in density, so as to separate into layers of different densities and thicknesses, placed at different distances from each other, and with the surfaces of each layer slowly changing in form. Further we must suppose that there is a power always intently watching each slight accidental alteration in the transparent layers; and carefully selecting each alteration which, under varied circumstances, may in any way, or in any degree, tend to produce a distincter image. We must suppose each new state of the instrument to be multiplied by the million; and each to be preserved till a better be produced, and then the old ones to be destroyed. In living bodies, variation will cause the slight alterations, generation will multiply them almost infinitely, and natural selection will pick out with unerring skill each improvement. Let this process go on for millions on millions of years; and during each year on millions of individuals of many kinds; and may we not believe that a living optical instrument might thus be formed as superior to one of glass, as the works of the Creator are to those of man?

If it could be demonstrated that any complex organ existed, which could not possibly have been formed by numerous, successive, slight modifications, my theory would absolutely break down. But I can find out no such case. No doubt many organs exist of which we do not know the transitional grades, more especially if we look to much-isolated species, round which, according to my theory, there has been much extinction. Or again, if we look to an organ common to all the members of a large class, for in this latter case the organ must have been first formed at an extremely remote period, since which all the many members of the class have been developed; and in order to discover the early transitional grades through which the organ has passed, we should have to look to very ancient ancestral forms, long since become extinct.

We should be extremely cautious in concluding that an organ could not have been formed by transitional gradations of some kind. Numerous cases could be given amongst the lower animals of the same organ performing at the same time wholly distinct functions; thus the alimentary canal respires, digests, and excretes in the larva of the dragon-fly and in the fish Cobites. In the Hydra, the animal may be turned inside out, and the exterior surface will then digest and the stomach respire. In such cases natural selection might easily specialise, if any advantage were thus gained, a part or organ, which had performed two functions, for one function alone, and thus wholly change its nature by insensible steps. Two distinct organs sometimes perform simultaneously the same function in the same individual; to give one instance, there are fish with gills or branchiae that breathe the air dissolved in the water, at the same time that they breathe free air in their swimbladders, this latter organ having a ductus pneumaticus for its supply, and being divided by highly vascular partitions. In these cases, one of the two organs might with ease be modified and perfected so as to perform all the work by itself, being aided during the process of modification by the other organ; and then this other organ might be modified for some other and quite distinct purpose, or be quite obliterated.

The illustration of the swimbladder in fishes is a good one, because it shows us clearly the highly important fact that an organ originally constructed for one purpose, namely flotation, may be converted into one for a wholly different purpose, namely respiration. The swimbladder has, also, been worked in as an accessory to the auditory organs of certain fish, or, for I do not know which view is now generally held, a part of the auditory apparatus has been worked in as a complement to the swimbladder. All physiologists admit that the swimbladder is homologous, or "ideally similar," in position and structure with the lungs of the higher vertebrate animals: hence there seems to me to be no great difficulty in believing that natural selection has actually converted a swimbladder into a lung, or organ used exclusively for respiration.

I can, indeed, hardly doubt that all vertebrate animals having true lungs have descended by ordinary generation from an ancient prototype, of which we know nothing, furnished with a floating apparatus or swimbladder. We can thus, as I infer from Professor Owen's interesting description of these parts, understand the strange fact that every particle of food and drink which we swallow has to pass over the orifice of the trachea, with some risk of falling into the lungs, notwithstanding the beautiful contrivance by which the glottis is closed. In the higher Vertebrata the branchiae have wholly disappeared—the slits on the sides of the neck and the loop-like course of the arteries still marking in the embryo their former position. But it is conceivable that the now utterly lost branchiae might have been gradually worked in by natural selection for some quite distinct purpose: in the same manner as, on the view entertained by some naturalists that the branchiae and dorsal scales of Annelids are homologous with the wings and wing-covers of insects, it is probable that organs which at a very ancient period served for respiration have been actually converted into organs of flight.

In considering transitions of organs, it is so important to bear in mind the probability of conversion from one function to another, that I will give one more instance. Pedunculated cirripedes have two minute folds of skin, called by me the ovigerous frena, which serve, through the means of a sticky secretion, to retain the eggs until they are hatched within the sack. These cirripedes have no branchiae, the whole surface of the body and sack, including the small frena, serving for respiration. The Balanidae or sessile cirripedes, on the other hand, have no ovigerous frena, the eggs lying loose at the bottom of the sack, in the well-enclosed shell; but they have large folded branchiae. Now I think no one will dispute that the ovigerous frena in the one family are strictly homologous with the branchiae of the other family; indeed, they graduate into each other. Therefore I do not doubt that little folds of skin, which originally served as ovigerous frena, but which, likewise, very slightly aided the act of respiration, have been gradually converted by natural selection into branchiae, simply through an increase in their size and the obliteration of their adhesive glands. If all pedunculated cirripedes had become extinct, and they have already suffered far more extinction than have sessile cirripedes, who would ever have imagined that the branchiae in this latter family had originally existed as organs for preventing the ova from being washed out of the sack?

Although we must be extremely cautious in concluding that any organ could not possibly have been produced by successive transitional gradations, yet, undoubtedly, grave cases of difficulty occur, some of which will be discussed in my future work.

One of the gravest is that of neuter insects, which are often very differently constructed from either the males or fertile females; but this case will be treated of in the next chapter. The electric organs of fishes offer another case of special difficulty; it is impossible to conceive by what steps these wondrous organs have been produced; but, as Owen and others have remarked, their intimate structure closely resembles that of common muscle; and as it has lately been shown that Rays have an organ closely analogous to the electric apparatus, and yet do not, as Matteuchi asserts, discharge any electricity, we must own that we are far too ignorant to argue that no transition of any kind is possible.

The electric organs offer another and even more serious difficulty; for they occur in only about a dozen fishes, of which several are widely remote in their affinities.

Generally when the same organ appears in several members of the same class, especially if in members having very different habits of life, we may attribute its presence to inheritance from a common ancestor; and its absence in some of the members to its loss through disuse or natural selection. But if the electric organs had been inherited from one ancient progenitor thus provided, we might have expected that all electric fishes would have been specially related to each other. Nor does geology at all lead to the belief that formerly most fishes had electric organs, which most of their modified descendants have lost. The presence of luminous organs in a few insects, belonging to different families and orders, offers a parallel case of difficulty. Other cases could be given; for instance in plants, the very curious contrivance of a mass of pollen-grains, borne on a foot-stalk with a sticky gland at the end, is the same in Orchis and Asclepias,—genera almost as remote as possible amongst flowering plants. In all these cases of two very distinct species furnished with apparently the same anomalous organ, it should be observed that, although the general appearance and function of the organ may be the same, yet some fundamental difference can generally be detected. I am inclined to believe that in nearly the same way as two men have sometimes independently hit on the very same invention, so natural selection, working for the good of each being and taking advantage of analogous variations, has sometimes modified in very nearly the same manner two parts in two organic beings, which owe but little of their structure in common to inheritance from the same ancestor.

Although in many cases it is most difficult to conjecture by what transitions an organ could have arrived at its present state; yet, considering that the proportion of living and known forms to the extinct and unknown is very small, I have been astonished how rarely an organ can be named, towards which no transitional grade is known to lead. The truth of this remark is indeed shown by that old canon in natural history of "Natura non facit saltum." We meet with this admission in the writings of almost every experienced naturalist; or, as Milne Edwards has well expressed it, nature is prodigal in variety, but niggard in innovation. Why, on the theory of Creation, should this be so? Why should all the parts and organs of many independent beings, each supposed to have been separately created for its proper place in nature, be so invariably linked together by graduated steps? Why should not Nature have taken a leap from structure to structure? On the theory of natural selection, we can clearly understand why she should not; for natural selection can act only by taking advantage of slight successive variations; she can never take a leap, but must advance by the shortest and slowest steps.

Organs of Little Apparent Importance

As natural selection acts by life and death,—by the preservation of individuals with any favourable variation, and by the destruction of those with any unfavourable deviation of structure,—I have sometimes felt much difficulty in understanding the origin of simple parts, of which the importance does not seem sufficient to cause the preservation of successively varying individuals. I have sometimes felt as much difficulty, though of a very different kind, on this head, as in the case of an organ as perfect and complex as the eye.

In the first place, we are much too ignorant in regard to the whole economy of any one organic being, to say what slight modifications would be of importance or not. In a former chapter I have given instances of most trifling characters, such as the down on fruit and the colour of the flesh, which, from determining the attacks of insects or from being correlated with constitutional differences, might assuredly be acted on by natural selection. The tail of the giraffe looks like an artificially constructed fly-flapper; and it seems at first incredible that this could have been adapted for its present purpose by successive slight modifications, each better and better, for so trifling an object as driving away flies; yet we should pause before being too positive even in this case, for we know that the distribution and existence of cattle and other animals in South America absolutely depends on their power of resisting the attacks of insects: so that individuals which could by any means defend themselves from these small enemies, would be able to range into new pastures and thus gain a great advantage. It is not that the larger quadrupeds are actually destroyed (except in some rare cases) by the flies, but they are incessantly harassed and their strength reduced, so that they are more subject to disease, or not so well enabled in a coming dearth to search for food, or to escape from beasts of prey.

Organs now of trifling importance have probably in some cases been of high importance to an early progenitor, and, after having been slowly perfected at a former period, have been transmitted in nearly the same state, although now become of very slight use; and any actually injurious deviations in their structure will always have been checked by natural selection. Seeing how important an organ of locomotion the tail is in most aquatic animals, its general presence and use for many purposes in so many land animals, which in their lungs or modified swimbladders betray their aquatic origin, may perhaps be thus accounted for. A well-developed tail having been formed in an aquatic animal, it might subsequently come to be worked in for all sorts of purposes, as a fly-flapper, an organ of prehension, or as an aid in turning, as with the dog, though the aid must be slight, for the hare, with hardly any tail, can double quickly enough.

In the second place, we may sometimes attribute importance to characters which are really of very little importance, and which have originated from quite secondary causes, independently of natural selection. We should remember that climate, food, etc., probably have some little direct influence on the organisation; that characters reappear from the law of reversion; that correlation of growth will have had a most important influence in modifying various structures; and finally, that sexual selection will often have largely modified the external characters of animals having a will, to give one male an advantage in fighting with another or in charming the females. Moreover when a modification of structure has primarily arisen from the above or other unknown causes, it may at first have been of no advantage to the species, but may subsequently have been taken advantage of by the descendants of the species under new conditions of life and with newly acquired habits.

To give a few instances to illustrate these latter remarks. If green woodpeckers alone had existed, and we did not know that there were many black and pied kinds, I dare say that we should have thought that the green colour was a beautiful adaptation to hide this tree-frequenting bird from its enemies; and consequently that it was a character of importance and might have been acquired through natural selection; as it is, I have no doubt that the colour is due to some quite distinct cause, probably to sexual selection. A trailing bamboo in the Malay Archipelago climbs the loftiest trees by the aid of exquisitely constructed hooks clustered around the ends of the branches, and this contrivance, no doubt, is of the highest service to the plant; but as we see nearly similar hooks on many trees which are not climbers, the hooks on the bamboo may have arisen from unknown laws of growth, and have been subsequently taken advantage of by the plant undergoing further modification and becoming a climber. The naked skin on the head of a vulture is generally looked at as a direct adaptation for wallowing in putridity; and so it may be, or it may possibly be due to the direct action of putrid matter; but we should be very cautious in drawing any such inference, when we see that the skin on the head of the clean-feeding male turkey is likewise naked. The sutures in the skulls of young mammals have been advanced as a beautiful adaptation for aiding parturition, and no doubt they facilitate, or may be indispensable for this act; but as sutures occur in the skulls of young birds and reptiles, which have only to escape from a broken egg, we may infer that this structure has arisen from the laws of growth, and has been taken advantage of in the parturition of the higher animals.

We are profoundly ignorant of the causes producing slight and unimportant variations; and we are immediately made conscious of this by reflecting on the differences in the breeds of our domesticated animals in different countries,—more especially in the less civilized countries where there has been but little artificial selection. Careful observers are convinced that a damp climate affects the growth of the hair, and that with the hair the horns are correlated. Mountain breeds always differ from lowland breeds; and a mountainous country would probably affect the hind limbs from exercising them more, and possibly even the form of the pelvis; and then by the law of homologous variation, the front limbs and even the head would probably be affected. The shape, also, of the pelvis might affect by pressure the shape of the head of the young in the womb. The laborious breathing necessary in high regions would, we have some reason to believe, increase the size of the chest; and again correlation would come into play. Animals kept by savages in different countries often have to struggle for their own subsistence, and would be exposed to a certain extent to natural selection, and individuals with slightly different constitutions would succeed best under different climates; and there is reason to believe that constitution and colour are correlated. A good observer, also, states that in cattle susceptibility to the attacks of flies is correlated with colour, as is the liability to be poisoned by certain plants; so that colour would be thus subjected to the action of natural selection. But we are far too ignorant to speculate on the relative importance of the several known and unknown laws of variation; and I have here alluded to them only to show that, if we are unable to account for the characteristic differences of our domestic breeds, which nevertheless we generally admit to have arisen through ordinary generation, we ought not to lay too much stress on our ignorance of the precise cause of the slight analogous differences between species. I might have adduced for this same purpose the differences between the races of man, which are so strongly marked; I may add that some little light can apparently be thrown on the origin of these differences, chiefly through sexual selection of a particular kind, but without here entering on copious details my reasoning would appear frivolous.

The foregoing remarks lead me to say a few words on the protest lately made by some naturalists, against the utilitarian doctrine that every detail of structure has been produced for the good of its possessor. They believe that very many structures have been created for beauty in the eyes of man, or for mere variety. This doctrine, if true, would be absolutely fatal to my theory. Yet I fully admit that many structures are of no direct use to their possessors. Physical conditions probably have had some little effect on structure, quite independently of any good thus gained. Correlation of growth has no doubt played a most important part, and a useful modification of one part will often have entailed on other parts diversified changes of no direct use. So again characters which formerly were useful, or which formerly had arisen from correlation of growth, or from other unknown cause, may reappear from the law of reversion, though now of no direct use. The effects of sexual selection, when displayed in beauty to charm the females, can be called useful only in rather a forced sense. But by far the most important consideration is that the chief part of the organisation of every being is simply due to inheritance; and consequently, though each being assuredly is well fitted for its place in nature, many structures now have no direct relation to the habits of life of each species. Thus, we can hardly believe that the webbed feet of the upland goose or of the frigate-bird are of special use to these birds; we cannot believe that the same bones in the arm of the monkey, in the fore leg of the horse, in the wing of the bat, and in the flipper of the seal, are of special use to these animals. We may safely attribute these structures to inheritance. But to the progenitor of the upland goose and of the frigate-bird, webbed feet no doubt were as useful as they now are to the most aquatic of existing birds. So we may believe that the progenitor of the seal had not a flipper, but a foot with five toes fitted for walking or grasping; and we may further venture to believe that the several bones in the limbs of the monkey, horse, and bat, which have been inherited from a common progenitor, were formerly of more special use to that progenitor, or its progenitors, than they now are to these animals having such widely diversified habits. Therefore we may infer that these several bones might have been acquired through natural selection, subjected formerly, as now, to the several laws of inheritance, reversion, correlation of growth, &c. Hence every detail of structure in every living creature (making some little allowance for the direct action of physical conditions) may be viewed, either as having been of special use to some ancestral form, or as being now of special use to the descendants of this form—either directly, or indirectly through the complex laws of growth.

Natural selection cannot possibly produce any modification in any one species exclusively for the good of another species; though throughout nature one species incessantly takes advantage of, and profits by, the structure of another. But natural selection can and does often produce structures for the direct injury of other species, as we see in the fang of the adder, and in the ovipositor of the ichneumon, by which its eggs are deposited in the living bodies of other insects. If it could be proved that any part of the structure of any one species had been formed for the exclusive good of another species, it would annihilate my theory, for such could not have been produced through natural selection. Although many statements may be found in works on natural history to this effect, I cannot find even one which seems to me of any weight. It is admitted that the rattlesnake has a poison-fang for its own defence and for the destruction of its prey; but some authors suppose that at the same time this snake is furnished with a rattle for its own injury, namely, to warn its prey to escape. I would almost as soon believe that the cat curls the end of its tail when preparing to spring, in order to warn the doomed mouse. But I have not space here to enter on this and other such cases.

Natural selection will never produce in a being anything injurious to itself, for natural selection acts solely by and for the good of each. No organ will be formed, as Paley has remarked, for the purpose of causing pain or for doing an injury to its possessor. If a fair balance be struck between the good and evil caused by each part, each will be found on the whole advantageous. After the lapse of time, under changing conditions of life, if any part comes to be injurious, it will be modified; or if it be not so, the being will become extinct, as myriads have become extinct.

Natural selection tends only to make each organic being as perfect as, or slightly more perfect than, the other inhabitants of the same country with which it has to struggle for existence. And we see that this is the degree of perfection attained under nature. The endemic productions of New Zealand, for instance, are perfect one compared with another; but they are now rapidly yielding before the advancing legions of plants and animals introduced from Europe. Natural selection will not produce absolute perfection, nor do we always meet, as far as we can judge, with this high standard under nature. The correction for the aberration of light is said, on high authority, not to be perfect even in that most perfect organ, the eye. If our reason leads us to admire with enthusiasm a multitude of inimitable contrivances in nature, this same reason tells us, though we may easily err on both sides, that some other contrivances are less perfect. Can we consider the sting of the wasp or of the bee as perfect, which, when used against many attacking animals, cannot be withdrawn, owing to the backward serratures, and so inevitably causes the death of the insect by tearing out its viscera?

If we look at the sting of the bee, as having originally existed in a remote progenitor as a boring and serrated instrument, like that in so many members of the same great order, and which has been modified but not perfected for its present purpose, with the poison originally adapted to cause galls subsequently intensified, we can perhaps understand how it is that the use of the sting should so often cause the insect's own death: for if on the whole the power of stinging be useful to the community, it will fulfill all the requirements of natural selection, though it may cause the death of some few members. If we admire the truly wonderful power of scent by which the males of many insects find their females, can we admire the production for this single purpose of thousands of drones, which are utterly useless to the community for any other end, and which are ultimately slaughtered by their industrious and sterile sisters? It may be difficult, but we ought to admire the savage instinctive hatred of the queen-bee, which urges her instantly to destroy the young queens her daughters as soon as born, or to perish herself in the combat; for undoubtedly this is for the good of the community; and maternal love or maternal hatred, though the latter fortunately is most rare, is all the same to the inexorable principle of natural selection. If we admire the several ingenious contrivances, by which the flowers of the orchis and of many other plants are fertilised through insect agency, can we consider as equally perfect the elaboration by our fir-trees of dense clouds of pollen, in order that a few granules may be wafted by a chance breeze on to the ovules?

On the Origin of the Species by Charles Darwin. Published in 1859, this work meets the criteria for fair use.

1. What are the key aspects of Darwin's theory of evolution?

2. How much of Darwin's theory was based on fact and how much was based on faith?

3. What was one thing that Darwin said would completely destroy his case for evolution?

4. What are some of the areas in which Darwin admitted ignorance or doubt?

5. Is there any place for evolution in the Christian worldview?

▶ "Myths of Evolution" Video

With Darwinian evolution asserted as truth in nearly every corner of academia, Sean McDowell dares to evaluate the evidence and systematically exposes five of the myths that have been passed off as settled scientific facts. Evolution is "change over time" and is categorized as microevolution and macroevolution. But the evidence cited for both types can also point to intelligent design, depending on your worldview.

To access this video, go to www.summitu.com/utt and enter the passcode found in the back of your manual.

_____ is a search for the truth about the natural world. Scientists begin with observations, then look for a theory that best accounts for the most data. Many worldviews begin with materialism and naturalism, so they can't see anything but evolution because they've dismissed the possibility of creation at the outset.

If Darwinian evolution is true, there is nothing special or unique about humans. We are just another type of primate, and it's okay to act like primates. But if we are made in the image of God according to a plan, there is a purpose to creation; it's not an unguided process.

Evolution is change over time.

_____ is the change within a specific species. It may be caused by natural selection and is not controversial.

_____ is Darwin's grand theory of how all organisms came about from a common ancestor by blind chance. It has two components:

1. _____: All life came from a common ancestor. This was believed before Darwin, but it couldn't be explained apart from an intelligent agent.

2. _____: Life evolved through an unguided process of random mutation.

Five "proofs" of evolution that turn out to be myths:

1. **Miller Urey experiment:** This produced amino acids, but it was totally designed, not a random process. There is no evidence this "prebiotic soup" ever existed, and the amino acids produced weren't living cells.

2. **Darwin's Tree of Life:** Geology doesn't show the fine iterations in this theory. The biggest division and range of animal types should come later but they're at the beginning during times like the Cambrian era, 520 million years ago.

3. _____: Different species have similar structure that transcends organism. Darwin says this shows common ancestry that has adapted to different needs. But it also can be seen as evidence for intelligent design (e.g., the iPad, iPod, and iPhone are similar because they were made by the same designers, not because they evolved from each other).

4. **Haeckel's Embryos:** The premise was that similar embryos become widely different as they develop, mirroring the process of evolution. But Haeckel's embryos were faked. This is one of the most famous hoaxes in biology.

5. **Bacterial** _____: Bacteria show creative potential to adapt to life-threatening changes, but when the antibiotic is removed the bacteria revert to their original state. Adaption is short-lived and doesn't prove long-term, positive adaptation.

1. What is the difference between microevolution and macroevolution? Do creationists reject both types?

2. Is Darwinism a more valid explanation of creation than intelligent design?

3. Was "common descent" a new idea introduced by Darwin to explain where all life came from?

4. What are the five myths McDowell debunks in this lecture? Pick one to explain in front of the class.

5. How can you show that belief in Darwinian evolution is driven more by worldview than by the data?

Chapter 11 Key Points

Key Questions:

1. What is biology?
2. How do the six dominant Western worldviews approach biology?

Key Terms:

1. Anti-essentialism*
2. Biology*
3. Collective Consciousness
4. Eugenics
5. Gene Flow
6. Genetic Drift
7. Intelligent Design Movement
8. Irreducible Complexity
9. Macroevolution
10. Microevolution
11. Mutation
12. Natural Selection
13. Neo-Darwinism*
14. Progressive Creationism
15. Punctuated Equilibrium*
16. Selective Breeding
17. Special Creation*
18. Spiritual Evolution*
19. Spontaneous Generation
20. Theistic Evolution
21. Young Age Creationism

Key Verses:

1. Genesis 1:1
2. John 1:1–3
3. Colossians 1:16–17
4. Hebrews 11:3

Key Players:

1. Charles Darwin
2. Carl Sagan
3. Niles Eldredge
4. Stephen Jay Gould
5. Daniel Dennett

Key Works:

1. *Darwin's Dangerous Idea* by Daniel Dennett
2. *The Dragons of Eden* by Carl Sagan
3. *On the Origin of the Species* by Charles Darwin
4. *Punctuated Equilibrium* by Stephen Jay Gould

Short answer or essay question on the exam

Hello there!

Well, school has started back, and today is the first day. I am really going to miss sleeping in every day! It is nice to get back to a routine though: up at 8:30 a.m., grab a cup of coffee (or three), and run to catch the bus. It is awesome getting to see Sarah and the gang again. We are probably going to meet up for coffee this week to finally decide on a book. I'll let you know if we actually pick something!

I've seen a lot of flyers up around campus advertising different clubs and organizations to get involved in throughout the semester. Did you know we have a sky diving club and a scuba club? It is pretty awesome. Apparently student government elections are going to be held at the end of the semester. It might be neat to run for office! Obviously, I wouldn't be able to be president or anything like that, but maybe I could be a senator. Getting involved with major decisions affecting the campus would be an amazing opportunity. Who knows? I might even decide to be a political science major. Politics could use some Christian involvement, huh?

My class schedule is pretty great this semester. I am taking Intro to Psychology, Political Theory 101, History of Western Civilization, biology, and macro-economics. Right now, I am really jazzed about biology. The professor is cool, but she actually lectured and assigned us homework for the first day of class. She began talking about evolution and how it is responsible for producing everything we see around us. It was weird to hear her call humans just another animal. She said that anyone who believes differently is ignoring the scientific evidence; evolution is a fact, and she will not teach "religious views" in her class. I know that, as Christians, we believe that God created us after his image, which separates us from the animals. Yet my professor claims that evolution is undeniably true and everything else is merely religion.

Maybe you can help me! Sarah didn't seem to be affected by what the professor said. In fact, Sarah seemed to agree with her wholeheartedly. **What do Secularists believe about the theory of evolution?** I asked Mark what he thought since he usually seems to agree with Sarah. He said something about the traditional theory of evolution operating too slowly. I'm not completely sure how else it could work. **What do Marxists believe about the theory of evolution?** I also asked Nathan what he thought since he believes everything is divine. He began to talk about evolution in a "spiritual" sense instead of a biological one. Given Nathan's theology, I guess this makes sense. Then again, I'm still a bit fuzzy on the concept. **How does New Spirituality view evolution?** Finally, if evolution is treated as an undeniable fact, **why is it important for Christians to focus on origins?**

Good thing you are in a worldview class! I wish I had taken one while I was in high school. Maybe then I wouldn't have all these questions in college! Anyway, I hope you are doing well. It was great seeing you over Christmas. Hopefully we can hang out over spring break!

See you later!
–Doug

UNIT

12

10c

PSYCHOLOGY

CHAPTER 12 LEARNING OBJECTIVES

Students will be able to:

1. define psychology. [12.1]

2. discuss why understanding the nature of the soul is important to psychology. [12.2]

3. explain Secularism's approach to psychology. [12.3]

4. explain Marxism's approach to psychology. [12.4]

5. explain Postmodernism's approach to psychology. [12.5]

6. explain New Spirituality's approach to psychology. [12.6]

7. explain Islam's approach to psychology. [12.7]

8. explain Christianity's approach to psychology. [12.8]

9. list four advantages to the Christian approach to psychology. [12.8]

1. What is psychology and what questions does it seek to answer? [12.1]

2. Where does psychology focus its attention? [12.2]

3. Does modern psychology see a difference between the "soul" and the "self"? [12.2]

4. What assumptions shape secular psychology? [12.3]

5. What are the three forces that combined to shape secular psychology? [12.3]

6. What are the main assumptions of third force psychology? [12.3]

7. What is self-actualization and how is it achieved? [12.3]

8. What did Pavlov's experiments prove?

9. What assumptions shape Marxist psychology? [12.4]

10. How does classical conditioning support the Marxist belief in dialectical materialism? [12.4]

11. What assumptions shape postmodern psychology? [12.5]

12. The idea of multiple selves creates multiple problems. Can you name a few? [12.5]

13. **What assumptions shape New Spiritualist psychology? [12.6]**

14. **What is the New Spiritualist view of psychological health and how does it differ from other worldviews? [12.6]**

15. **What assumptions shape Islamic psychology? [12.7]**

16. **How do Islam and Christianity differ when it comes to understanding human nature? [12.7]**

17. **What assumptions shape Christian psychology? [12.8]**

18. **How does Christianity's view of the soul differ from other worldviews?" [12.8]**

19. **What does Christianity identify as the source of all psychological problems?" [12.8]**

20. **What therapeutic possibilities does Christianity have that are unavailable to materialism? [12.8]**

21. **What is transmodern psychology? [12.9]**

22. **In what way is every person offered the same choice as Adam and Eve? [12.9]**

In this excerpt from Francis Schaeffer's book *Pollution and the Death of Man*, Schaeffer reveals what he believes to be four broken relationships as a result of the fall:

- humanity and God
- humanity and self
- humanity and humanity
- humanity and nature

These relationships, Schaeffer argues, are broken and will remain so without Christ's grace and aid. The good news is that Christ's work on the cross is sufficient to begin the healing process, and that upon his return, all will be reconciled back to God.

As you read through this material, consider these four types of relationships in your own life and then consider them in the lives of others. How can you help bring healing in your life and in the lives of others?

A Substantial Healing

by Francis Schaeffer

In Romans 8 Paul looks ahead to what is going to happen when Jesus Christ comes back again. He writes: "For the earnest expectation of the creation waiteth for the manifestation of the sons of God [the Christians]. For the creation was made subject to vanity [i.e., frustration], not willingly, but by reason of him who hath subjected the same in hope. Because the creation itself also shall be delivered from the bondage of corruption into the glorious liberty of the children of God. For we know that the whole creation groaneth and travaileth in pain together until now. And not only they, but ourselves also, who have the first fruits of the Spirit [i.e., the Christians], even we ourselves groan within ourselves, waiting for the adoption, that is, the redemption of our body."

What Paul says there is that when our bodies are raised from the dead, at that time nature too will be redeemed. The blood of the Lamb will redeem man and nature together. There is a parallel here to the time of Moses in Egypt when the blood applied to the doorposts saved not only the sons of the Hebrews, but also their animals.

As we stressed in the last chapter, the Bible has no place at all for Platonic distinctions about nature. As Christ's death redeems men, including their bodies, from the consequences of the Fall, so His death will redeem all nature from the Fall's evil consequences at the time when we are raised from the dead.

In Romans 6 Paul applies this future principle to our present situation. It is the great principle of Christian spirituality. Christ died, Christ is our Savior, Christ is coming back again to raise us from the dead. So by faith—because this is true to what has been in Christ's death and to what will be when He comes again, by faith, in the power of the Holy Spirit—we are to live this way substantially now. "Now if we be dead with Christ, we believe that we shall also live with him. Likewise, reckon ye also yourselves to be dead indeed unto sin, but alive unto God through Jesus Christ, our Lord." So we look forward to this, and one day it will be perfect. But we should be looking now, on the basis of the work of Christ, for substantial healing in every area affected by the Fall.

We must understand that even in our relationship with God, a distinction has to be made here. By justification our guilt was completely removed, in a forensic way, as God declared our guilt gone when we accepted Christ as our Savior. But in practice, in our lives between becoming a Christian and the second coming of Christ or our death, we are not in a perfect relationship to God. Therefore, real spirituality lies in the existential, moment-by-moment looking to the work of Christ—seeking and asking God in faith for a substantial reality in our relationship with Him at the present moment. I must be doing this so that substantially, in practice, at this moment, there will be a reality in my relationship with the personal God who is there.

This is also true in other areas, because the Fall, as the Reformation theology has always emphasized, not only separated man from God, but also caused other deep separations. It is interesting that almost the whole "curse" in Genesis 3 is centered upon the outward manifestations. It is the earth that is going to be cursed for man's sake. It is the woman's body that is involved in the pain of childbirth.

So there are other divisions. Man was divided from God, first; and then, ever since the Fall, man is separated from himself. These are the psychological divisions. I am convinced that this is the basic psychosis: that the individual man is divided from himself as a result of the Fall.

The next division is that man is divided from other men; these are the sociological divisions. And then man is divided from nature, and nature is divided from nature. So there are these multiple divisions, and one day, when Christ comes back, there is going to be a complete healing of all of them, on the basis of the "blood of the Lamb."

But Christians who believe the Bible are not simply called to say that "one day" there will be healing, but that by God's grace, upon the basis of the work Of Christ, substantial healing can be a reality here and now.

Here the church—the orthodox, Bible believing church—has been really poor. What have we done to heal sociological divisions? Often our churches are a scandal; they are cruel not only to the man "outside," but also to the man "inside."

The same thing is true psychologically. We load people with psychological problems by telling them that "Christians don't have breakdowns," and that is a kind of murder.

On the other hand, what we should have, individually and corporately, is a situation where, on the basis of the work of Christ, Christianity is seen to be not just "pie in the sky," but something that has in it the possibility of substantial healing now in every area where there are divisions because of the Fall. First of all, my division from God is healed by justification, but then there must be the "existential reality" of this moment by moment. Second, there is the psychological division of man from himself. Third, the sociological divisions of man from other men. And lastly, the division of man from nature, and nature from nature. In all of these areas we should do what we can to bring forth substantial healing.

I took a long while to settle on that word "substantially," but it is, I think, the right word. It conveys the idea of a healing that is not perfect, but nevertheless is real and evident. Because of past history and future history, we are called upon to live this way now by faith.

When we carry these ideas over into the area of our relationship to nature, there is an exact parallel. On the basis of the fact that there is going to be total redemption in the future, not only of man but of all creation, the Christian who believes the Bible should be the man who—with God's help and in the power of the Holy Spirit—is treating nature now in the direction of the way nature will be then. It will not now be perfect, but there should be something substantial or we have missed our calling. God's calling to the Christian now, and to the Christian community, in the area of nature (just as it is in the area of personal Christian living in true spirituality) is that we should exhibit a substantial healing here and now, between man and nature and nature and itself, as far as Christians can bring it to pass.

In *Novum Organum Scientiarum* Francis Bacon wrote: "Man by the fall fell at the same time from his state of innocence and from his dominion over nature. Both of these losses, however, even in this life, can in some part be repaired; the former by religion and faith, the latter by the arts and sciences." It is a tragedy that the church, including the orthodox, evangelical church, has not always remembered that. Here, in this present life, it is possible for the Christian to have some share, through sciences and the arts, in returning nature to its proper place.

Taken from *Pollution and the Death of Man* by Francis A. Schaeffer, © 1970, originally published by Tyndale House, Wheaton, Illinois. This edition published by Crossway. pp. 63–68. Used by permission of Crossway, a publishing ministry of Good News Publishers, Wheaton, IL 60187, www.crossway.org.

1. What does Romans 8 teach will happen *when* Christ returns?

2. What does Romans 6 teach needs to happen *until* Christ returns?

3. What is the difference between our "position" in Christ and our "practice" of the Christian life?

4. The Fall described in Genesis 3 brought about what kinds of divisions in creation?

5. If all creation will be healed, how should we be treating the natural world today?

Abdu Murray addresses the arguments of Freud and others, showing that atheism is as much of a crutch as theism. Everyone has a crutch to get through life, the question is, which crutch is sturdier? Human crutches rely on ingenuity, self-actualization, and personal efforts that are woefully inadequate. Christianity is a more reliable crutch because it depends on a savior who is more than human. Murray demonstrates that Christianity has empirical adequacy, logical consistency, and historical evidence—especially of the resurrection—to prove its trustworthiness.

To access this video, go to www.summitu.com/utt and enter the passcode found in the back of your manual.

▶ "Is Christianity Just a Crutch?" Video Outline

Some people believe Christianity is a crutch to get through life. After all, if things are going well and they are fulfilled, why would they need God? They think Christianity is a _____ crutch for those who are too weak to face reality.

_____ taught that Christianity is a defense mechanism to deal with what terrifies us or was a way to resolve father issues. Christians invented a sky daddy as a neurosis to deal with the problems in their lives.

But Freud's argument can be turned on atheists as well. They get rid of God because they want autonomy and have daddy issues of their own. _____ is as much a crutch as Christianity. In fact, everyone needs a crutch. The question isn't whether they have a crutch but whether their crutch strong.

A sturdy crutch needs to have empirical adequacy, logical consistency, and personal relevance. We can't be our own crutch. If we are the problem, how can we be the solution? We need someone who is not us to save us from ourselves.

Other religions aren't good crutches for the same reason. Every religious system but Christianity says we are our own _____:

1. We are divine beings who need to realize our own perfection.
2. We need to lean on our own wisdom and ingenuity.
3. We need to work harder to make ourselves worthy of mercy.

Christianity is a reliable crutch because of Jesus Christ. He paid the price for our sins. He has credibility because of the resurrection. This is a historical fact that's empirically verifiable. Most scholars agree there is a strong "CASE" for the resurrection:

- **C**—The _____ happened in a specific time and place with thousands of witnesses.
- **A**—**Appearances** of the risen Christ changed the disciples from cowards to martyrs.
- **S**—_____ like Paul and James were converted and converted others.
- **E**—The _____ was never refuted by enemies with every reason and resource to do so.

There are good reasons to believe in Jesus that are factual, logically consistent, and relevant to our lives. Faith isn't about belief when there is no evidence. Faith is the _____ of things not seen (Hebrews 11:1). Faith means trusting because we have good reason to believe.

Christianity is a crutch worthy of our trust.

1. Is it a sign of weakness to need an emotional or spiritual crutch to get through life?

2. Why did Sigmund Freud see Christianity as a harmful neurosis?

3. How is the "Christian crutch" different from what other religious systems offer by way of support?

4. What makes Christianity a sturdier crutch than other worldviews or religious systems?

5. Is true faith based on reason or contrary to it?

Chapter 12 Key Points

Key Questions:

1. What is psychology?
2. How do the six dominant Western worldviews approach psychology?

Key Terms:

1. Behaviorism
2. Classical Conditioning*
3. Cognitive Behaviorism
4. Decentered Self*
5. Epiphenomenalism
6. *Fitrah*
7. Fourth Force Psychology*
8. Higher Consciousness
9. Mind/Body Monism*
10. Mind/Body Dualism*
11. Positive Psychology
12. Psychoanalysis
13. Psychology*
14. Self-actualization*
15. Third Force Psychology
16. Visualization

Key Verses:

1. Genesis 2:7
2. Jeremiah 17:9
3. Matthew 10:28
4. Ephesians 2:1–3

Key Players:

1. Sigmund Freud
2. Erich Fromm
3. Jacques Lacan
4. Abraham Maslow
5. Ivan Pavlov
6. Carl Rogers
7. B. F. Skinner
8. L. S. Vygotsky

Key Works:

1. *Ecrits* by Jacques Lacan
2. *A Theory of Human Motivation* by Abraham Maslow
3. *Civilization and Its Discontents* by Sigmund Freud
4. *The Interpretation of Dreams* by Sigmund Freud
5. *Conditioned Reflexes* by Ivan Pavlov
6. *On Becoming a Person* by Carl Rogers
7. *About Behaviorism* by B.F. Skinner
8. *Beyond Freedom and Dignity* by B.F. Skinner
9. *Science and Human Behavior* by B.F. Skinner

Short answer or essay question on the exam

Hello there!

This weekend was *awesome*! The gang met up at the front lawn to play some ultimate Frisbee while we still have a warm spell. I was not expecting so many really good players here, but boy was I wrong! We had three different teams, so each team alternated games. After about four hours, everyone was wiped out. Sarah didn't play, so she brought smoothies for everyone. We really needed them after all that running. Nathan and I had an epic moment where he threw the Frisbee over the head of the tallest guy, and I miraculously caught it while running into the in-zone. Paige was taking pictures during all the games, and she managed to capture that play on camera. Needless to say, that picture will be on my wall as soon as she prints it. Overall, we placed second, but it was still a blast. If it doesn't snow next weekend, we might meet up again for round two.

School has not been busy lately, so I have had more time to just relax and catch up on some reading. I finished C. S. Lewis's Space Trilogy last week. Have you read it? If not, you definitely should. C. S. Lewis is a fantastic author. My favorite was the last book, *That Hideous Strength*. All of the bioethics stuff was really interesting, especially since I am taking biology. It is crazy to imagine what science could do without the ethical boundaries like we talked about a few weeks ago.

In my Intro to Psychology class, we have been learning about theories of human behavior. This week, the class focused specifically on behaviorism. Behaviorism is basically an approach in psychology that sees humans as stimulus receptors who respond in predetermined ways to their environment. B.F. Skinner, the founder of behaviorism, taught that everything is learned through interactions with the environment. We are shaped solely by the world around us. Apparently this is not as prominent now as it used to be.

Sarah, Mark, Paige, and I were talking about it over coffee. I guess Sarah took the class last semester. She began talking about the third-force psychology. In an effort to avoid looking ignorant, I didn't bother asking her what "third force psychology" was. Mark went on to say that behaviorism doesn't make sense because it cannot account for free will. He mentioned Pavlov and tied his research to the dialectic. **How does Secularism view psychology?** And **how does Marxism view psychology?** Paige chimed into the conversation saying we cannot understand the self as a unified entity. Instead, we have a multiplicity of selves. I don't really understand what that means. **How does Postmodernism view psychology?** As I was talking with Mark and Paige, I began to wonder how Nathan, as a New Spiritualist, would think about the soul. **How does New Spirituality view the concept of the self?** I know the Bible teaches that human beings are fallen and composed of immaterial souls. I bet this affects how we practice psychology. **What is the Christian view of psychology?**

Well it is already past midnight here. I guess that means I should get some sleep before my 8:30 a.m. class tomorrow. Thanks again for all your help! You're the best.

Talk to you soon,
–Doug

UNIT **13**

SOCIOLOGY

CHAPTER 13 LEARNING OBJECTIVES

Students will be able to:

1. describe the history of sociology. [13.1]

2. identify reasons why sociology is important. [13.2]

3. explain Secularism's approach to sociology. [13.3]

4. explain Marxism's approach to sociology. [13.4]

5. explain Postmodernism's approach to sociology. [13.5]

6. explain New Spirituality's approach to sociology. [13.6]

7. explain Islam's approach to sociology. [13.7]

8. explain Christianity's approach to sociology. [13.8]

9. list seven unique implications of the Christian approach to sociology. [13.8]

1. What is Sociology and how did it get its start? [13.1]

2. Why has our social situation today been likened to a civil war of values? [13.1]

3. Is the idea of Christian sociology an oxymoron? [13.2]

4. What is the starting point of secular sociology? [13.3]

5. What issues does determinism raise for secular sociology? [13.3]

6. If there's no personal sin, how does secular sociology explain bad behavior? [13.3]

7. What alternatives to the traditional family does secular sociology propose? What are the dangers of such alternatives? [13.3]

8. How familiar are you with LGBT (lesbian, gay, bisexual, transgender) issues? What are some examples of their impact upon American society?

9. What is the starting point of Marxist sociology? [13.4]

10. Why are religion and family such problem for Marxist sociology? [13.4]

11. How does Marxist sociology treat the traditional family? [13.4]

12. What is the starting point of Postmodernist sociology? [13.5]

13. What are some of the stumbling blocks Postmodernist sociology seeks to remove? [13.5]

14. Why is Postmodernist sociology so obsessed with sex? [13.5]

15. What is the starting point of New Spiritualist sociology? [13.6]

16. What are some of the old "limits" New Spiritualist sociology seeks to overcome? [13.6]

17. What is the starting point of Islamic sociology? [13.7]

18. Can you identify some of the inequities built into traditional Islamic society? [13.7]

19. Does Islam make a distinction between social institutions and the state? [13.7]

20. What is the starting point of Christian sociology? [13.8]

21. What is sphere sovereignty and how does it produce a healthy society? [13.8]

22. How does Christian sociology understand free will and individual responsibility? [13.8]

23. What makes Christian sociology radically different from its secular counterpart? [13.9]

24. What do you think are the specific tasks Christ assigned his church?

Charles Moore draws on the New Testament and his own experience to paint a picture of Christian community as it is meant to be, not how it often is in today's church. Christians are connected to one another in Christ, and what that means practically is spelled out in the "one-another" verses, of which Moore lists twenty-one. To live these out requires a commitment of time, space, resources, accountability, and forgiveness.

Moore gives examples from the early church of what it means to live in authentic community in such a way that the world is convinced of the truthfulness of the gospel. He quotes Stanley Hauerwas, who says, "What is crucial is not that Christians know the truth, but that they be the truth," and insists that the strongest argument for Christianity's truthfulness consists of the lives (and communities) it produces.

Doing Life Together
by Charles Moore

> Fellowship is life, and lack of fellowship is death;
> fellowship is heaven, and lack of fellowship is hell;
> and the deeds that ye do upon the earth
> it is for fellowship's sake that ye do them.
> — William Morris

If I've read the New Testament right, as followers of Christ, we are members of Christ's body (1 Cor. 12:14–21), and hence, by definition, we belong to each other. We cannot intentionally follow Christ solo. Interdependence, not independence, is God's pattern. In other words, there is no such thing as a lone-ranger Christian. When we fail to connect with each other we are failing to connect with Jesus.

But what does it mean to *connect* with one another? Sadly, superficiality is a disease of our time. Shallow friendships and fragile relationships mark not only our society but also the church. Even our language betrays such superficiality. Consider how we use the word "fellowship" in Christian gatherings. In Acts 2:42 we read that the early Christians "devoted themselves to the fellowship." They did not occasionally have fellowship (verb). They *were* the fellowship (noun); marked by a shared life together. They were devoted *to each other*, and so they were being woven together in mutual care. It involved a common, daily, material life of unity and sharing. The early church experienced daily life *together* in Christ, and this was how they were constituted as a fellowship.

Biblically speaking, therefore, fellowship is far more than spilling coffee on one another on Sunday morning. It extends far beyond "getting together" and experiencing a rush of relational warm fuzzies during hyped-up religious happenings. Sadly, very few of us experience our life together as did the early Christians. They did not consider what they had as their own. Theirs was a common, daily, material life of unity and sharing. We, however, assemble and associate and meet at regular intervals, but our lives and pocket books are still very much our own. Our lives really don't intersect. We share commonly very little.

Re-Membering the Body

From what I have read and heard, right after the collapse of the Twin Towers, one might inadvertently come across a human body part, like a finger or a toe. The thought of dismemberment both shocks and repulses us. It not only is incongruous, but a severed body part is not quite human; removed from the body it is horrendously out of place.

Now if we would but step back and actually see how fractured and dismembered our country has become, how severed and alienated, and how conflicted and fearful we are of each other, if we could but see how frightfully alone we have become, we might become more repulsed and begin to see what it is that ails us both individually and socially. We might also discover anew the plan and purpose of God revealed in Christ's prayer for unity: "That they may be one, Father, as you and I are one …" (John 17:21ff).

Herein lies the gift and witness of Christ's body: the church on earth. God's people can, by their manner of life together, be the very thing the world cannot achieve on its own steam. But it is important to grasp that following Jesus is nothing if it is not a way, a life, a living, and a living together. It's all about *togetherness*. Consider, for example, the reciprocal pronoun "one another" (*allelon*) in the New Testament. This one word alone highlights the significance of doing life together:

- Outdo one another in showing honor (Rom. 12:10)
- Live in harmony with one another (Rom. 12:16)
- Admonish one another (Rom. 15:14)
- Greet one another with a holy kiss (Rom. 16:16)
- Wait for one another (1 Cor. 11:33)
- Have the same care for one another (1 Cor. 12:25)
- Be servants of one another (Gal. 5:13)
- Bear one another's burdens (Gal. 6:2)
- Comfort one another (1 Thess. 5:11)
- Build one another up (1 Thess. 5:11)
- Be at peace with one another (1 Thess. 5:13)
- Do good to one another (1 Thess. 5:15)
- Put up with one another in love (Eph. 4:2)
- Be kind and compassionate to one another (Eph. 4:32)
- Submit to one another (Eph. 5:21)

- Forgive one another (Col. 3:13)
- Confess your sins to one another (James 5:16)
- Pray for one another (James 5:16)
- Love one another from the heart (1 Pet. 1:22)
- Be hospitable to one another (1 Pet. 4:9)
- Meet one another with humility (1 Pet. 5:5)

Now when we reflect on the above list, one thing is clear: Virtually none of the above exhortations make sense without a serious level of *commitment* to one another. How are we to bear another person's burden unless the burden is known and unless we are willing to actually carry it? How are we to "put up with each other" unless we relate closely enough to get on each other's nerves? How are we to forgive one another unless we are in each other's lives enough to hurt and let down one another? How can we learn to submit to one another unless we struggle with differences? In other words, if we are to connect (or reconnect) our lives with one another, it will demand much more of us than we normally give. To be the church, and not just go to church, demands a great deal more than many of us are willing to give.

Few of us are ready to build up a common, committed life with others on a daily level, especially if it costs us a pay raise or causes us to forgo our personal preferences. If we are honest, we take our primary social cues from the broader culture. We consider our lives as "ours," independent of or above the church in some way. But experiencing genuine Christian community will never happen if you are hanging on to your own life or if your schedule only allows for a couple of "religious" meetings a week. New lifestyle habits will have to form. Sacrifices of convenience and of giving up private spaces and personal preferences will have to be made. It will involve making concerted choices so that others can more naturally and easily be in, and not just around, your life.

Doing life together demands commitment. But it involves more than this. Without engaging in some very concrete practices, life together, instead of being a joy, may be hell.

Life Together

Commitment is the basis, but community in Christ is the aim. What might this look like in more concrete terms? What are the marks that signify authentic Christian fellowship beyond going to church on Sundays? What does a shared life really look like in which the Spirit bears its fruit?

Time: Perhaps the first fruit of commitment is *time.* Those who love one another spend time with each other. When I was in college and seminary I purposely took fewer credits than I could handle, just so I could make more time for others. As the years have gone by, finding time for others has become more difficult. A stark example of this occurred when I was living in an intentional Christian community in downtown Denver. A group of us, mostly in our thirties, lived in four duplexes right next to each other. We wanted to go on a back-packing trip together, but wouldn't you know, there was not one available weekend in the summer where we could all be together. Though we managed to share "space" together, our time was another matter.

Time is important because without being available to each other, fulfilling the biblical "one anothers" is virtually impossible. Take the construction metaphor of "building one another up." Building is a process that requires effort and persistence. Leaving a project undone will do damage to the materials. And if it is not done together who knows what will result? Or take the command to "do good to one another." It takes time to discern what is good for another person. I remember very well when I accidentally put a young college student into an emotional tailspin. I gave her a very strong challenge that completely backfired. I didn't realize she had been severely abused as a child and constantly struggled with suicidal feelings. If I had taken the time to know her better, I would have handled things very differently.

Time is crucial if we are really to "serve one another." Interestingly, the New Testament concept of service means performing lowly, thankless deeds—as a slave would do. This is what Jesus modeled when he washed his disciples' feet. The slave serves the master as he has need. Our gifts are less important than our readiness to serve. This hit home to me while I was in seminary. Jake, a fellow seminarian, and his wife Sharon were struggling to keep their home sane. They had two small boys, and Sharon had several medical needs. Their house, especially their kitchen, was a disaster. I was busy myself, but not at 10:30 PM. That was downtime before bed. I felt a nudge inside me that I should offer to do their dishes at that time. Did I want to? No. But a slave of Christ doesn't have the luxury of choosing which service to perform and when. They accepted my offer, and for two years this is what I did. Jake has been a life-long friend ever since.

Space: As important as time is, so is sharing space. This may or may not mean living with one another under the same roof. But it will mean finding practical ways of becoming more proximate with each other. The notion of a commuter marriage is an oxymoron. So is a commuter church. Unless we are physically present in each other's lives, unless our personal spaces are made available to one another, sharing life will only be skin deep.

Throughout history believers have found various ways of sanctifying space together. The earliest Christians formed neighborhoods within cities. The Celtic church created entire villages, sharing everything in common. Then there were various monastic orders, and during the Reformation radical reformers, like the Anabaptists, formed outright communities, some consisting of as many as 2,000 people. Today there are churches that revolve around cluster groups and there are groups like Jesus People USA in Chicago, or Community of Sojourners in San Francisco, or the Community of Jesus on Cape Cod, who have forged their own unique ways of drawing together in close proximity. Whatever its size, shape, or form, a living fellowship will seek very physical ways to share life together.

Of course, community demands more than sharing time and space. A fellowship of Christians is not the same things as a *Christian* fellowship. Doing life together must be done *in Christ*—in other words, in a way where Christ's authority holds sway. For this to happen, we must learn to listen to the Word—both in the Bible and as the Spirit speaks through others—and obey it *together*. Personal study of the Scriptures is vital, but God's Word has always been primarily addressed to his people—as a people! Interestingly, almost all the New Testament Epistles are written to churches! And when we think about the various "one another" commands, they can be fulfilled only if they are accomplished with others. Being under the Word is not just a matter of listening to a sermon together, but seeking with each other, by way of dialogue and prayer, what it means to obey Christ together. In my own church community, for instance, we regularly read the Scriptures together and then ask: "What must we do?" Recently, we felt convicted by how much unnecessary "stuff" we all had. So on a Saturday we all went through our houses, and with feedback from each other, got rid of piles of things that we really didn't need. We brought everything to one place to be either hauled away or sold. We did this all together in order to show God that we were serious about doing his Word. And by doing it together, we dealt a deathblow to the spirit of Mammon that wreaks so much havoc in our world. This was obviously not easy to do, but discipleship certainly isn't easy, and it definitely involves discipline (1 Cor. 9:24–27).

Resources: Another mark of life together is being open-handed with the excess that we have. "*Koinonia*" is not solely translated as "fellowship." In fact, its predominate use denotes the sharing of resources. The Macedonian and Achaian churches, for example, set up a common fund (*koinonian*) for the impoverished church in Jerusalem. Since the Gentiles shared (*ekoinonesan*) in the Jews' spiritual blessing, they in turn served their material need (Rom. 15:26,27; also 12:13). Out of their extreme poverty, they urgently pleaded with the apostles for the privilege of taking part (*koinonian*) in this service to the saints (2 Cor. 8:4). Such generosity marked a liberality of fellowship (*aploteti tes koinonias*—2 Cor. 9:13). It demonstrated the effectual working of God's grace (2 Cor. 8:1). On this basis and for this reason, Paul commands those of material means to generously extend their fellowship (*einai koinonikous*) by sharing with those in need (1 Tim. 6:17–19).[1]

For Paul, the right hand of fellowship (*koinonias*) authenticated his apostolic mission: he was committed to taking the gospel to the Gentiles and to obtaining funds for the needy in Jerusalem (Gal. 2:9,10). This sacrifice of sharing (*koinonias*), according to Paul, is what pleases God (Heb. 13:16).[2] Similarly, those receiving instruction in the gospel were to share (*koinoneito*) the good things of this life with their instructor (Gal. 6:6). For this reason Paul praises the Philippian church as ones who partook (*sugkoinonous*) in God's grace, who shared (*koinonia*) in the work of the gospel, and who were partners (*sugkononesantes*) in his troubles, for only they shared (*ekoinonesen eis logon*—lit. "opened an account") in giving to him and his companions the aid they needed (Phil. 1:5,7;4:14–16). This was indeed a "fragrant offering, an acceptable sacrifice, pleasing to God" (4:18).

The fellowship of the early church, therefore, was marked by how it shared material life together. It was this very practical expression of love that so impressed pagan society. Their love for one another was not in words, but in deeds—demanding real, physical sacrifices. It was assumed that those who belonged to Christ would have their material needs met (Acts 4:34; 2 Cor. 8:13–15). What a contrast to how we practice church today, where money matters are almost entirely private and personal.

This "none of your business" attitude can work both ways: for those who give and those who receive. Many years ago Cheryl, a good friend of mine who was a part of our local fellowship, lost her job. When she came to tell my wife and I about it, she was literally shaking, in tears, gripped with fear. After sharing with us it dawned on me: Cheryl feels alone because, in terms of money, she was. It would be up to her to fend for herself. *She* lost her job, and *she* would have to find another. We as a fellowship hadn't lost a source of income; she had, and it was her welfare, not ours, that was on the line. She was no more willing to ask the church for help, than the church was willing to supply it. We were far from being a New Testament community.

I am currently a member of a community movement that consists of several intentional communities throughout the world. One thing we've vowed together is that amongst ourselves we will never charge each other money. Our services to each other are free. Why? Because we don't want money issues to divide or distract us. Nor do we want to be caught up in the snares of the world, which can so easily choke the inner life. Jesus said that we cannot serve both God and Mammon, and that if we seek first the kingdom of God and his justice, all our needs will be provided for (Matt. 6:33). We know which god the world worships; the church, by contrast, must do everything it can to show that it worships a very different God. What better way is there then to be free of the love of money?[3]

What so many Christians seem to miss is how it is possible to shape everyday life itself—including one's work—on the basis of faith. *In Christ*, all things can be made new, including those areas that tend to have a momentum all their own, as they especially do when it comes to career or business. If God's people would join together and redeem the workplace itself, both in terms of what is done and how, then a corporate work—a "Kingdom work"—of transformation can be achieved. A different social-spiritual-material reality would emerge, one woven together by the diverse strands of everyday life where Jesus is proclaimed Lord, not just in word, but in deed.

Money and business matters are one thing, our homes are another. We mustn't forget how significant the injunction to "show hospitality to one another" is. It's a resource we often fail to use. It demands a different kind of personal investment—one that is often more telling. Showing hospitality is more than entertaining one another at our convenience. It means providing for each other's needs by offering what is most intimately "yours." Writing a check is easy compared to providing a night's lodging for someone who needs it. Eating at a restaurant with friends may be "fun," but what about taking the time and effort to prepare an equally nice meal? Giving hospitality communicates that you are giving your life, not just your possessions.

Accountability: Now all of this—be it our time, our space, our resources—demands a great deal of trust. Invariably, life together means not only building each other up, but letting each other down. For the struggle against sin, both within ourselves and how we are with each other, is an on-going one. Life together requires that we be our brother's and sister's keeper.

At the very minimum, holding each other accountable demands that we speak the truth in love. Jesus instructed us clearly on this matter: if a brother is in sin, go to him. If he doesn't listen, get help. If he still doesn't listen, then bring the matter to the whole church (Matt. 18:15–20). His point? Don't let sin destroy your brother or sister, nor let it mar my Body.

We have a "rule" in our community. It is paramount for experiencing real joy together. It goes as follows:

> There is no law but that of love (1 John 4:7–8). Love means having joy in others. Then what does being annoyed with them mean? It is thus out of the question to speak about another person in a spirit of irritation or vexation (Eph. 4:29–32). There must never be talk, either in open remarks or by insinuation, against another, against their individual characteristics—under no circumstances behind the person's back. Talking in one's own family is no exception.

> Without this rule of silence there can be no loyalty, no community. Direct address is the only way possible; it is the spontaneous service of love we owe anyone whose weaknesses cause a negative reaction in us (Eph. 4:2–3). An open word spoken directly to the other person deepens friendship and is not resented.

A truthful word spoken in love can be extremely powerful. A few years ago I met two fellow members of my community in a rather heated argument—right in the middle of work. Keith, one of our shop foremen, had made a bad machining mistake and had gotten overly defensive (and excited) about it. A few minutes later a couple of co-workers came over to try and sort things out. Then, all of a sudden, they all walked out of the factory. Later I learned that the whole scene was a result of something deeper, unrelated to work. Keith and his wife had been struggling in their marriage and it was starting to take its toll on Keith's general attitude on the floor. Fortunately, with the help of different ones in the community, they were able to find each other's hearts again.

To cite another example, some members of our community once spent a fair amount of money on hotel accommodations while on a mission trip. My wife and I got upset. Why hadn't that money, which we helped to earn, been put to better use? But in the course of our confrontation, and after several others had spoken honestly to us, we realized that our so-called concern was a cover up for cold-heartedness and self-righteousness. We weren't really interested in understanding their situation or their needs. We were more concerned with principles than with warm-blooded, everyday people. I'm glad we were called up short.

Having open, free and honest relationships demands work. And speaking the truth in love doesn't always work out. When Jim fell in love with Karen, who was married to Sean in our community in Denver, it was a burden to bear. But when they began to spend time together alone, and when Karen began to have feelings toward Jim, then something needed to be done. Neither, however, wanted Sean or others to know what was happening. And neither was willing to humble themselves to get help or to ask forgiveness. Sadly, two years later Karen and Sean divorced.

Karen and Jim were not solely to blame. If our community had been more committed to them, and had brought them up short and battled for their relationship openly, then the alluring power of sin might have been nipped in the bud. Recently, when some friends of mine inadvertently discovered a six-pack of beer in Greg's room, they right away talked to him about it. When it happened again, our whole fellowship confronted Greg. In so doing, we came to realize that it wasn't just drinking Greg struggled with, but a whole host of other things: vanity, sexual impurity, and loneliness. Fortunately, Greg wanted things to be different, and so he unburdened his conscience and heart with one of our pastors. He's been a new person ever since!

Forging life together in Christ with others is never easy. We fail each other—and God—all the time. This is why speaking truth in love must always be accompanied by forgiving one another. The Christian fellowship, the community, the church, or whatever one may call life together in Christ is ultimately the place of forgiveness. It is here that the cross comes alive. As Jean Vanier of the L'Arche Community, writes: "In spite of all the trust we may have in each other, there are always words that wound, self-promoting attitudes, situations where susceptibilities clash. That is why living together implies a certain cross, a constant effort, and an acceptance which is daily and mutual forgiveness."[4]

There's a reason why Jesus told his disciples to forgive seventy times seven times. Forgiveness is perhaps the most essential quality necessary for an on-going and vibrant life with others. Without it our worship is not only false (Matt. 5:23–26), but we violate the very Body of Christ (1 Cor. 11:17ff). We actually make a mockery of the cross. For in the cross, Jesus came to mend what is broken, and reconcile estranged relationships (Eph. 2:11ff). Harboring judgment, grudges, mistrust, and fear of each other denies the mystery of why Jesus came.

There are many other attributes one could list that mark being church together. But to reiterate the following point again, because disciples of Jesus follow a different road map than that of the world, the way in which we live and relate to each other will be markedly different. The path we are on is meant to be traveled together, for our destination is towards a kingdom the first fruits of which can already be felt and seen. Coming together in Christ, if it is real, can show the world that Jesus is Lord both in heaven and on earth.

Becoming an Apologetic

It is a misnomer to think that a highly committed fellowship is an "exclusive" or a "reclusive" one. In fact, there is no greater witness to the reality of God's coming kingdom than a biblically formed life together. A fully functioning fellowship of love demonstrates the truth of the gospel far better than apologetic arguments over abstract ideas. As Stanley Hauerwas argues, "What is crucial is not that Christians know the truth, but that they be the truth." The strongest argument for Christianity's truthfulness consists of the lives it produces. Jesus was quite clear about this when he said, "All people will know that you are my disciples if you love one another" (John 13:35). What the world needs most is not words, but living testaments who embody the power of his love. Only our unity will convince the world of Christ's reality (John 17:22–23). For Jesus, the medium and the message are one.

As scientific theories are judged by the fruitfulness of the activities they generate, so is the Christian story. Christian truth is ultimately to be judged by the richness of moral character and the authenticity of relationship it generates. How else can the power of the gospel be *known* (1 Cor. 4:20)?

Therefore, it is how we are together, not just how smart or intellectually astute we are, that vindicates Christ. This is what characterized the witness of the early Christians and permeated the writing of all the early apologists. Athenagoras, for example, wrote:

> Among us you will find uneducated persons, and artisans, and old women, who, though in words are unable to prove the benefit of our doctrine, by their deeds exhibit the benefit arising from their persuasion of its truth. They do not rehearse speeches, but exhibit good works. When struck, they do not strike again; when robbed, they do not go to law. They give to those that ask of them, and love their neighbors as themselves.[5]

Athenagoras' words are not exaggerated. For example, the type of care the early Christians had for one another, revolutionary in comparison with pagan society, extended to all its members: to widows, orphans, the elderly and sick, those incapable of working and the unemployed, prisoners and exiles, Christians on a journey and all other members of the church who had fallen into special need. Care was also taken that the poor received a decent burial. Those no longer able to work received the support of the community.

Such care extended beyond the community's own ranks to include those abandoned and rejected by the unbelieving. For this reason, Christian compassion often received high praise, even from enemies of the faith. The Roman Emperor Julian writes:

> Why don't we notice that it is their [the Christians'] benevolence to strangers, their care for the graves of the dead and the pretended holiness of their lives that have done the most to increase atheism [i.e. Christianity]? … When these impious Galileans support not only their own poor but ours as well, everyone sees that our people lack aid from us.[6]

This failure, combined with the church's deeds, is what convinced the ancient world of Christianity's truth. The church's life together was its logic. Hence, Origen did not hesitate to say, "The evidences of Jesus' divinity are the Churches of people who have been helped."[7] It was not the rationality of its beliefs per se, but the lives the early church produced that persuaded the world. It was the church's ethical transformation that silenced her critics and their desperate accusations. This is how it always is. Christ's truth is both validated and vindicated when it is being lived out. A moral revolution, set in motion, not argument set in propositions, is what convinces.

Consider again the early church and the extraordinary role healing miracles played. For example, the apologist Origen takes for granted the healing power of Christ as he regularly saw with his own eyes those who were miraculously cured. And Cyprian, in his letter to Demetrianus, describes how the Spirit whips demons and drives them away from the believing. He thus challenges Demetrianus: "Come yourself and see how true it is what we say. You will see how we are entreated by those (i.e. the demons) whom you entreat and feared by those whom you fear and worship." In this vein, the church fathers repeatedly pointed out that the most profound miracles did not consist in people being healed of their infirmities but in their ability—against all human striving and expectation—to break with their pagan past and to embark on a new life.

In other words, the early Christians did not just believe in the power of Christ's resurrection, they lived in and by this power. C.S. Lewis writes, concerning the New Testament's resurrection narratives, that they "are not a picture of survival after death; they record how a totally new mode of being has arisen in the Universe. Something new had appeared in the Universe: as new as the first coming of organic life." A new mode of being has arisen, the first fruits of which were given to the Church to partake. For this reason, Clarence Jordan declares: "The crowning evidence that Jesus was alive was not a vacant grave, but a spirit-filled fellowship. Not a rolled-away stone, but a carried-away church." Such people were the direct evidence of the kingdom—the God movement.

While there is a place for demonstrating Christianity's truthfulness and historicity on certain documentary and experiential "facts," believers ultimately need to become the evidence—a living epistle—necessary to support its claims. Are the scriptures reliable? How can this ever be answered unless there exists a people who consistently live by them and bear good fruit? Are miracles possible? Jesus' reply to John the Baptist was: "Look and see! ..." Do we live in such a way that the only satisfactory explanation for its existence is the power of God in its midst? Was Christ raised from the dead? Did he actually die for the world's sin? Well, are there or are there not communities of faith marked by the new life of the Spirit who reconciles all things?

Conclusion

In his book, *Life Together*, Deitrich Bonhoeffer writes: "It is grace, nothing but grace, that we are allowed to live in community with Christian brothers and sisters." This but echoes the words of the Psalmist who wrote: "How good and pleasant it is when brothers live together in unity!" (Psalm 133:1). This gift of life together opens up the way to God and to our brother and sister.

This gift of community is not simply Christians who are really nice to their friends and the people they go to church with. In the end, Christian community is not even living together and sharing cars, money, and bagels. Genuine community is more like a movement where groups of people have been set free by Christ to pursue radically different agendas with their life and lifestyles.

The Apostle Paul reminds us that love is the greatest gift. This is precisely why Jesus gave up his body on the Cross and gave it back again in the Church. Doing life together in a way where we really need each other brings Christ and his kingdom very close to this earth. For Jesus once dwelt among us as a humble servant; and he continues to dwell among us in this same way. As Paul writes in *Philippians*, Jesus takes up residence in brothers and sisters, his corporate body, who, "being like-minded, having the same love, being one in spirit and purpose," consider others better than themselves and look to the interests of others above their own. It is they who "shine like stars in the universe" and hold out the word of life.

. . . .

Reproduction rights granted by Charles Moore.

[1] It was only because of who the early church was as a *fellowship* that Paul could literally *command* the wealthier members to give generously. To hold back was a denial of their common life.

[2] The contribution for the needy Jewish Christians in Jerusalem, taken up by the Gentile Christians in the Hellenistic world was "a theological expression of the validity of his [Paul's] work among Gentiles, a sure sign that they had been completely accepted into God's work among the Jews." J.R. McRay, "Fellowship" in *Evangelical Dictionary of Theology*, ed. by Walter E. Elwell (Grand Rapids, MI.: Baker Book House, 1984), p. 414.

[3] One very practical way to show this is to find common ways to work together. Rondout House, in New York, consists of a group of Christians who run a cleaning and maintenance business together. Norwood Community, outside of Cincinnati, operates a café. Danthonia Community, in Australia, makes and sells custom signs together. Rose Creek Community in Tennessee runs a restaurant and a business in solar tinting, construction, and home improvement. Shepherdfield's Community, in Missouri, earns part of its living through organic homemade goods. And in my own community, Catskill Bruderhof, we manufacture specialized handicap equipment.

[4] Jean Vanier, *Community and Growth* (New York: Paulist Press, 1979), p. 10.

[5] *The Ante-Nicene Fathers*, vol. II, edited by A. Roberts and J. Donaldson (Grand Rapids: Wm. B. Eerdmans), p. 134.

[6] W.C. Wright, *The Works of the Emperor Julian*, vol. 3 (LCL, 1923), pp. 69, 71.

[7] Henry Chadwick, *Origen: Contra Celsum* (Cambridge: Cambridge University Press, 1953), p. 150.

1. What's the difference between fellowship as a verb and as a noun?

2. How many of the "one another" verses can you quote from memory? Which would you say are the three most important ones?

3. Why is a commitment of time crucial to building strong community?

4. Can we experience authentic Christian community without sharing our resources?

5. What characterized the early church's community in Christ?

Christians are not called to be tolerant but to be loving. Love involves standing for the truth even if people misunderstand and dislike us for it. Nowhere is this more evident than in the debate over same-sex marriage. Frank Turek explains what the same-sex marriage debate is *not* about and exposes what its proponents are really after: validation and normalization. He shows how traditional marriage differs from same-sex marriage and why they shouldn't be treated as though they are the same.

To access this video, go to www.summitu.com/utt and enter the passcode found in the back of your manual.

Christians are not called to be _____ but to be *loving*. Sometimes this involves telling people the truth, even when they don't want to hear it. Love involves standing for the truth even if people misunderstand and dislike us for it.

Nowhere is this more evident in our society than in the debate over same-sex marriage. Many heterosexuals approve of same-sex marriage for some fallacious reasons:

1. **Intellectually** they don't understand why the state supports marriage.
2. **Morally** they've been duped into believing this is a civil rights issue.
3. **Emotionally** they are loving people who want others to be happy.

Here are some things the debate is *not* about:

- Equality or equal rights
- _____ against a class of people
- Denying homosexuals the ability to commit to one another
- Love or private relationship
- Tolerance or intolerance
- Bigotry or homophobia
- Sexual orientation or being born a certain way
- Separation of church and state
- _____

Same-sex marriage isn't about marriage; it's about *validation* and *normalization*. The force of the law will be used to make those who disagree comply or suffer the consequences.

The Four Ps

For what *purpose* does a government promote traditional marriage (between a man and a woman)? It's not because two people love one another. It is because of the many benefits to society that come from such a union:

- Creates and nurtures _____
- _____ men
- Protects women and children from uncommitted men
- Perpetuates and preserves society

Government has three options toward the behavior of its citizens: to **promote**, to **prohibit**, or to **prevent**. This is not a matter of discrimination. Everyone has the same rights as a person, but not all _____ are allowed under the law. All laws prohibit behavior for the good of society.

There is no such thing as a civil right to marriage. The state should promote only those marriages that help society. Virtually every social problem we have can be traced back to a problem in the family. *Every child deserves a mother and a father.* If this is true, then same-sex marriage can't benefit society. Traditional marriage and same-sex marriage aren't the same and shouldn't be treated as though they are.

_____ is a great teacher. Many think that if something is legal, it's moral and if it's illegal, it's immoral. The goal of the gay agenda is to get same-sex marriage accepted legally in order to radically transform the idea of family and the fabric of society.

1. Same-sex marriage may be about love on the personal level, but what is it trying to accomplish on the societal level?

2. Why do many heterosexuals approve of same-sex marriage?

3. For what purpose should a government promote traditional marriage (between a man and a woman)?

4. Christians are called to be tolerant, so why shouldn't we accept sexual preferences that differ from our own?

5. How would you use the argument that every child deserves a mother and a father to oppose same-sex marriage?

Chapter 13 Key Points

Key Questions:

1. What is sociology?
2. How do the six dominant Western worldviews approach sociology?

Key Terms:

1. Biological Determinism
2. Collective Consciousness*
3. Deviance
4. Pan-Islam
5. Patriarchal Society
6. Personal Autonomy*
7. Proletariat Society*
8. Social Constructionism*
9. Sociological Determinism
10. Sociology*
11. Sphere Sovereignty*
12. Subsidiarity
13. *Ummah**

Key Verses:

1. Genesis 2:23–24
2. Ephesians 4:11–16
3. Ephesians 5:25

Key Players:

1. Emile Durkheim
2. Abraham Kuyper
3. Karl Marx
4. Pitirim Sorokin
5. Max Weber

Key Works:

1. "Sphere Sovereignty"
   by Abraham Kuyper
2. *Social and Cultural Dynamics*
   by Pitirim Sorokin

Short answer or essay question on the exam

Hello!

Sorry I haven't written lately. Classes picked up pretty quickly with the first round of exams. Thankfully, midterms are still a few weeks off. That still doesn't stop us from dreaming about spring break though! Nathan, Sarah, and Paige invited me to go skiing with them in Colorado, but Mark and Muhammad are going hiking in the Appalachians. I haven't been skiing or hiking in several years, so both options sound like awesome adventures. What are your plans for the break?

Over the last few weeks, I have been trying out the fencing team here at the university. After watching a lot of pirate movies with my little brother over Christmas break, I decided to learn how to sword fight. Let me tell you, it is a lot more difficult than you would think. Thankfully, Mark has been going with me, and he is just as bad as I am! It is a great stress reliever after all that studying. If you come up to visit, maybe I can take you to a practice and show you the ropes!

While walking to practice the other day, Mark and I ran into Sarah. She and some other students were passing out flyers in the quad. They were advertising a student government debate about the role of family in society and the state. Obviously, Mark was really interested, so we began to discuss the topic. Sarah said we should encourage alternative lifestyles and family structures. According to her, society should be free from arbitrary constraints that religion places on progress. I assume that her views on the family are grounded in her Secularist views, but I don't know exactly how. **What does Secularism have to say about sociology?** Mark agreed that the traditional idea of the family hinders the progress of society, but he said it was because the family causes the "illicit hording of capital and wealth." To be honest, I have no idea what he meant. Mark mentioned Karl Marx's sociological views frequently, so I am assuming that Marxism has a lot to say about the relationship between people and society. **What is the Marxist view of sociology?**

In the middle of the conversation, Muhammad rode up on his bike and joined the discussion. At first I thought our views would be similar since we both believe in a God, but I was just as confused when he began talking about removing the separation of church and state. Unfortunately, Mark and I had to run to fencing practice, so I didn't hear the rest of what Muhammad was saying. Maybe you can help. **What is the role of sociology in Islam?** And **what is the Christian view of sociology?**

Well, the break between classes is almost over. I can't wait to hear back from you!

See you later!
–Doug

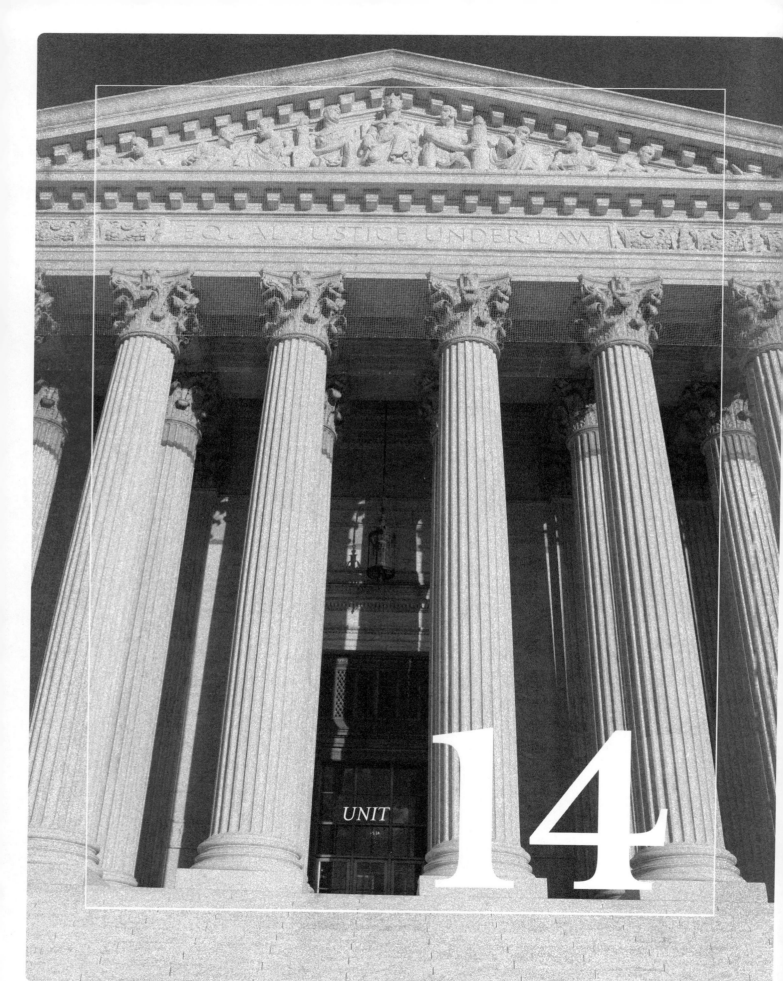

EQUAL JUSTICE UNDER LAW

UNIT

14

LAW

CHAPTER 14 LEARNING OBJECTIVES

Students will be able to:

1. express why law is important. [14.2]

2. identify why order and justice are necessary for creating good laws. [14.3]

3. explain Secularism's approach to law. [14.4]

4. explain Marxism's approach to law. [14.5]

5. explain Postmodernism's approach to law. [14.6]

6. explain New Spirituality's approach to law. [14.7]

7. explain Islam's approach to law. [14.8]

8. explain Christianity's approach to law. [14.9]

1. What is the role of law in human society? [14.2]

2. What constitutes orderly and just governance? [14.3]

3. What does the Law of Moses, given thousands of years ago, have to do with our laws today? [14.3]

4. Is there a distinction between what is legal and what is right? [14.3]

5. According to the natural law view, what kinds of rules lead to just laws? [14.3]

6. What is distributive justice and what kind of shift does it represent? [14.3]

7. What assumptions shape the Secularist understanding of law? [14.4]

8. If laws aren't based on the laws of nature and nature's God, where do they come from? [14.4]

9.   What assumptions shape the Marxist understanding of law? [14.5]

10. What is proletariat law and what purpose does it serve? [14.5]

11. What assumptions shape the Postmodernist understanding of law? [14.6]

12. What is social constructionism and what role does it play in Postmodernist legal thinking? [14.6]

13. Do you agree or disagree with this statement by Justice Sotomayor: "I would hope that a wise Latina woman with the richness of her experiences would more often than not reach a better conclusion than a white male who hasn't lived that life."

14. What assumptions shape the New Spiritualist understanding of law? [14.7]

15. How does the idea of self-law shape the New Spiritualist understanding of law? [14.7]

16. What assumptions shape the Islamic understanding of law? [14.8]

17. If the constitution guarantees religious freedom, do you think Muslims should be allowed to practice shariah law in America?

18. Why do nations with large Muslim populations tend toward dictatorship or monarchy? [14.8]

19. What assumptions shape the Christian understanding of law? [14.9]

20. Where do general revelation and natural law come from? [14.9]

21. Where do special revelation and divine law come from? [14.9]

22. What is the goal of Christian law? [14.9]

In this 1850 excerpt from *The Law*, Frédéric Bastiat defines what law is: the collective organization of the individual right to lawful defense. What we have the right to do as individuals—defend our person, liberty, and property—a society has the collective right and responsibility to do.

Bastiat explains that the role of government in enacting laws is to protect and preserve the natural rights of its citizens, which include the right to enjoy the fruits of their labor and protection from unjust attack. He then identifies two kinds of plunder: illegal and legal. Illegal plunder (theft, swindling) is punishable by law and is why police and judicial systems exist. Legal plunder is when the state takes from some individuals what belongs to them and gives what it takes to other individuals to whom it does not belong.

Illegal plunder exists because of greed. This flaw has its origin in the sinful nature of man, which impels him to satisfy his desires with the least possible effort. The law is often perverted by the influence of greed. Those in power make and use laws to limit the personal freedom of the citizens and to legally take property in ways that benefit those who make the laws.

Finally, Bastiat touches on the relationship between law and justice. To most people they are synonymous. They erroneously hold that things are "just" because law makes them so. When law and justice contradict each other, citizens will either lose their moral sense or lose their respect for law. Examples of law and justice contradicting each other include slavery, discrimination, and political or economic monopolies.

No society can exist for long unless its laws are respected to a certain degree. The safest way to make laws respected is to make them just.

A SELECTION FROM "THE LAW"
by Frédéric Bastiat

The law perverted! And the police powers of the state perverted along with it! The law, I say, not only turned from its proper purpose but made to follow an entirely contrary purpose! The law become the weapon of every kind of greed! Instead of checking crime, the law itself guilty of the evils it is supposed to punish!

If this is true, it is a serious fact, and moral duty requires me to call the attention of my fellow-citizens to it.

Life Is a Gift from God

We hold from God the gift which includes all others. This gift is life—physical, intellectual, and moral life.

But life cannot maintain itself alone. The Creator of life has entrusted us with the responsibility of preserving, developing, and perfecting it. In order that we may accomplish this, He has provided us with a collection of marvelous faculties. And He has put us in the midst of a variety of natural resources. By the application of our faculties to these natural resources we convert them into products, and use them. This process is necessary in order that life may run its appointed course.

Life, faculties, production—in other words, individuality, liberty, property—this is man. And in spite of the cunning of artful political leaders, these three gifts from God precede all human legislation, and are superior to it. Life, liberty, and property do not exist because men have made laws. On the contrary, it was the fact that life, liberty, and property existed beforehand that caused men to make laws in the first place.

What Is Law? What, then, is law? It is the collective organization of the individual right to lawful defense.

Each of us has a natural right—from God—to defend his person, his liberty, and his property. These are the three basic requirements of life, and the preservation of any one of them is completely dependent upon the preservation of the other two. For what are our faculties but the extension of our individuality? And what is property but an extension of our faculties? If every person has the right to defend even by force—his person, his liberty, and his property, then it follows that a group of men have the right to organize and support a common force to protect these rights constantly. Thus the principle of collective right—its reason for existing, its lawfulness—is based on individual right. And the common force that protects this collective right cannot logically have any other purpose or any other mission than that for which it acts as a substitute. Thus, since an individual cannot lawfully use force against the person, liberty, or property of another individual, then the common force—for the same reason—cannot lawfully be used to destroy the person, liberty, or property of individuals or groups.

Such a perversion of force would be, in both cases, contrary to our premise. Force has been given to us to defend our own individual rights. Who will dare to say that force has been given to us to destroy the equal rights of our brothers? Since no individual acting separately can lawfully use force to destroy the rights of others, does it not logically follow that the same principle also applies to the common force that is nothing more than the organized combination of the individual forces?

If this is true, then nothing can be more evident than this: The law is the organization of the natural right of lawful defense. It is the substitution of a common force for individual forces. And this common force is to do only what the individual forces have a natural and lawful right to do: to protect persons, liberties, and properties; to maintain the right of each, and to cause *justice* to reign over us all.

A Just and Enduring Government

If a nation were founded on this basis, it seems to me that order would prevail among the people, in thought as well as in deed. It seems to me that such a nation would have the most simple, easy to accept, economical, limited, nonoppressive, just, and enduring government imaginable—whatever its political form might be.

Under such an administration, everyone would understand that he possessed all the privileges as well as all the responsibilities of his existence. No one would have any argument with government, provided that his person was respected, his labor was free, and the fruits of his labor were protected against all unjust attack. When successful, we would not have to thank the state for our success. And, conversely, when unsuccessful, we would no more think of blaming the state for our misfortune than would the farmers blame the state because of hail or frost. The state would be felt only by the invaluable blessings of safety provided by this concept of government.

It can be further stated that, thanks to the non-intervention of the state in private affairs, our wants and their satisfactions would develop themselves in a logical manner. We would not see poor families seeking literary instruction before they have bread. We would not see cities populated at the expense of rural districts, nor rural districts at the expense of cities. We would not see the great displacements of capital, labor, and population that are caused by legislative decisions.

The sources of our existence are made uncertain and precarious by these state-created displacements. And, furthermore, these acts burden the government with increased responsibilities.

The Complete Perversion of the Law

But, unfortunately, law by no means confines itself to its proper functions. And when it has exceeded its proper functions, it has not done so merely in some inconsequential and debatable matters. The law has gone further than this; it has acted in direct opposition to its own purpose. The law has been used to destroy its own objective: It has been applied to annihilating the justice that it was supposed to maintain; to limiting and destroying rights which its real purpose was to respect. The law has placed the collective force at the disposal of the unscrupulous who wish, without risk, to exploit the person, liberty, and property of others. It has converted plunder into a right, in order to protect plunder. And it has converted lawful defense into a crime, in order to punish lawful defense.

How has this perversion of the law been accomplished? And what have been the results?

The law has been perverted by the influence of two entirely different causes: stupid greed and false philanthropy. Let us speak of the first.

A Fatal Tendency of Mankind

Self-preservation and self-development are common aspirations among all people. And if everyone enjoyed the unrestricted use of his faculties and the free disposition of the fruits of his labor, social progress would be ceaseless, uninterrupted, and unfailing.

But there is also another tendency that is common among people. When they can, they wish to live and prosper at the expense of others. This is no rash accusation. Nor does it come from a gloomy and uncharitable spirit. The annals of history bear witness to the truth of it: the incessant wars, mass migrations, religious persecutions, universal slavery, dishonesty in commerce, and monopolies. This fatal desire has its origin in the very nature of man—in that primitive, universal, and insuppressible instinct that impels him to satisfy his desires with the least possible pain.

Property and Plunder

Man can live and satisfy his wants only by ceaseless labor; by the ceaseless application of his faculties to natural resources. This process is the origin of property.

But it is also true that a man may live and satisfy his wants by seizing and consuming the products of the labor of others. This process is the origin of plunder.

Now since man is naturally inclined to avoid pain—and since labor is pain in itself—it follows that men will resort to plunder whenever plunder is easier than work. History shows this quite clearly. And under these conditions, neither religion nor morality can stop it.

When, then, does plunder stop? It stops when it becomes more painful and more dangerous than labor.

It is evident, then, that the proper purpose of law is to use the power of its collective force to stop this fatal tendency to plunder instead of to work. All the measures of the law should protect property and punish plunder.

But, generally, the law is made by one man or one class of men. And since law cannot operate without the sanction and support of a dominating force, this force must be entrusted to those who make the laws.

This fact, combined with the fatal tendency that exists in the heart of man to satisfy his wants with the least possible effort, explains the almost universal perversion of the law. Thus it is easy to understand how law, instead of checking injustice, becomes the invincible weapon of injustice. It is easy to understand why the law is used by the legislator to destroy in varying degrees among the rest of the people, their personal independence by slavery, their liberty by oppression, and their property by plunder. This is done for the benefit of the person who makes the law, and in proportion to the power that he holds.

Victims of Lawful Plunder

Men naturally rebel against the injustice of which they are victims. Thus, when plunder is organized by law for the profit of those who make the law, all the plundered classes try somehow to enter—by peaceful or revolutionary means—into the making of laws. According to their degree of enlightenment, these plundered classes may propose one of two entirely different purposes when they attempt to attain political power: Either they may wish to stop lawful plunder, or they may wish to share in it.

Woe to the nation when this latter purpose prevails among the mass victims of lawful plunder when they, in turn, seize the power to make laws! Until that happens, the few practice lawful plunder upon the many, a common practice where the right to participate in the making of law is limited to a few persons. But then, participation in the making of law becomes universal. And then, men seek to balance their conflicting interests by universal plunder. Instead of rooting out the injustices found in society, they make these injustices general. As soon as the plundered classes gain political power, they establish a system of reprisals against other classes. They do not abolish legal plunder. (This objective would demand more enlightenment than they possess.) Instead, they emulate their evil predecessors by participating in this legal plunder, even though it is against their own interests.

It is as if it were necessary, before a reign of justice appears, for everyone to suffer a cruel retribution—some for their evilness, and some for their lack of understanding.

The Results of Legal Plunder

It is impossible to introduce into society a greater change and a greater evil than this: the conversion of the law into an instrument of plunder.

What are the consequences of such a perversion? It would require volumes to describe them all. Thus we must content ourselves with pointing out the most striking.

In the first place, it erases from everyone's conscience the distinction between justice and injustice.

No society can exist unless the laws are respected to a certain degree. The safest way to make laws respected is to make them respectable. When law and morality contradict each other, the citizen has the cruel alternative of either losing his moral sense or losing his respect for the law. These two evils are of equal consequence, and it would be difficult for a person to choose between them.

The nature of law is to maintain justice. This is so much the case that, in the minds of the people, law and justice are one and the same thing. There is in all of us a strong disposition to believe that anything lawful is also legitimate. This belief is so widespread that many persons have erroneously held that things are "just" because law makes them so. Thus, in order to make plunder appear just and sacred to many consciences, it is only necessary for the law to decree and sanction it. Slavery, restrictions, and monopoly find defenders not only among those who profit from them but also among those who suffer from them.

The Fate of Non-Conformists

If you suggest a doubt as to the morality of these institutions, it is boldly said that "You are a dangerous innovator, a utopian, a theorist, a subversive; you would shatter the foundation upon which society rests." If you lecture upon morality or upon political science, there will be found official organizations petitioning the government in this vein of thought: "That science no longer be taught exclusively from the point of view of free trade (of liberty, of property, and of justice) as has been the case until now, but also, in the future, science is to be especially taught from the viewpoint of the facts and laws that regulate French industry (facts and laws which are contrary to liberty, to property, and to justice). That, in government-endowed teaching positions, the professor rigorously refrain from endangering in the slightest degree the respect due to the laws now in force."

Thus, if there exists a law which sanctions slavery or monopoly, oppression or robbery, in any form whatever, it must not even be mentioned. For how can it be mentioned without damaging the respect which it inspires? Still further, morality and political economy must be taught from the point of view of this law; from the supposition that it must be a just law merely because it is a law. …

Two Kinds of Plunder

Mr. de Montalembert [politician and writer] adopting the thought contained in a famous proclamation by Mr. Carlier, has said: "We must make war against socialism." According to the definition of socialism advanced by Mr. Charles Dupin, he meant: "We must make war against plunder."

But of what plunder was he speaking? For there are two kinds of plunder: legal and illegal.

I do not think that illegal plunder, such as theft or swindling—which the penal code defines, anticipates, and punishes—can be called socialism. It is not this kind of plunder that systematically threatens the foundations of society. Anyway, the war against this kind of plunder has not waited for the command of these gentlemen. The war against illegal plunder has been fought since the beginning of the world. Long before the Revolution of February 1848—long before the appearance even of socialism itself—France had provided police, judges, gendarmes, prisons, dungeons, and scaffolds for the purpose of fighting illegal plunder. The law itself conducts this war, and it is my wish and opinion that the law should always maintain this attitude toward plunder.

The Law Defends Plunder

But it does not always do this. Sometimes the law defends plunder and participates in it. Thus the beneficiaries are spared the shame, danger, and scruple which their acts would otherwise involve. Sometimes the law places the whole apparatus of judges, police, prisons, and gendarmes at the service of the plunderers, and treats the victim—when he defends himself—as a criminal. In short, there is a *legal plunder*, and it is of this, no doubt, that Mr. de Montalembert speaks.

This legal plunder may be only an isolated stain among the legislative measures of the people. If so, it is best to wipe it out with a minimum of speeches and denunciations—and in spite of the uproar of the vested interests.

How to Identify Legal Plunder

But how is this legal plunder to be identified? Quite simply. See if the law takes from some persons what belongs to them, and gives it to other persons to whom it does not belong. See if the law benefits one citizen at the expense of another by doing what the citizen himself cannot do without committing a crime.

Then abolish this law without delay, for it is not only an evil itself, but also it is a fertile source for further evils because it invites reprisals. If such a law—which may be an isolated case—is not abolished immediately, it will spread, multiply, and develop into a system.

The person who profits from this law will complain bitterly, defending his *acquired rights*. He will claim that the state is obligated to protect and encourage his particular industry; that this procedure enriches the state because the protected industry is thus able to spend more and to pay higher wages to the poor workingmen.

Do not listen to this sophistry by vested interests. The acceptance of these arguments will build legal plunder into a whole system. In fact, this has already occurred. The present-day delusion is an attempt to enrich everyone at the expense of everyone else; to make plunder universal under the pretense of organizing it.

Legal Plunder Has Many Names

Now, legal plunder can be committed in an infinite number of ways. Thus we have an infinite number of plans for organizing it: tariffs, protection, benefits, subsidies, encouragements, progressive taxation, public schools, guaranteed jobs, guaranteed profits, minimum wages, a right to relief, a right to the tools of labor, free credit, and so on, and so on. All these plans as a whole—with their common aim of legal plunder—constitute socialism.

Now, since under this definition socialism is a body of doctrine, what attack can be made against it other than a war of doctrine? If you find this socialistic doctrine to be false, absurd, and evil, then refute it. And the more false, the more absurd, and the more evil it is, the easier it will be to refute. Above all, if you wish to be strong, begin by rooting out every particle of socialism that may have crept into your legislation. This will be no light task.

Socialism Is Legal Plunder

Mr. de Montalembert has been accused of desiring to fight socialism by the use of brute force. He ought to be exonerated from this accusation, for he has plainly said:

"The war that we must fight against socialism must be in harmony with law, honor, and justice."

But why does not Mr. de Montalembert see that he has placed himself in a vicious circle? You would use the law to oppose socialism? But it is upon the law that socialism itself relies. Socialists desire to practice *legal* plunder, not *illegal* plunder. Socialists, like all other monopolists, desire to make the law their own weapon. And when once the law is on the side of socialism, how can it be used against socialism? For when plunder is abetted by the law, it does not fear your courts, your gendarmes, and your prisons. Rather, it may call upon them for help. To prevent this, you would exclude socialism from entering into the making of laws? You would prevent socialists from entering the Legislative Palace? You shall not succeed, I predict, so long as legal plunder continues to be the main business of the legislature. It is illogical—in fact, absurd—to assume otherwise.

The Choice before Us

This question of legal plunder must be settled once and for all, and there are only three ways to settle it:

1. The few plunder the many.
2. Everybody plunders everybody.
3. Nobody plunders anybody.

We must make our choice among limited plunder, universal plunder, and no plunder. The law can follow only one of these three.

Limited legal plunder: This system prevailed when the right to vote was restricted. One would turn back to this system to prevent the invasion of socialism.

Universal legal plunder: We have been threatened with this system since the franchise was made universal. The newly enfranchised majority has decided to formulate law on the same principle of legal plunder that was used by their predecessors when the vote was limited.

No legal plunder: This is the principle of justice, peace, order, stability, harmony, and logic. Until the day of my death, I shall proclaim this principle with all the force of my lungs (which alas! is all too inadequate).

The Law by Frédéric Bastiat. Translation by Dean Russell. Reproduction rights granted by the FEE Foundation for Economic Education.

1. What is law and upon what is it based?

2. What is the role of government in making and enforcing laws?

3. What's the difference between illegal plunder and legal plunder?

4. How is the law perverted from its proper function?

5. What is the relationship between law and justice?

Frank Beckwith, who holds PhDs in both philosophy and law, explains the conceptual and foundational issues dealing with law. The two dominant approaches are *legal positivism* (whoever is in charge of the community determines the law) and *natural law theory* (human law get its justification from natural law).

Beckwith then unpacks the famous definition of law given by Thomas Aquinas: "Law is an ordinance of reason for the common good made by him who has care of the community and is promulgated." He concludes with some of the common questions addressed by the philosophy of law: 1) What is law and how is it justified? 2) Must the law depend on morality? 3) Should the law enforce private morality as normative for all citizens? 4) How should judges interpret constitutions and statutes? 5) Are contracts moral promises or just efficient means to best facilitate economic transactions?

To access this video, go to www.summitu.com/utt and enter the passcode found in the back of your manual.

"THE PHILOSOPHY OF LAW" VIDEO OUTLINE

Philosophy is "the love of wisdom" and has to do with the first principles or fundamental beliefs in a discipline. The philosophy of law has to do with the conceptual and foundational issues dealing with law.

The two most prominent theories of law:

1. _____: Whoever is in charge of the community determines the law. The law is no more and no less than what is posited by those in authority. What the leaders in a community say is the law becomes the law. Morality is not necessary for the legitimacy of law.

2. _____: Human law gets its justification from natural law. The law is more than what is posited by those in authority. There are principles behind the law, such as fairness and equity, that aren't legislated; they just are.

Thomas Aquinas's definition of law:

1. An ordinance of _____: Reasons are offered for its existence.
2. For the common good: It benefits everyone without harming anyone and is not for private gain.
3. Made by him who has care of the community: This refers to the government on various levels and administrative agencies.
4. _____: Something well known in principle, even if people don't know all the details.

Two kinds of law not allowed in our current system:

1. _____: Laws passed after the fact, then applied to specific people or situations.
2. _____: Laws passed to target specific individuals.

Questions dealt with by the philosophy of law:

1. What is law and how is it justified?
2. Must the law depend on _____?
3. Should the law enforce private morality as normative for all citizens?
4. How should judges interpret constitutions and statutes?
5. Are _____ moral promises or just efficient means to best facilitate economic transactions?

1. What is the philosophy of law?

2. What is the definition of law as put forth by Thomas Aquinas?

3. What are some differences between legal positivism and natural law theory?

4. Can you give some examples of laws that have been part of the European legal system but aren't part of the American system?

5. Can you give some examples of the fundamental questions dealt with by the philosophy of law?

Chapter 14 Key Points

Key Questions:

1. What is law?
2. How do the six dominant Western worldviews approach law?

Key Terms:

1. Common Law
2. Critical Legal Studies*
3. General Revelation
4. Justice
5. Law*
6. Legal Positivism*
7. Natural Law*
8. Order
9. Proletariat Law*
10. Self-law*
11. Shariah Law*
12. Social Constructionism
13. Social Justice
14. Special Revelation
15. Tort Law
16. Utilitarianism

Key Verses:

1. Acts 17:30–31
2. 2 Corinthians 5:10

Key Players:

1. Ahmad ibn Naqib al-Misri
2. William Blackstone
3. Friedrich Engels
4. Stanley Fish
5. Oliver Wendell Holmes, Jr.
6. John Rawls

Key Works:

1. *Commentaries on the Laws of England* by William Blackstone
2. *There's No Such Things As Free Speech* by Stanley Fish
3. *A Theory of Justice* by John Rawls
4. *The Origin of the Family, Private Property, and the State* by Friedrich Engels

Short answer or essay question on the exam

Hello there!

I have to tell you about the festival on campus yesterday. Several of the engineering groups host an event every year where students can get free food, compete on obstacle courses, and watch movies. Apparently, it is a promotion for exercise and mental health awareness. It was awesome! Mark and I battled each other in the gladiator games. I had a blast! Oh, I almost forgot to mention that they had a petting zoo of sorts. Some local farmers brought lambs and horses, and a few animal shelters brought puppies and kittens for the college students to play with. Sarah and Paige spent most of their time with the animals while Mark and I were busy running through the obstacles. I needed a fun-filled day with midterms looming in the near future!

Speaking of midterms and classes, my Political Theory course has been discussing the foundations of governmental forms and the histories behind many of them. We have been reading a good deal of Locke, Hobbes, Montesquieu, and Rousseau. The theme this week has been on the foundation of law. I can't believe how many different theories there are for explaining what law is and why it exists! I hadn't really thought about it much. As part of the class, students are required to give a presentation on one of these theories, and Muhammad presented yesterday. His talk was about the Islamic perspective on law and the value of shariah law.

After class, Muhammad, Sarah, and I grabbed coffee to talk more about it. Muhammad explained that Islamic law is divine law and is coeternal with Allah. He said there are a great deal of similarities between shariah and the laws in Christianity. Sarah explained her view of law was based on something called positivism. According to her, natural law cannot exist because God does not exist. As she sees it, laws are only man-made constructions that emerged from the cultural, economic, political, and social institutions of each society. I guess I was quiet throughout the conversation because Muhammad and Sarah asked me what I thought about law and its construction. To be honest, I didn't really know what to say. I mumbled something about obeying God, but it didn't seem to satisfy them. Muhammad pointed out how we both agree on divine law, but I feel like there must be something different between Christian and Islamic views on law.

I left the conversation a bit befuddled. Maybe you can help me. After listening to Sarah speak, I would like to know more about her worldview. **What is the basis of law in Secularist thought?** I am assuming that Mark would agree with her, but I am not sure. **How does Marxism view law?** Paige always describes Postmodernism as the rejection of metanarratives and absolute truth. I bet that shapes what her view of the role of law in society. **What is the foundation of law in Postmodernism?** Perhaps most confusing for me is the relationship between Christianity and Islam. **What are the differences between Islam and Christianity's view of law?**

Thank you so much for your help. I don't know what I would do without you!

Later!
—Doug

UNIT

15

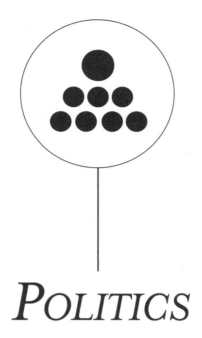

POLITICS

CHAPTER 15 LEARNING OBJECTIVES

Students will be able to:

1. state why politics is important. [15.1]

2. identify the history and philosophy of politics. [15.2]

3. explain Secularism's approach to politics. [15.3]

4. explain Marxism's approach to politics. [15.4]

5. explain Postmodernism's approach to politics. [15.5]

6. explain New Spirituality's approach to politics. [15.6]

7. explain Islam's approach to politics. [15.7]

8. explain Christianity's approach to politics. [15.8]

9. list five different approaches Christians have taken to politics. [15.9]

10. answer common questions Christians ask about politics. [15.10]

CHAPTER 15 DISCUSSION QUESTIONS

1. What is the key question politics asks and seeks to answer? [15.1]

2. Why is political engagement necessary to a healthy society? [15.2]

3. What social contract view influences American politics today? [15.2]

4. What assumptions does distributive justice make about society? [15.2]

5. Which of the assumptions made by distributive justice do you agree with and which do you reject? [15.2]

6. What assumptions shape the Secularist understanding of politics? [15.3]

7. Why does economics play such a key role in Secularist politics? [15.3]

8. How does Secularist thinking lead to a utopian vision of one world government? [15.3]

9. What assumptions shape the Marxist understanding of politics? [15.4]

10. What are the three steps in the transition from capitalism to communism? [15.4]

11. What assumptions shape the Postmodernist understanding of politics? [15.5]

12. Why do some Postmodernists get excited about identity politics? [15.5]

13. **What assumptions shape the New Spiritualist understanding of politics? [15.6]**

14. **How does the new world order of New Spiritualism differ from that of Secularism, Marxism or Islam? [15.6]**

15. **What assumptions shape the Islamic understanding of politics? [15.7]**

16. **What consequences would follow successful jihad? [15.7]**

17. What assumptions shape the Christian understanding of politics? [15.8]

18. Can you name five common Christian positions on political involvement and give a brief synopsis of each? [15.9]

19. How would you respond to the claim that Jesus didn't get involved in politics, so neither should we? [15.10]

20. Why is political involvement necessary for Christians? [15.10]

21. What do Christians see as the purpose and responsibilities of government? [15.10]

22. Would Christian involvement in politics lead to theocracy? [15.10]

23. Are Christians responsible to submit to an evil government or obey bad laws?

The Declaration of Independence is one of the most important and influential documents ever written. The logic is sound and the language is clear. The colonies' rebellion against England is based on the idea that governments "[derive] their just powers from the consent of the governed," and that they are free to choose a new government when the old one "fails in its duties. At such times, the people have the right to withhold their consent and establish a new government."

Having listed multiple grievances against the king in the first part of the Declaration and stated that their repeated protests had been ignored,

> We, therefore, the Representatives of the united States of America, in General Congress, Assembled, appealing to the Supreme Judge of the world for the rectitude of our intentions, do, in the Name, and by Authority of the good People of these Colonies, solemnly publish and declare That these united Colonies are, and of Right ought to be Free and Independent States; that they are Absolved from all Allegiance to the British Crown and that all political connection between them and the State of Great Britain, is and ought to be totally dissolved and that as Free and Independent States, they have full Power to levy War, conclude Peace, contract Alliances, establish Commerce, and to do all other Acts and Things which Independent States may of right do.

In short, having become convinced that England would continue to abuse them rather than protect them, the colonies declared their sovereignty as an independent nation. The new nation backed up its declaration with a war that lasted more than eight years and cost thousands of lives.

IN CONGRESS, JULY 4, 1776
A DECLARATION

by the Representatives of the
United States of America
In General Congress assembled

When in the Course of human events it becomes necessary for one people to dissolve the political bands which have connected them with another and to assume among the powers of the earth, the separate and equal station to which the Laws of Nature and of Nature's God entitle them, a decent respect to the opinions of mankind requires that they should declare the causes which impel them to the separation.

We hold these truths to be self-evident, that all men are created equal, that they are endowed by their Creator with certain unalienable Rights, that among these are Life,

Liberty and the pursuit of Happiness.—That to secure these rights, Governments are instituted among Men, deriving their just powers from the consent of the governed,—That whenever any Form of Government becomes destructive of these ends, it is the Right of the People to alter or to abolish it, and to institute new Government, laying its foundation on such principles and organizing its powers in such form, as to them shall seem most likely to effect their Safety and Happiness. Prudence, indeed, will dictate that Governments long established should not be changed for light and transient causes; and accordingly all experience hath shewn that mankind are more disposed to suffer, while evils are sufferable than to right themselves by abolishing the forms to which they are accustomed. But when a long train of abuses and usurpations, pursuing invariably the same Object evinces a design to reduce them under absolute Despotism, it is their right, it is their duty, to throw off such Government, and to provide new Guards for their future security.—Such has been the patient sufferance of these Colonies; and such is now the necessity which constrains them to alter their former Systems of Government. The history of the present King of Great Britain is a history of repeated injuries and usurpations, all having in direct object the establishment of an absolute Tyranny over these States. To prove this, let Facts be submitted to a candid world.

He has refused his Assent to Laws, the most wholesome and necessary for the public good.

He has forbidden his Governors to pass Laws of immediate and pressing importance, unless suspended in their operation till his Assent should be obtained; and when so suspended, he has utterly neglected to attend to them.

He has refused to pass other Laws for the accommodation of large districts of people, unless those people would relinquish the right of Representation in the Legislature, a right inestimable to them and formidable to tyrants only.

He has called together legislative bodies at places unusual, uncomfortable, and distant from the depository of their Public Records, for the sole purpose of fatiguing them into compliance with his measures.

He has dissolved Representative Houses repeatedly, for opposing with manly firmness his invasions on the rights of the people.

He has refused for a long time, after such dissolutions, to cause others to be elected, whereby the Legislative Powers, incapable of Annihilation, have returned to the People at large for their exercise; the State remaining in the mean time exposed to all the dangers of invasion from without, and convulsions within.

He has endeavoured to prevent the population of these States; for that purpose obstructing the Laws for Naturalization of Foreigners; refusing to pass others to encourage their migrations hither, and raising the conditions of new Appropriations of Lands.

He has obstructed the Administration of Justice by refusing his Assent to Laws for establishing Judiciary Powers.

He has made Judges dependent on his Will alone for the tenure of their offices, and the amount and payment of their salaries.

He has erected a multitude of New Offices, and sent hither swarms of Officers to harass our people and eat out their substance.

He has kept among us, in times of peace, Standing Armies without the Consent of our legislatures.

He has affected to render the Military independent of and superior to the Civil Power.

He has combined with others to subject us to a jurisdiction foreign to our constitution, and unacknowledged by our laws; giving his Assent to their Acts of pretended Legislation:

For quartering large bodies of armed troops among us:

For protecting them, by a mock Trial from punishment for any Murders which they should commit on the Inhabitants of these States:

For cutting off our Trade with all parts of the world:

For imposing Taxes on us without our Consent:

For depriving us in many cases, of the benefit of Trial by Jury:

For transporting us beyond Seas to be tried for pretended offences:

For abolishing the free System of English Laws in a neighbouring Province, establishing therein an Arbitrary government, and enlarging its Boundaries so as to render it at once an example and fit instrument for introducing the same absolute rule into these Colonies.

For taking away our Charters, abolishing our most valuable Laws and altering fundamentally the Forms of our Governments:

For suspending our own Legislatures, and declaring themselves invested with power to legislate for us in all cases whatsoever.

He has abdicated Government here, by declaring us out of his Protection and waging War against us.

He has plundered our seas, ravaged our coasts, burnt our towns, and destroyed the lives of our people.

He is at this time transporting large Armies of foreign Mercenaries to compleat the works of death, desolation, and tyranny, already begun with circumstances of Cruelty & Perfidy scarcely paralleled in the most barbarous ages, and totally unworthy the Head of a civilized nation.

He has constrained our fellow Citizens taken Captive on the high Seas to bear Arms against their Country, to become the executioners of their friends and Brethren, or to fall themselves by their Hands.

He has excited domestic insurrections amongst us, and has endeavoured to bring on the inhabitants of our frontiers, the merciless Indian Savages whose known rule of warfare, is an undistinguished destruction of all ages, sexes and conditions.

In every stage of these Oppressions We have Petitioned for Redress in the most humble terms: Our repeated Petitions have been answered only by repeated injury. A Prince, whose character is thus marked by every act which may define a Tyrant, is unfit to be the ruler of a free people.

Nor have We been wanting in attentions to our British brethren. We have warned them from time to time of attempts by their legislature to extend an unwarrantable jurisdiction over us. We have reminded them of the circumstances of our emigration and settlement here. We have appealed to their native justice and magnanimity, and we have conjured them by the ties of our common kindred to disavow these usurpations, which would inevitably interrupt our connections and correspondence. They too have been deaf to the voice of justice and of consanguinity. We must, therefore, acquiesce in the necessity, which denounces our Separation, and hold them, as we hold the rest of mankind, Enemies in War, in Peace Friends.

We, therefore, the Representatives of the united States of America, in General Congress, Assembled, appealing to the Supreme Judge of the world for the rectitude of our intentions, do, in the Name, and by Authority of the good People of these Colonies, solemnly publish and declare, That these united Colonies are, and of Right ought to be Free and Independent States, that they are Absolved from all Allegiance to the British Crown, and that all political connection between them and the State of Great Britain, is and ought to be totally dissolved; and that as Free and Independent States, they have full Power to levy War, conclude Peace, contract Alliances, establish Commerce, and to do all other Acts and Things which Independent States may of right do.—And for the support of this Declaration, with a firm reliance on the protection of Divine Providence, we mutually pledge to each other our Lives, our Fortunes, and our sacred Honor.

New Hampshire:
Josiah Bartlett, William Whipple, Matthew Thornton

Massachusetts:
John Hancock, Samuel Adams, John Adams, Robert Treat Paine, Elbridge Gerry

Rhode Island:
Stephen Hopkins, William Ellery

Connecticut:
Roger Sherman, Samuel Huntington, William Williams, Oliver Wolcott

New York:
William Floyd, Philip Livingston, Francis Lewis, Lewis Morris

New Jersey:
Richard Stockton, John Witherspoon, Francis Hopkinson, John Hart, Abraham Clark

Pennsylvania:
Robert Morris, Benjamin Rush, Benjamin Franklin, John Morton, George Clymer, James Smith, George Taylor, James Wilson, George Ross

Delaware:
Caesar Rodney, George Read, Thomas McKean

Maryland:
Samuel Chase, William Paca, Thomas Stone, Charles Carroll of Carrollton

Virginia:
George Wythe, Richard Henry Lee, Thomas Jefferson, Benjamin Harrison, Thomas Nelson, Jr., Francis Lightfoot Lee, Carter Braxton

North Carolina:
William Hooper, Joseph Hewes, John Penn

South Carolina:
Edward Rutledge, Thomas Heyward, Jr., Thomas Lynch, Jr., Arthur Middleton

Georgia:
Button Gwinnett, Lyman Hall, George Walton

Published in 1776, this work meets the criteria for fair use.

1. Why does government exist and from where does it derive its power?

2. Can you recall some of the reasons the colonists sought independence even though many of them saw themselves as loyal English subjects?

3. What does the Declaration of Independence actually state the colonists would do?

4. What evidence from the Declaration proves its signers were men of faith?

5. How do you think the Declaration of Independence was viewed in England?

Mike Adams uses his own experiences on college campuses to illustrate what's happening with free speech in America. (One instance even went viral and made the national news.) He touches on the right to privacy and what happens when local laws and the Constitution are in conflict. Today Mike speaks nationally and is involved in litigation to change free-speech laws on campuses. He talks about how to use the First Amendment to restore the First Amendment and how to use the courts when that fails.

To access this video, go to www.summitu.com/utt and enter the passcode found in the back of your manual.

As a professor, Mike Adams got involved with free-speech issues on college campuses even before he was a Christian. He eventually came to realize that college administrators pick and choose which ideas they oppose, and among their most consistent targets are conservative traditions and Christian morals.

After 9/11, Mike responded to an e-mail from a student saying the United States deserved to be attacked. This resulted in a conflict with his university. At issue was whether a college could limit freedom of speech guaranteed in the Constitution.

His story was picked up by *U.S. News & World Report* and Fox News and went viral. The university reversed itself but Mike got involved in free speech issues across the country. He has become a recognized expert, has spoken on national TV, has written a book, and has been in demand on college campuses.

Christians can fight and win battles in the court of public opinion using the First Amendment to restore the First Amendment. But sometimes Christians must resort to the courts of law as well. As a result of recent legal battles, the number of colleges with restrictive free-speech codes has shrunk from 90 percent to 58 percent.

1. Should Christians read what opponents of Christianity have to say?

2. How should you respond if your free speech rights are violated on your high school or college campus?

3.   What did Oliver Wendell Holmes mean when he said, "Every idea is an incitement?"

4.   Is it ever right for Christians to resort to a court of law when asserting their rights?

Chapter 15 Key Points

Key Questions:

1. What is politics?
2. How do the six dominant Western worldviews approach politics?

Key Terms:

1. Anarchism
2. Anarchy
3. Autarchy*
4. Capitalism
5. Civil Disobedience
6. Communism
7. Distributive Justice
8. *Dhimmi*
9. Identity Politics
10. Islamic Theocracy*
11. Jihad
12. *Jizya*
13. Libertarianism
14. Neo-Marxism
15. Political Conservatism
16. Political Correctness
17. Political Liberalism*
18. Political Pessimism*
19. Politics*
20. Power
21. Progressivism*
22. Pure Nature View
23. Sin Nature View
24. Social Contract
25. Socialism
26. Sphere Sovereignty
27. Statism*
28. Subsidiarity*
29. Theocracy

Key Verses:

1. Matthew 22:15–22
2. Acts 5:27–29
3. Romans 13:1–7
4. 1 Peter 2:13–14

Key Players:

1. Edmund Burke
2. Milton Friedman
3. Thomas Hobbes
4. Abraham Kuyper
5. John Locke
6. Robert Nozick
7. Ayn Rand
8. John Rawls
9. Jean Jacques Rousseau

Key Works:

1. *Reflections on the Revolution in France* by Edmund Burke
2. *Leviathan* by Thomas Hobbes
3. "Sphere Sovereignty" by Abraham Kuyper
4. *Of Civil Government* by John Locke
5. *Two Treatises on Government* by John Locke
6. *Anarchy, State, and Utopia* by Robert Nozick
7. *Manual for a Perfect Government* by John Hagelin
8. *A Theory of Justice* by John Rawls

Short answer or essay question on the exam

Hello there!

Sorry I haven't written in a while. I thought classes would slow down after midterms. Boy, was I wrong! Student Government elections are coming up in a few weeks, so the gang and I have been making flyers and planning speeches for the debates between the candidates. I can't believe I am actually running for a senate position! I have already been passing out flyers in my classes, and I even gave a speech in front of my Political Theory class about my platform: campus-wide free speech zone, increasing dining hall hours, and a library that is open 24/7. So far, other students have seemed really interested in these policy changes, and others people have actually suggested more of them! I am excited and all, but it is a bit weird seeing my face on flyers around campus. I'll let you know more about what happens in the next few weeks!

Other than campaigning, I haven't been doing too much outside of school. Mark and I have been running in the morning consistently. I don't want to put on the freshman forty! It has been a good experience getting to know Mark better. We have been talking a lot about the elections on campus and all the changes students have been promoting. Through our talks, I began to think seriously about what I was running for and what effects my changes would have at the university. To be honest, I never really paid too much attention during elections at home. It seemed like whoever spent the most money on their campaign won, regardless of their platform. Now, I have an appreciation for politics that I didn't have before. One person can make a difference, and it is important to stand for the right things in life.

Anyway, Mark brought up some interesting ideas about politics. As a Marxist, he spoke rather harshly about the "democracy" of capitalists. He said communism is "true" democracy. Since Sarah and Mark tend to agree, I wonder what she would say in comparison with Mark. **What is the Secularist view of politics?** Also **how does Marxism view politics?** I am meeting with Paige later on this week to talk about campaign strategies, so I will probably learn more about her views on politics as well. Of course, I would like to be prepared to ask questions. **What role does politics play in Postmodernism?** I know from your last letter that Islam adheres to shariah law. I bet this has implications on their political views, but I am not sure how exactly. **What is the Islamic view of politics?**

During my conversations, I began wondering what Christianity thinks about politics. Growing up, I heard people say Christians shouldn't be involved in politics because the world is a lost cause. Mark seems to agree. He said Christians should to stick to the immaterial world and keep religion out of politics. What do you think? **Should Christians be involved in politics and, if so, how?**

Thanks for all your help! Your worldview class has helped me out a lot. Hopefully we can talk more soon.

See you later!
–Doug

UNIT

16

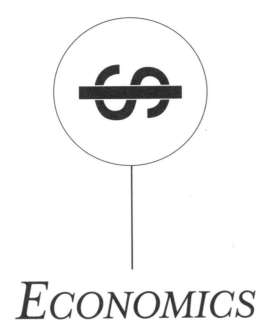

ECONOMICS

CHAPTER 16 LEARNING OBJECTIVES

Students will be able to:

1. describe why economics is important. [16.2]

2. identify the basics of economics. [16.3]

3. list the five building blocks of economic success. [16.4]

4. explain Secularism's approach to economics. [16.5]

5. explain Marxism's approach to economics. [16.6]

6. explain Postmodernism's approach to economics. [16.7]

7. explain New Spirituality's approach to economics. [16.8]

8. explain Islam's approach to economics. [16.9]

9. explain Christianity's approach to economics. [16.10]

1. What is economics and why does it matter? [16.2]

2. Where is humanity on the continuum of poverty to prosperity? [16.2]

3. What is meant by the terms "microeconomics," "macroeconomics," and "free market economics"? [16.3]

4. Are economists more concerned with the present or the future"? [16.3]

5. What are the building blocks necessary for a well-functioning economy? [16.4]

6. What role does the rule of law play in a healthy economy? [16.4]

7. Do you believe that digital property rights are among the rights guaranteed by the Constitution (article 1, section 8)? Do you think people's ideas, not just their physical property, should be protected from theft?

8. What role does limited government play in a healthy economy? [16.4]

9. What role does the freedom of ideas play in a healthy economy? [16.4]

10. What role does participation play in a healthy economy? [16.4]

11. What role does sustainability play in a healthy economy? [16.4]

12. How did the US get into its current debt predicament? [16.4]

13. How do you feel about the government running up debt that you and your children will be responsible to pay?

14. What economic system do Secularists prefer? [16.5]

15. Why do most Secularists embrace socialism? [16.5]

16. What is economic interventionism? [16.5]

17. Why do Marxists favor socialism over capitalism? [16.6]

18. What is the goal of Marxism and the transitional phase needed to get there? [16.6]

19. How does Postmodernism view economics? [16.7]

20. How does New Spirituality view economics? [16.8]

21. How does Islam view economics? [16.9]

22. What are some economic implications of Islamic law? [16.9]

23. How does Christianity view economics? [16.10]

24. What biblical principles and ideas have helped shape capitalism? [16.10]

George Orwell, though a socialist, looked with disgust at the new Communist government in Russia and was convinced it would be disastrous for the country and the rest of the world. He published *Animal Farm* in 1945 when Stalin was at the height of his power and his allegory helped millions to see what was really going on.

The story begins with Major, a boar, giving a stirring speech about the tyranny of their master, Mr. Jones. Two pigs, Napoleon and Snowball, lead a revolt and take over the farm. They establish a new order that is supposed to be fair to all. However, the pigs are favored as time goes on. Snowball and Napoleon assert themselves as leaders until Napoleon exiles Snowball and takes over as a dictator. The story ends with the animals miserable, while Napoleon walks on two legs, wears the same clothes, and sleeps in the same bed as the original farmer. The last chapter finds him playing cards with his human neighbors and the animals can't tell the species apart.

All the changes Old Major called for have been subverted and the Seven Commandments the revolution began with have been abandoned. All that's left is the new Golden Rule: "All animals are equal, but some animals are more equal than others." This is the most famous line in the book.

As you read the first and last chapters of this story, look for parallels between the farm and totalitarian governments in today's world.

A SELECTION FROM *ANIMAL FARM*
by George Orwell

Chapter 1

Mr. Jones, of the Manor Farm, had locked the hen-houses for the night, but was too drunk to remember to shut the pop-holes. With the ring of light from his lantern dancing from side to side, he lurched across the yard, kicked off his boots at the back door, drew himself a last glass of beer from the barrel in the scullery, and made his way up to bed, where Mrs. Jones was already snoring.

As soon as the light in the bedroom went out there was a stirring and a fluttering all through the farm buildings. Word had gone round during the day that old Major, the prize Middle White boar, had had a strange dream on the previous night and wished to communicate it to the other animals. It had been agreed that they should all meet in the big barn as soon as Mr. Jones was safely out of the way. Old Major (so he was always called, though the name under which he had been exhibited was

Willingdon Beauty) was so highly regarded on the farm that everyone was quite ready to lose an hour's sleep in order to hear what he had to say.

At one end of the big barn, on a sort of raised platform, Major was already ensconced on his bed of straw, under a lantern which hung from a beam. He was twelve years old and had lately grown rather stout, but he was still a majestic-looking pig, with a wise and benevolent appearance in spite of the fact that his tushes had never been cut. Before long the other animals began to arrive and make themselves comfortable after their different fashions. First came the three dogs, Bluebell, Jessie, and Pincher, and then the pigs, who settled down in the straw immediately in front of the platform. The hens perched themselves on the window-sills, the pigeons fluttered up to the rafters, the sheep and cows lay down behind the pigs and began to chew the cud. The two cart-horses, Boxer and Clover, came in together, walking very slowly and setting down their vast hairy hoofs with great care lest there should be some small animal concealed in the straw. Clover was a stout motherly mare approaching middle life, who had never quite got her figure back after her fourth foal. Boxer was an enormous beast, nearly eighteen hands high, and as strong as any two ordinary horses put together. A white stripe down his nose gave him a somewhat stupid appearance, and in fact he was not of first-rate intelligence, but he was universally respected for his steadiness of character and tremendous powers of work. After the horses came Muriel, the white goat, and Benjamin, the donkey. Benjamin was the oldest animal on the farm, and the worst tempered. He seldom talked, and when he did, it was usually to make some cynical remark—for instance, he would say that God had given him a tail to keep the flies off, but that he would sooner have had no tail and no flies. Alone among the animals on the farm he never laughed. If asked why, he would say that he saw nothing to laugh at. Nevertheless, without openly admitting it, he was devoted to Boxer; the two of them usually spent their Sundays together in the small paddock beyond the orchard, grazing side by side and never speaking.

The two horses had just lain down when a brood of ducklings, which had lost their mother, filed into the barn, cheeping feebly and wandering from side to side to find some place where they would not be trodden on. Clover made a sort of wall round them with her great foreleg, and the ducklings nestled down inside it and promptly fell asleep. At the last moment Mollie, the foolish, pretty white mare who drew Mr. Jones's trap, came mincing daintily in, chewing at a lump of sugar. She took a place near the front and began flirting her white mane, hoping to draw attention to the red ribbons it was plaited with. Last of all came the cat, who looked round, as usual, for the warmest place, and finally squeezed herself in between Boxer and Clover; there she purred contentedly throughout Major's speech without listening to a word of what he was saying.

All the animals were now present except Moses, the tame raven, who slept on a perch behind the back door. When Major saw that they had all made themselves comfortable and were waiting attentively, he cleared his throat and began:

"Comrades, you have heard already about the strange dream that I had last night. But I will come to the dream later. I have something else to say first. I do not think, comrades, that I shall be with you for many months longer, and before I die, I feel it my duty to pass on to you such wisdom as I have acquired. I have had a long life, I have had much time for thought as I lay alone in my stall, and I think I may say that I understand the nature of life on this earth as well as any animal now living. It is about this that I wish to speak to you.

"Now, comrades, what is the nature of this life of ours? Let us face it: our lives are miserable, laborious, and short. We are born, we are given just so much food as will keep the breath in our bodies, and those of us who are capable of it are forced to work to the last atom of our strength; and the very instant that our usefulness has come to an end we are slaughtered with hideous cruelty. No animal in England knows the meaning of happiness or leisure after he is a year old. No animal in England is free. The life of an animal is misery and slavery: that is the plain truth.

"But is this simply part of the order of nature? Is it because this land of ours is so poor that it cannot afford a decent life to those who dwell upon it? No, comrades, a thousand times no! The soil of England is fertile, its climate is good, it is capable of affording food in abundance to an enormously greater number of animals than now inhabit it. This single farm of ours would support a dozen horses, twenty cows, hundreds of sheep—and all of them living in a comfort and a dignity that are now almost beyond our imagining. Why then do we continue in this miserable condition? Because nearly the whole of the produce of our labour is stolen from us by human beings. There, comrades, is the answer to all our problems. It is summed up in a single word—Man. Man is the only real enemy we have. Remove Man from the scene, and the root cause of hunger and overwork is abolished for ever.

"Man is the only creature that consumes without producing. He does not give milk, he does not lay eggs, he is too weak to pull the plough, he cannot run fast enough to catch rabbits. Yet he is lord of all the animals. He sets them to work, he gives back to them the bare minimum that will prevent them from starving, and the rest he keeps for himself. Our labour tills the soil, our dung fertilises it, and yet there is not one of us that owns more than his bare skin. You cows that I see before me, how many thousands of gallons of milk have you given during this last year? And what has happened to that milk which should have been breeding up sturdy calves? Every drop of it has gone down the throats of our enemies. And you hens, how many eggs have you laid in this last year, and how many of those eggs ever hatched into chickens? The rest have all gone to market to bring in money for Jones and his men. And you, Clover, where are those four foals you bore, who should have been the support and pleasure of your old age? Each was sold at a year old—you will never see one of them again. In return for your four confinements and all your labour in the fields, what have you ever had except your bare rations and a stall?

"And even the miserable lives we lead are not allowed to reach their natural span. For myself I do not grumble, for I am one of the lucky ones. I am twelve years old and have had over four hundred children. Such is the natural life of a pig. But no animal escapes the cruel knife in the end. You young porkers who are sitting in front of me, every one of you will scream your lives out at the block within a year. To that horror we all must come—cows, pigs, hens, sheep, everyone. Even the horses and the dogs have no better fate. You, Boxer, the very day that those great muscles of yours lose their power, Jones will sell you to the knacker, who will cut your throat and boil you down for the foxhounds. As for the dogs, when they grow old and toothless, Jones ties a brick round their necks and drowns them in the nearest pond.

"Is it not crystal clear, then, comrades, that all the evils of this life of ours spring from the tyranny of human beings? Only get rid of Man, and the produce of our labour would be our own. Almost overnight we could become rich and free. What then must we do? Why, work night and day, body and soul, for the overthrow of the human race! That is my message to you, comrades: Rebellion! I do not know when that Rebellion will come, it might be in a week or in a hundred years, but I know, as surely as I see this straw beneath my feet, that sooner or later justice will be done. Fix your eyes on that, comrades, throughout the short remainder of your lives! And above all, pass on this message of mine to those who come after you, so that future generations shall carry on the struggle until it is victorious.

"And remember, comrades, your resolution must never falter. No argument must lead you astray. Never listen when they tell you that Man and the animals have a common interest, that the prosperity of the one is the prosperity of the others. It is all lies. Man serves the interests of no creature except himself. And among us animals let there be perfect unity, perfect comradeship in the struggle. All men are enemies. All animals are comrades."

At this moment there was a tremendous uproar. While Major was speaking four large rats had crept out of their holes and were sitting on their hindquarters, listening to him. The dogs had suddenly caught sight of them, and it was only by a swift dash for their holes that the rats saved their lives. Major raised his trotter for silence.

"Comrades," he said, "here is a point that must be settled. The wild creatures, such as rats and rabbits—are they our friends or our enemies? Let us put it to the vote. I propose this question to the meeting: Are rats comrades?"

The vote was taken at once, and it was agreed by an overwhelming majority that rats were comrades. There were only four dissentients, the three dogs and the cat, who was afterwards discovered to have voted on both sides. Major continued:

"I have little more to say. I merely repeat, remember always your duty of enmity towards Man and all his ways. Whatever goes upon two legs is an enemy. Whatever goes upon four legs, or has wings, is a friend. And remember also that in fighting against Man, we must not come to resemble him. Even when you have conquered him, do not adopt his vices. No animal must ever live in a house, or sleep in a bed, or wear clothes, or drink alcohol, or smoke tobacco, or touch money, or engage in trade. All the habits of Man are evil. And, above all, no animal must ever tyrannise over his own kind. Weak or strong, clever or simple, we are all brothers. No animal must ever kill any other animal. All animals are equal.

"And now, comrades, I will tell you about my dream of last night. I cannot describe that dream to you. It was a dream of the earth as it will be when Man has vanished. But it reminded me of something that I had long forgotten. Many years ago, when I was a little pig, my mother and the other sows used to sing an old song of which they knew only the tune and the first three words. I had known that tune in my infancy, but it had long since passed out of my mind. Last night, however, it came back to me in my dream. And what is more, the words of the song also came back-words, I am certain, which were sung by the animals of long ago and have been lost to memory for generations. I will sing you that song now, comrades. I am old and my voice is hoarse, but when I have taught you the tune, you can sing it better for yourselves. It is called 'Beasts of England.'"

Old Major cleared his throat and began to sing. As he had said, his voice was hoarse, but he sang well enough, and it was a stirring tune, something between "Clementine" and "La Cucaracha." The words ran:

> Beasts of England, beasts of Ireland,
> Beasts of every land and clime,
> Hearken to my joyful tidings
> Of the golden future time.
>
> Soon or late the day is coming,
> Tyrant Man shall be o'erthrown,
> And the fruitful fields of England
> Shall be trod by beasts alone.
>
> Rings shall vanish from our noses,
> And the harness from our back,
> Bit and spur shall rust forever,
> Cruel whips no more shall crack.
>
> Riches more than mind can picture,
> Wheat and barley, oats and hay,
> Clover, beans, and mangel-wurzels
> Shall be ours upon that day.
>
> Bright will shine the fields of England,
> Purer shall its waters be,
> Sweeter yet shall blow its breezes
> On the day that sets us free.
>
> For that day we all must labour,
> Though we die before it break;
> Cows and horses, geese and turkeys,
> All must toil for freedom's sake.
>
> Beasts of England, beasts of Ireland,
> Beasts of every land and clime,
> Hearken well and spread my tidings
> Of the golden future time.

The singing of this song threw the animals into the wildest excitement. Almost before Major had reached the end, they had begun singing it for themselves. Even the stupidest of them had already picked up the tune and a few of the words, and as for the clever ones, such as the pigs and dogs, they had the entire song by heart within a few minutes. And then, after a few preliminary tries, the whole farm burst out into 'Beasts of England' in tremendous unison. The cows lowed it, the dogs whined it, the sheep bleated it, the horses whinnied it, the ducks quacked it. They were so delighted with the song that they sang it right through five times in succession, and might have continued singing it all night if they had not been interrupted.

Unfortunately, the uproar awoke Mr. Jones, who sprang out of bed, making sure that there was a fox in the yard. He seized the gun which always stood in a corner of his bedroom, and let fly a charge of number 6 shot into the darkness. The pellets buried themselves in the wall of the barn and the meeting broke up hurriedly. Everyone fled to his own sleeping-place. The birds jumped on to their perches, the animals settled down in the straw, and the whole farm was asleep in a moment.

Chapter 10

Years passed. The seasons came and went, the short animal lives fled by. A time came when there was no one who remembered the old days before the Rebellion, except Clover, Benjamin, Moses the raven, and a number of the pigs.

Muriel was dead; Bluebell, Jessie, and Pincher were dead. Jones too was dead—he had died in an inebriates' home in another part of the country. Snowball was forgotten. Boxer was forgotten, except by the few who had known him. Clover was an old stout mare now, stiff in the joints and with a tendency to rheumy eyes. She was two years past the retiring age, but in fact no animal had ever actually retired. The talk of setting aside a corner of the pasture for superannuated animals had long since been dropped. Napoleon was now a mature boar of twenty-four stone. Squealer was so fat that he could with difficulty see out of his eyes. Only old Benjamin was much the same as ever, except for being a little greyer about the muzzle, and, since Boxer's death, more morose and taciturn than ever.

There were many more creatures on the farm now, though the increase was not so great as had been expected in earlier years. Many animals had been born to whom the Rebellion was only a dim tradition, passed on by word of mouth, and others had been bought who had never heard mention of such a thing before their arrival. The farm possessed three horses now besides Clover. They were fine upstanding beasts, willing workers and good comrades, but very stupid. None of them proved able to learn the alphabet beyond the letter B. They accepted everything that they were told about the Rebellion and the principles of Animalism, especially from Clover, for whom they had an almost filial respect; but it was doubtful whether they understood very much of it.

The farm was more prosperous now, and better organised: it had even been enlarged by two fields which had been bought from Mr. Pilkington. The windmill had been successfully completed at last, and the farm possessed a threshing machine and a hay elevator of its own, and various new buildings had been added to it. Whymper had bought himself a dogcart. The windmill, however, had not after all been used for generating electrical power. It was used for milling corn, and brought in a handsome money profit. The animals were hard at work building yet another windmill;

when that one was finished, so it was said, the dynamos would be installed. But the luxuries of which Snowball had once taught the animals to dream, the stalls with electric light and hot and cold water, and the three-day week, were no longer talked about. Napoleon had denounced such ideas as contrary to the spirit of Animalism. The truest happiness, he said, lay in working hard and living frugally.

Somehow it seemed as though the farm had grown richer without making the animals themselves any richer—except, of course, for the pigs and the dogs. Perhaps this was partly because there were so many pigs and so many dogs. It was not that these creatures did not work, after their fashion. There was, as Squealer was never tired of explaining, endless work in the supervision and organisation of the farm. Much of this work was of a kind that the other animals were too ignorant to understand. For example, Squealer told them that the pigs had to expend enormous labours every day upon mysterious things called "files," "reports," "minutes," and "memoranda." These were large sheets of paper which had to be closely covered with writing, and as soon as they were so covered, they were burnt in the furnace. This was of the highest importance for the welfare of the farm, Squealer said. But still, neither pigs nor dogs produced any food by their own labour; and there were very many of them, and their appetites were always good.

As for the others, their life; so far as they knew, was as it had always been. They were generally hungry, they slept on straw, they drank from the pool, they laboured in the fields; in winter they were troubled by the cold, and in summer by the flies. Sometimes the older ones among them racked their dim memories and tried to determine whether in the early days of the Rebellion, when Jones's expulsion was still recent, things had been better or worse than now. They could not remember. There was nothing with which they could compare their present lives: they had nothing to go upon except Squealer's lists of figures, which invariably demonstrated that everything was getting better and better. The animals found the problem insoluble; in any case, they had little time for speculating on such things now. Only old Benjamin professed to remember every detail of his long life and to know that things never had been, nor ever could be much better or much worse—hunger, hardship, and disappointment being, so he said, the unalterable law of life.

And yet the animals never gave up hope. More, they never lost, even for an instant, their sense of honour and privilege in being members of Animal Farm. They were still the only farm in the whole county—in all England!—owned and operated by animals. Not one of them, not even the youngest, not even the newcomers who had been brought from farms ten or twenty miles away, ever ceased to marvel at that. And when they heard the gun booming and saw the green flag fluttering at the masthead, their hearts swelled with imperishable pride, and the talk turned always towards the old heroic days, the expulsion of Jones, the writing of the Seven Commandments, the great battles in which the human invaders had been defeated. None of the old dreams had been abandoned. The Republic of the Animals which Major had foretold, when the green fields of England should be untrodden by human feet, was still believed in. Some day it was coming: it might not be soon, it might not be with in the lifetime of any animal now living, but still it was coming. Even the tune of Beasts of England was perhaps hummed secretly here and there: at any rate, it was a fact that every animal on the farm knew it, though no one would have dared to sing it aloud. It might be that their lives were hard and that not all of their hopes had been fulfilled; but they were conscious that they were not as other animals. If they went hungry, it was not from feeding tyrannical human beings; if they worked hard, at least they worked for themselves. No creature among them went upon two legs. No creature called any other creature "Master." All animals were equal.

One day in early summer Squealer ordered the sheep to follow him, and led them out to a piece of waste ground at the other end of the farm, which had become overgrown with birch saplings. The sheep spent the whole day there browsing at the leaves under Squealer's supervision. In the evening he returned to the farmhouse himself, but, as it was warm weather, told the sheep to stay where they were. It ended by their remaining there for a whole week, during which time the other animals saw nothing of them. Squealer was with them for the greater part of every day. He was, he said, teaching them to sing a new song, for which privacy was needed.

It was just after the sheep had returned, on a pleasant evening when the animals had finished work and were making their way back to the farm buildings, that the terrified neighing of a horse sounded from the yard. Startled, the animals stopped in their tracks. It was Clover's voice. She neighed again, and all the animals broke into a gallop and rushed into the yard. Then they saw what Clover had seen.

It was a pig walking on his hind legs.

Yes, it was Squealer. A little awkwardly, as though not quite used to supporting his considerable bulk in that position, but with perfect balance, he was strolling across the yard. And a moment later, out from the door of the farmhouse came a long file of pigs, all walking on their hind legs. Some did it better than others, one or two were even a trifle unsteady and looked as though they would have liked the support of a stick, but every one of them made his way right round the yard successfully. And finally there was a tremendous baying of dogs and a shrill crowing from the black cockerel, and out came Napoleon himself, majestically upright, casting haughty glances from side to side, and with his dogs gambolling round him.

He carried a whip in his trotter.

There was a deadly silence. Amazed, terrified, huddling together, the animals watched the long line of pigs march slowly round the yard. It was as though the world had turned upside-down. Then there came a moment when the first shock had worn off and when, in spite of everything—in spite of their terror of the dogs, and of the habit, developed through long years, of never complaining, never criticising, no matter what happened—they might have uttered some word of protest. But just at that moment, as though at a signal, all the sheep burst out into a tremendous bleating of—

"Four legs good, two legs better! Four legs good, two legs better! Four legs good, two legs better!"

It went on for five minutes without stopping. And by the time the sheep had quieted down, the chance to utter any protest had passed, for the pigs had marched back into the farmhouse.

Benjamin felt a nose nuzzling at his shoulder. He looked round. It was Clover. Her old eyes looked dimmer than ever. Without saying anything, she tugged gently at his mane and led him round to the end of the big barn, where the Seven Commandments were written. For a minute or two they stood gazing at the tatted wall with its white lettering.

"My sight is failing," she said finally. "Even when I was young I could not have read what was written there. But it appears to me that that wall looks different. Are the Seven Commandments the same as they used to be, Benjamin?"

For once Benjamin consented to break his rule, and he read out to her what was written on the wall. There was nothing there now except a single Commandment. It ran:

ALL ANIMALS ARE EQUAL

BUT SOME ANIMALS ARE MORE EQUAL THAN OTHERS

After that it did not seem strange when next day the pigs who were supervising the work of the farm all carried whips in their trotters. It did not seem strange to learn that the pigs had bought themselves a wireless set, were arranging to install a telephone, and had taken out subscriptions to "John Bull," "TitBits," and the "Daily Mirror." It did not seem strange when Napoleon was seen strolling in the farmhouse garden with a pipe in his mouth—no, not even when the pigs took Mr. Jones's clothes out of the wardrobes and put them on, Napoleon himself appearing in a black coat, ratcatcher breeches, and leather leggings, while his favourite sow appeared in the watered silk dress which Mrs. Jones had been used to wear on Sundays.

A week later, in the afternoon, a number of dogcarts drove up to the farm. A deputation of neighbouring farmers had been invited to make a tour of inspection. They were shown all over the farm, and expressed great admiration for everything they saw, especially the windmill. The animals were weeding the turnip field. They worked diligently hardly raising their faces from the ground, and not knowing whether to be more frightened of the pigs or of the human visitors.

That evening loud laughter and bursts of singing came from the farmhouse. And suddenly, at the sound of the mingled voices, the animals were stricken with curiosity. What could be happening in there, now that for the first time animals and human beings were meeting on terms of equality? With one accord they began to creep as quietly as possible into the farmhouse garden.

At the gate they paused, half frightened to go on but Clover led the way in. They tiptoed up to the house, and such animals as were tall enough peered in at the dining-room window. There, round the long table, sat half a dozen farmers and half a dozen of the more eminent pigs, Napoleon himself occupying the seat of honour at the head of the table. The pigs appeared completely at ease in their chairs The company had been enjoying a game of cards but had broken off for the moment, evidently in order to drink a toast. A large jug was circulating, and the mugs were being refilled with beer. No one noticed the wondering faces of the animals that gazed in at the window.

Mr. Pilkington, of Foxwood, had stood up, his mug in his hand. In a moment, he said, he would ask the present company to drink a toast. But before doing so, there were a few words that he felt it incumbent upon him to say.

It was a source of great satisfaction to him, he said—and, he was sure, to all others present—to feel that a long period of mistrust and misunderstanding had now come to an end. There had been a time—not that he, or any of the present company, had shared such sentiments—but there had been a time when the respected proprietors of Animal Farm had been regarded, he would not say with hostility, but perhaps with a certain measure of misgiving, by their human neighbours. Unfortunate incidents had occurred, mistaken ideas had been current. It had been felt that the existence of a farm owned and operated by pigs was somehow abnormal and was liable to have an unsettling effect in the neighbourhood. Too many farmers had assumed, without due enquiry, that on such a farm a spirit of licence and indiscipline would prevail. They had been nervous about the effects upon their own animals, or even upon their human employees. But all such doubts were now dispelled. Today he and his friends had visited Animal Farm and inspected every inch of it with their own eyes, and what did they find? Not only the most up-to-date methods, but a discipline and an orderliness which should be an example to all farmers everywhere. He believed that he was right in saying that the lower animals on Animal Farm did more work and received less food than any animals in the county. Indeed, he and his fellow-visitors today had observed many features which they intended to introduce on their own farms immediately.

He would end his remarks, he said, by emphasising once again the friendly feelings that subsisted, and ought to subsist, between Animal Farm and its neighbours. Between pigs and human beings there was not, and there need not be, any clash of interests whatever. Their struggles and their difficulties were one. Was not the labour problem the same everywhere? Here it became apparent that Mr. Pilkington was about to spring some carefully prepared witticism on the company, but for a moment he was too overcome by amusement to be able to utter it. After much choking, during which his various chins turned purple, he managed to get it out: "If you have your lower animals to contend with," he said, "we have our lower classes!" This *bon mot* set the table in a roar; and Mr. Pilkington once again congratulated the pigs on the low rations, the long working hours, and the general absence of pampering which he had observed on Animal Farm.

And now, he said finally, he would ask the company to rise to their feet and make certain that their glasses were full. "Gentlemen," concluded Mr. Pilkington, "gentlemen, I give you a toast: To the prosperity of Animal Farm!"

There was enthusiastic cheering and stamping of feet. Napoleon was so gratified that he left his place and came round the table to clink his mug against Mr. Pilkington's before emptying it. When the cheering had died down, Napoleon, who had remained on his feet, intimated that he too had a few words to say.

Like all of Napoleon's speeches, it was short and to the point. He too, he said, was happy that the period of misunderstanding was at an end. For a long time there had been rumours—circulated, he had reason to think, by some malignant enemy—that there was something subversive and even revolutionary in the outlook of himself and his colleagues. They had been credited with attempting to stir up rebellion among the animals on neighbouring farms. Nothing could be further from the truth! Their sole wish, now and in the past, was to live at peace and in normal business relations with their neighbours. This farm which he had the honour to control, he added, was a co-operative enterprise. The title-deeds, which were in his own possession, were owned by the pigs jointly.

He did not believe, he said, that any of the old suspicions still lingered, but certain changes had been made recently in the routine of the farm which should have the effect of promoting confidence still further. Hitherto the animals on the farm had had a rather foolish custom of addressing one another as "Comrade." This was to be suppressed. There had also been a very strange custom, whose origin was unknown, of marching every Sunday morning past a boar's skull which was nailed to a post in the garden. This, too, would be suppressed, and the skull had already been buried. His visitors might have observed, too, the green flag which flew from the masthead. If so, they would perhaps have noted that the white hoof and horn with which it had previously been marked had now been removed. It would be a plain green flag from now onwards.

He had only one criticism, he said, to make of Mr. Pilkington's excellent and neighbourly speech. Mr. Pilkington had referred throughout to "Animal Farm." He could not of course know—for he, Napoleon, was only now for the first time announcing it—that the name "Animal Farm" had been abolished. Henceforward the farm was to be known as "The Manor Farm"—which, he believed, was its correct and original name.

"Gentlemen," concluded Napoleon, "I will give you the same toast as before, but in a different form. Fill your glasses to the brim. Gentlemen, here is my toast: To the prosperity of The Manor Farm!"

There was the same hearty cheering as before, and the mugs were emptied to the dregs. But as the animals outside gazed at the scene, it seemed to them that some strange thing was happening. What was it that had altered in the faces of the pigs? Clover's old dim eyes flitted from one face to another. Some of them had five chins, some had four, some had three. But what was it that seemed to be melting and changing? Then, the applause having come to an end, the company took up their cards and continued the game that had been interrupted, and the animals crept silently away.

But they had not gone twenty yards when they stopped short. An uproar of voices was coming from the farmhouse. They rushed back and looked through the window again. Yes, a violent quarrel was in progress. There were shoutings, bangings on the table, sharp suspicious glances, furious denials. The source of the trouble appeared to be that Napoleon and Mr. Pilkington had each played an ace of spades simultaneously.

Twelve voices were shouting in anger, and they were all alike. No question, now, what had happened to the faces of the pigs. The creatures outside looked from pig to man, and from man to pig, and from pig to man again; but already it was impossible to say which was which.

Animal Farm by George Orwell. Published in 1945, this work meets the criteria for fair use.

"ANIMAL FARM" DISCUSSION QUESTIONS

1. *Animal Farm* was an allegory that pointed to what country and historical figures of Orwell's time?

2. How is the original condition of the animals on the farm similar to that of the workers in Russia before the 1917 revolution?

3. Which animals were better off years after the rebellion and which were worse off? What are the parallels to the Soviet Union?

4. What is the significance of the pigs walking on their hind legs and playing cards with humans at the end of the book?

5. Can you name some other famous allegorical books that have had a significant influence and briefly summarize their messages?

Chad Connelly points out the differences between socialism (where the state controls the means of production) and a free market society (where people do the work they want and trade for the goods they want). He then contrasts the European economic model with the American model. The former tries to establish equality of *outcome*, which doesn't work except by force. The latter is based on equality of *opportunity*, which leads to freedom and prosperity.

Connelly touches briefly on the economic strategies of Communism and contrasts these with free enterprise, where material well-being comes about by natural resources, plus human energy (work), multiplied by the tools of production. He concludes by noting the stages of the world's greatest civilizations.

To access this video, go to www.summitu.com/utt and enter the passcode found in the back of your manual.

The differences between socialism and a free market society:

Socialism:

- The _____ controls the means of production.
- Central planning is in the hands of the state.
- The state forces participation and government dependency.
- The state solves problems, instead of focusing on people.

Free Market Society:

- People can do the work they want and trade for the goods and services they want.
- Material well-being comes about by natural resources plus _____(work) multiplied by the tools of production.
- There isn't a "_____" of resources but an expanding pie based on the goods and services people create.
- People solve their own problems and create their own opportunities.

The European economic model contrasted with the American model:

- **European Model:** God gives power to government (state), which gives power, rights, and resources to the people. Government tries to establish equality of _____, which doesn't work except by force.
- **American Model:** Our rights come from God, not the state. Government is committed to providing equality of _____, which leads to freedom and prosperity.

Economic strategies of Communism:

- _____ of (private) property
- Heavy progressive _____
- Abolition of rights of inheritance
- Confiscation of property from immigrants and rebels

Pillars of economic wisdom:

1. Nothing in the material world comes from nowhere, nor can it be free.
2. Everything in our economic lives has a source, a cost that must be paid.
3. Government is never a source of goods. Everything produced is produced by the people.

4. Everything government gives to the people it must first take from the
_____.

5. The greater the government the greater the poverty. The greater the freedom the greater the wealth.

Progression of the world's greatest civilizations:

- Bondage leads to spiritual faith
- Spiritual faith leads to great courage
- Great courage leads to liberty
- Liberty leads to abundance
- Abundance leads to selfishness
- Selfishness leads to complacency
- Complacency leads to apathy
- Apathy leads to dependency
- Dependency leads to _____

1. What are some of the differences between socialism and a free market society?

2. How do the European model and the American model of economics differ?

3. What is the "invisible hand" at work in the free market?

4. What economic steps does *The Communist Manifesto* call for on the way to worldwide Communism?

5. What is the common trajectory of great civilizations? Where does America fit on this timeline?

Chapter 16 Key Points

Key Questions:

1. What is economics?
2. How do the six dominant Western worldviews approach economics?

Key Terms:

1. Biblical Stewardship*
2. Capital
3. Capitalism
4. Communism
5. Decentered Self
6. Economic Competition
7. Economics*
8. Free Market Economy
9. Economic Interventionism*
10. *Jizyah*
11. Macroeconomics
12. Microeconomics
13. *Riba*
14. Say's Law
15. Shariah Economics*
16. Socialism*
17. Surplus Value Theory of Labor
18. *Ummah*
19. Universal Enlightened Production*
20. Usury
21. *Zakat*

Key Verses:

1. Genesis 2:15
2. Exodus 20:15
3. Exodus 20:17
4. Proverbs 10:4
5. Proverbs 14:23
6. Proverbs 16:8
7. Ephesians 4:28
8. 2 Thessalonians 3:10

Key Players:

1. Fredrick Engels
2. Erich Fromm
3. John Maynard Keynes
4. Karl Marx
5. Ayn Rand
6. Richard Rorty
7. Jean Baptiste Say
8. Adam Smith

Key Works:

1. *Das Capital* by Karl Marx
2. *Islam, Economics, and Society* by Syed Nawab Haider Naqvi
3. *Postmodern Moments in Modern Economics* by David Ruccio and Jack Amariglio
4. *Socialism* by Fredrick Engels
5. *The Wealth of Nations* by Adam Smith

Short answer or essay question on the exam

Hello there!

Best break idea ever? Hiking the Appalachian Trail with Mark, Nathan, and Muhammad. With backpacks, trail mix, and sleeping bags in tow, we spent about ten days on the trail. It was probably the most adventurous retreat I have ever taken. We caught our own food, cooked it over a campfire, and slept under the stars. It was an amazing bonding experience. We saw a lot of wildlife and flora that Nathan, our resident biologist, identified for us. Good thing he was there, because I almost ate poisonous berries! It was a welcome break from the stress of classes and campaigning.

Speaking of classes, my professors are already talking about final papers and exams. For my macroeconomics class, the students are required to write a paper on what they think is the ideal economic system. Before I began the class, I heard that the free market system was the most ideal. My professor, however, seemed to favor a lot of government intervention to help with the distribution of wealth. He didn't actually say he favored socialism, but I believe that is his leaning. He portrayed capitalism as a greedy, manipulative system where the rich oppress everyone else. Going into this final paper, I no longer have any idea which economic system is the most biblical. Nathan and I were talking about it for a while during the hike, but he didn't help me out too much. If I understood him correctly, he believed that we all have the potential to become rich and successful if we only ask the universe!

Hearing us talk about economics, Mark jumped right into the conversation. He said that a market-oriented economy, like capitalism, is a chaotic system only useful for exploiting the poor. He talked about socialism as the solution. Somehow, socialism will lead to the establishment of communism. Mark even suggested that socialism is consistent with the teachings of Christianity. I'm not sure how that works exactly, but we are called to care for the poor, right?

I know Sarah and Mark sometimes agree on these worldview matters. Have you heard anything about this in your worldview class? **What is the Secularist view of economics?** Also, **what is the Marxist view?**

Nathan's views were probably the most confusing. **What is the role of economics in New Spirituality?** Perhaps my biggest concern is not knowing which economic system is the most consistent with Christianity. I can't remember if economics is even addressed in the Bible. **Are there any biblical principles of economics, and if so, what are they?**

Thanks for all your help. You are a lifesaver! Boy, am I glad that you had a worldview class to help me out with all this. Hopefully I will have time to write again soon. With finals and elections coming up, I'm not sure I will even have time to sleep!

See ya later!
–Doug

UNIT

17

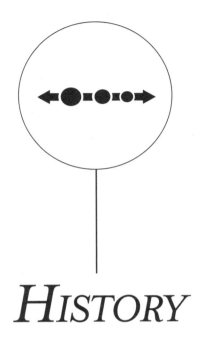

HISTORY

CHAPTER 17 LEARNING OBJECTIVES

Students will be able to:

1. articulate a synopsis of the history of history. [17.2]

2. describe what historians do. [17.3]

3. explain Secularism's approach to history. [17.4]

4. explain Marxism's approach to history. [17.5]

5. explain Postmodernism's approach to history. [17.6]

6. explain New Spirituality's approach to history. [17.7]

7. explain Islam's approach to history. [17.8]

8. explain Christianity's approach to history. [17.9]

1. What is history and why is it important to study it? [17.1]

2. Do you have a favorite period of history that interests you or a certain historical figure that has influenced you?

3. Who are some of the people who shaped our understanding of history? [17.2]

4. What are two dangers threatening the study of history today? [17.2]

5. Is Christianity based on fact or faith? [17.2]

6. What do historians do? [17.3]

7. What's the difference between historiography and historicism? [17.3]

8. What does Secularism assume about history? [17.4]

9.   Where do Secularists think history is headed? [17.4]

10. What does Marxism assume about history? [17.5]

11. How do Marxists view the study of history? [17.5]

12. What does Postmodernism assume about history? [17.6]

13. For Postmodernists, what is the task of the historian? [17.6]

14. What does New Spirituality assume about history? [17.7]

15. What form of religion does New Spirituality think is appropriate for the modern age? [17.7]

16. What does Islam assume about history? [17.8]

17. How does the Islamic view of history justify a global Islamic state? [17.8]

18. Can Islam and Christianity peacefully coexist in the twenty-first century?

19. What does Christianity assume about history? [17.9]

20. How does Christianity make sense of the past in light of Christ's sacrifice? [17.9]

21. How does Christianity make sense of the present in light of Christ's sacrifice? [17.9]

22. How does Christianity make sense of the future in light of Christ's sacrifice? [17.9]

Censorship is a mandate by the civil government which prohibits the publication, sale, or distribution of material it deems to be politically harmful. Legally, censorship in violation of the First Amendment can only take place when an agent or agency of the state suppresses speech.

But censorship is far broader and more dangerous in today's secular world. In *Censoring the Past*, Gary DeMar asks and answers some key questions about censorship:

- What is censorship?
- When is it appropriate?
- Who draws the line?

DeMar examines censorship in such places as libraries, public schools, the news media, and the entertainment business (Hollywood). He illustrates the anti-Christian bias of many self-appointed censors whose "editing" extends from rewriting history to the selective coverage of international news.

The removal of religion from textbooks is a major area of concern. DeMar notes, "Since the nineteenth century, secularists have been gradually chipping away at the historical record, denying the impact Christianity has had on the development of the moral character of the United States."

As you read this essay, what areas of censorship are the most troubling to you?

CENSORING THE PAST
by Gary DeMar

There is a lot of talk today about censorship. Recent art exhibits, funded by tax dollars and promoted by the National Endowment for the Arts, have come under severe attack. Many Americans rightly criticize these exhibits as inappropriate, certainly for viewing, but most assuredly for government support and funding. Museums, government-funded artists, Hollywood activists, homosexual groups, and the government-funded NEA (National Endowment for the Arts)[1] are crying "censorship" over such protests.

Another battle is raging over the selling of pornography in popularly trafficked bookstores. Rev. Donald Wildmon and his American Family Association have targeted Waldenbooks, a subsidiary of K-Mart, for selling pornography. Harry Hoffman, president of Waldenbooks, says that Wildmon and others like him "want to censor and stop the sales of constitutionally protected publications they deem objectionable."[2]

Protests against pornography and government-funded art are not acts of censorship. Censorship is a mandate by the civil government which prohibits the publication, sale, or distribution of material it deems to be politically harmful. As civil libertarian Nat Hentoff describes it, "Legally, censorship in violation of the First Amendment can only take place when an agent or agency of the state—a public school principal, a congressman, a President—suppresses speech."[3]

It is not censorship for a government to refuse to pay for objectionable material. In the case of pornographic "art," the protestors are only asking that their tax money not be used to fund the offensive material. Rev. Wildmon is not asking the government to prohibit Waldenbooks from selling *Playboy* and *Penthouse*; he is only calling on concerned citizens to stop doing business with K-Mart and its subsidiaries.[4] He wants the same freedoms that the pornographers are claiming belong only to them. Wildmon writes: "We don't want K-Mart, *Playboy* and *Penthouse* drawing the line for the rest of us. The First Amendment belongs to all Americans, not just to pornographers."[5]

The Censor Band Wagon

Literature of all types has been scrutinized by numerous groups from different ends of the political and religious spectrum. Those on the political left have denounced classic works like Charles Dickens' *Oliver Twist* as being "anti-semitic." William Shakespeare's *King Lear* has been condemned as "sexist." *Tom Sawyer*, Mark Twain's coming-of-age classic, has suffered a double blow with denouncements of "racism" and "sexism." Beatrix Potter's *Peter Rabbit* and *Benjamin Bunny* have been criticized "because they are about 'middle-class rabbits.'"[6]

In 1988, librarians in Cobb County, Georgia, removed *Nancy Drew* and *The Hardy Boys* from the library shelves. The librarians cited lack of shelf space as the reason for the exclusion of the popular mystery series. Mary Louis Rheay, director of the Cobb County Library System, tells a different story, saying that "series books are poorly written and do not meet library standards for book selection."[7] In 1994 the library board in Wellesley, Massachusetts, voted 5 to 1 to keep *Playboy* on the shelves. The board said the magazine, like all its material, is protected by free speech provisions. "There is something in the library to offend everyone," librarian Anne Reynolds said. "We cannot be in the position of censoring everything. Those days are gone." Trustee Carol Gleason, who voted to remove the magazine, said, "If minors cannot buy the magazine in a store, why should they be able to obtain it in the library?"[8]

Who Draws the Line?

An ad hoc public school committee supported the removal of books by Dr. James Dobson, a Christian psychologist, from the library of the Early Childhood Family Education Program of the Mankato, Minnesota, school system. They were removed because the staff "disagreed with Dobson's views on child discipline, which includes an endorsement of spanking, and because of the religious nature of his philosophy."[9]

Donated books are often refused by libraries because of religious content. *The Closing of the American Heart*, written by Dr. Ronald H. Nash, was donated to the Haggard

Library in Plano, Texas, by a group of concerned citizens. Nash is a former professor of religion and philosophy at Western Kentucky University who presently teaches at Reformed Theological Seminary in Orlando, Florida. He has also served as an advisor to the United States Civil Rights Commission. Why was his book refused? Certainly not because of his academic and professional credentials. Book donations had to pass the library's evaluation criteria.[10] *The Closing of the American Heart* did not pass because of its Christian perspective.

Each year People for the American Way (PAW), a liberal political advocacy group, publishes a report on censorship and "book banning." Most of the books which are brought into question deal with occultic themes, promiscuous sexual content, and advocacy of homosexuality. Most of the protestors are parents who send their children to government controlled (public) schools. PAW considers such parental concern over what children read "attacks on the freedom to learn."[11] What PAW does not tell its unsuspecting audience is that incidents of so-called censorship are negligible compared to the number of schools and libraries in existence. For example, the most challenged book, *Scary Stories to Tell in the Dark*, "was challenged only 7 times out of 84,000 public schools and never removed." In fact, Kristi Harrick, press secretary for the Family Research Council, reports that "none of the most challenged books were censored."[12]

Eric Buehrer, a former public-school teacher and president of Gateways to Better Education in Lake Forest, California, states that "PAW has confused the issues of material selection and censorship. What used to be called discernment is now called censorship."[13] Why is it called "censorship" when parents apply standards for book selection but called "meeting library standards" when a librarian evaluates a book?

Judgments are constantly made as to what children should read and what books should appear on library shelves. As we've seen, librarians appeal to "library standards" when selecting books. There is nothing wrong with having "standards."

Unfortunately, these "library standards" are neither applied consistently in libraries and schools nor always reported in the same way by the press.[14] It seems that when concerned Christian parents voice objections to the content of books, they are said to be censors. But when books with Christian themes are refused by libraries or when teachers are denied the right to read a Bible silently during a reading period,[15] we learn that the rejection is based upon the religious nature of the literature. Rarely are such actions by libraries and schools said to be "censorship" by even the strongest opponents of book banning.

Will the Real Censors Please Stand Up

It is instructive how one segment of our society screams "censorship" every time its views are questioned, but when Christians claim "censorship" of the facts of history, they are ignored by the guardians of the First Amendment.

Liberal media coverage of world events is just one example of the anti-Christian bias of mainstream contemporary society. Consider journalistic coverage of events in Eastern Europe. Rev. Laszlo Tokes, the Hungarian pastor who sparked the Romanian

Revolution, stated that "Eastern Europe is not just in a political revolution but a religious renaissance." How many people read in their local newspapers or saw on the evening news that Rev. Tokes believed he had been saved from execution through "divine intervention"? Explicitly Christian themes are regularly excluded from news articles: "References to 'Jesus,' the 'Christian spirit,' and Czechoslovakia's role as the 'spiritual crossroads of Europe' were omitted from excerpts of President Vaclav Havel's New Year's Day address. *The New York Times*, *The Washington Post*, and *Newsweek* were among the sinful censors."[16]

None of these examples should surprise the informed Christian. The present educational establishment, to cite just one group, has been obscuring the past so that our children have no way of comparing the facts of history with the distorted version promoted by biased secular historians.

Censorship at Work in the Classroom

Public school textbooks are fertile ground for the seeds of willful historical deception. Paul C. Vitz, professor of psychology at New York University, spent months of careful analysis of sixty textbooks used in elementary schools across the country. The study was sponsored by the National Institute on Education. The texts were examined in terms of their references to religion, either directly or indirectly. "In grades 1 through 4 these books introduce the child to U.S. society—to family life, community activities, ordinary economic transactions, and some history. *None of the books covering grades 1 through 4 contain one word referring to any religious activity in contemporary American life*."[17] Dr. Vitz offers an example of how this translates into the real world of classroom instruction:

> Some particular examples of the bias against religion are significant. One social studies book has thirty pages on the Pilgrims, including the first Thanksgiving. But there is not one word (or image) that referred to religion as even a part of the Pilgrims' life. One mother whose son is in a class using this book wrote me to say that he came home and told her that "Thanksgiving was when the Pilgrims gave thanks to the Indians." The mother called the principal of this suburban New York City school to point out that Thanksgiving was when the Pilgrims thanked God. The principal responded by saying "that was her opinion"—the schools could only teach what was in the books![18]

In 1986 school children in Seattle, Washington, were given a large dose of revisionist history in the booklet *Teaching about Thanksgiving*. The children were told that "the Pilgrims were narrow-minded bigots who survived initially only with the Indian's help, but turned on them when their help wasn't needed anymore." The Pilgrims "had something up their sleeves other than friendship when they invited the Indians to a Thanksgiving feast, and it was the Indians who ended up bringing most of the food, anyway."[19] The booklet has obvious biases and is filled with historical inaccuracies. For example, supposedly Increase Mather preached a sermon in 1623 where he reportedly "gave special thanks to God for the plague of smallpox which had wiped out the majority of Wampanoag Indians, praising God for destroying 'chiefly young men and children, the very seeds of increase, thus clearing the forests for a better growth."[20] This sermon could not have been preached by Increase Mather, at least not in 1623, because he was not born until 1639.

The rewriting of history has even reached the pages of the Sunday comics. A story recently appeared about "Squanto and the First Thanksgiving." As all children know, Squanto was a great help to the Pilgrims. But was Squanto so much of a help that the first Thanksgiving was given in his honor? According to the author of the Squanto column, we learn that "the Pilgrims so appreciated Squanto's generosity that they had a great feast to show their thanks."[21] William Bradford, governor of Plymouth and the colony's first historian, continually makes reference to "the Lord Who never fails," "God's blessing," and "the Providence of God," in times of both plenty and want.[22] How uncharacteristic it would have been for the Plymouth settlers to ignore thanking God during a time of harvest. Edward Winslow, in his important chronicle of the history of Plymouth, reports the following eyewitness account of the colony's thanksgiving celebration:

> Our harvest being gotten in, our governor sent four men out fowling, that so we might, after a special manner, rejoice together after we had gathered the fruit of our labors. They four in one day killed as much fowl as, with a little help beside, served the company almost a week. At which time, among other recreations, we exercised our arms, many of the Indians coming among us, and among the rest their greatest king, Massasoit, with some ninety men, whom for three days we entertained and feasted; and they went out and killed five deer, which they brought to the plantation, and bestowed on our governor, and upon the captain and others. And although it be not always so plentiful as it was at this time with us, *yet by the goodness of God* we are so far from want, that we often wish you partakers of our plenty.[23]

Squanto was an example of God's providential care of the Pilgrims. He taught them how to farm in the New World and led them on trading expeditions. There is no doubt that these early Christian settlers thanked the "Indians" in general and Squanto in particular for their generosity in supplying venison to supplement the Pilgrims' meager Thanksgiving rations. As the historical record shows, however, thanksgiving was ultimately made to God. "Governor Bradford, with one eye on divine Providence, proclaimed a day of thanksgiving to God, and with the other eye on the local political situation, extended an invitation to neighboring Indians to share in the harvest feast. . . . This 'first Thanksgiving' was a feast called to suit the needs of the hour, which were to celebrate the harvest, thank the Lord for His goodness, and regale and impress the Indians."[24]

Censorship through Creative Editing

Dr. Vitz is not the only person to uncover the way public school texts minimize the role that Christianity played in the founding of our nation. Consider how a teacher's guide for the high school history text *Triumph of the American Nation*, published in 1986, omits material from the Mayflower Compact without informing the teacher that the document has been edited. Students in discussing the document are left with an incomplete understanding of what motivated these early founders because they do not have all the facts. The Mayflower Compact is depicted solely as a political document with its more striking religious elements deleted. Here is the document as presented by the textbook company. The **bold face** portions are missing from the textbook version:

> In the name of God, Amen. We whose names are underwritten, **the loyal subjects of our dread sovereign lord, King James, by the grace of God, of Great Britain, France, and Ireland, King, Defender of the Faith, etc.,** having undertaken **for the glory of God and advancement of the Christian faith and honor of our king and country,** a voyage to plant the first colony in the northern parts of Virginia, do **by these presents** solemnly and in the presence of God, and one another, covenant and combine ourselves together into a civil body politic. . . .[25]

These brave men and women had more on their minds than political freedom. Missionary zeal and the advancement of the Christian faith were their primary motivations as they risked life and property to carve out a new home in an uncertain wilderness.

The critics of America's early Christian origins have steadily removed such references from textbooks and have created a tense legal environment that frightens many teachers from even raising evidence contradicting the censored texts. Will a member of the ACLU threaten legal action against a teacher who decides to cite original source material to support a view that differs from the historical perspective of the textbook?

Hollywood History

The entertainment industry has entered the field of creative editing in an animated version of the story of Pocahontas, the Native American woman who pleaded with her father to spare the life of John Smith. Pocahontas later became a Christian and married another colonist, John Rolfe. But this episode will all be deleted from an animated retelling of the story. Kendall Hamilton of *Newsweek* offers the following report on the newly designed and politically correct Pocahontas:

> The film's P.C. prospects are . . . helped by the exclusion of Pocahontas's potentially, er, problematic later years, in which she was kidnapped by settlers and, after converting to Christianity, married one of her captors. Male-domination fantasy! Subversion of morally superior indigenous culture! Well, maybe, but [Producer James] Pentecost says such considerations weren't a factor: "We didn't really sidestep any of it for any reason other than this was the most direct way to tell the story and the clearest." Pass the peace pipe.[26]

While this might be the *official* explanation from Disney, my guess is that the studio was pressured by Native Americans to hide Pocahontas's "mistake" of rejecting her native religion.

William Holmes McGuffey's Eclectic Readers

A study of the historical record reveals that religion played a major role in the development of the public school curriculum. "Textbooks referred to God without embarrassment, and public schools considered one of their major tasks to be the development of character through the teaching of religion. For example, the *New England Primer* opened with religious admonitions followed by the Lord's Prayer, the Apostles' Creed, the Ten Commandments, and the names of the books of the Bible."[27]

The most widely used textbook series in public schools from 1836 to 1920 were William Holmes McGuffey's *Eclectic Readers*. More than 120 million *Readers* were sold during this period. The *Readers* stressed religion and its relationship to morality and the proper use of knowledge. In an introduction for a reissue of the *Fifth Reader*, historian Henry Steele Commager writes:

> What was the nature of the morality that permeated the *Readers*? It was deeply religious, and… religion then meant a Protestant Christianity. … The world of the *McGuffeys* was a world where no one questioned the truths of the Bible or their relevance to everyday contact. … The *Readers*, therefore, are filled with stories from the Bible, and tributes to its truth and beauty.[28]

Competing textbooks of the same era contained varying amounts of biblical material, but *McGuffey's* contained the greatest amount—"more than three times as much as any other text of the period."[29] Subsequent editions of the *Readers*—1857 and 1879—showed a reduction in the amount of material devoted to biblical themes. Even so, the 1879 edition contained the Sermon on the Mount, two selections from the Book of Psalms, the Lord's Prayer, the story of the death of Absalom (2 Samuel 18), and Paul's speech on the Areopagus (Acts 17). The Bible was still referred to as "'the Book of God,' 'a source of inspiration,' 'an important basis for life,' and was cited in support of particular moral issues."[30]

Antiseptic Texts

Since the nineteenth century, secularists have been gradually chipping away at the historical record, denying the impact Christianity has had on the development of the moral character of the United States. In 1898 Bishop Charles Galloway delivered a series of messages in the Chapel at Emory College in Georgia. In his messages he noted that "books on the making of our nation have been written, and are the texts in our colleges, in which the Christian religion, as a social and civil factor, has only scant or apologetic mention. This is either a fatal oversight or a deliberate purpose, and both alike to be deplored and condemned. A nation ashamed of its ancestry will be despised by its posterity."[31]

The 1980s saw an even greater expurgation of the impact the Christian religion has had on our nation. So much so that even People for the American Way had to acknowledge that religion is often overlooked in history textbooks: "Religion is simply not treated as a significant element in American life—it is not portrayed as an integrated part of the American value system or as something that is important to individual Americans."[32] A 1994 study of history textbooks commissioned by the federal government and drafted by the National Center for History in the Schools at UCLA concluded that religion "was foolishly purged from many recent textbooks."[33] In 1990, Warren A. Nord of the University of North Carolina wrote:

> What cannot be doubted is that our ways of thinking about nature, morality, art, and society were once (and for many people still are) fundamentally religious, and

still today in our highly secular world it is difficult even for the non-religious to extricate themselves entirely from the webs of influence and meaning provided by our religious past. . . . To understand history and (historical) literature one must understand a great deal about religion: on this all agree. Consequently, the relative absence of religion from history textbooks is deeply troubling.[34]

The removal of the topic of religion from textbooks is not always motivated by a desire to slam Christianity. Textbook publishers fear special interest groups that scrutinize the material for any infraction, whether it be religious, racial, sexual, or ethnic. For example, "the 1990 Houghton Mifflin elementary series first made special efforts to include material (and in state hearings received savage criticism from militant Jews, Muslims, and fundamentalist Christians)."[35] The easiest way to placate these diverse groups is to remove all discussion of the topic. This deletion of material is either outright censorship or else a reluctance to fight ideological wars, but whatever the case, failure to deal factually with the past distorts a student's historical perspective. This has happened to such an extent that even when religious themes are covered "their treatments are uniformly antiseptic and abstract."[36]

This essay originally appeared as a chapter in Gary DeMar, *America's Christian History: The Untold Story*, (Atlanta: American Vision, 1994), pp. 21–34. Reproduction rights granted by Gary DeMar and American Vision.

[1] Miriam Horn with Andy Plattner, "Should Congress censor art?," *U.S. News and World Report* (September 25, 1989), 22, 24; Bo Emerson, "Civil War over Censorship: Morality is the Issue on Battlefield of Culture," *Atlanta Journal/Constitution* (July 25, 1990), D1; and "Four artists to NEA: Who are you to judge?," *The Atlanta Constitution* (March 19, 1991), B6.

[2] Harry Hoffman, "Protect the Right to Buy and Sell Books," *USA Today* (April 25, 1990), 10A.

[3] Nat Hentoff, *Free Speech for Me—But Not for Thee: How the American Left and Right Relentlessly Censor Each Other* (New York: HarperCollins, 1992), 2.

[4] Those who promote liberal causes are not opposed to boycotts of companies and products they deem objectionable from their perspective. Ultra-liberal leftist groups promote "Working Assets Long Distance Service" as a way of funding radical groups such as Planned Parenthood, Greenpeace, Rainforest Action Network, and over 100 other action groups. One of their tactics is the promotion of "boycotts and buycotts." See Cathy Lynn Grossman, "Boycotting is popular resort for activists," *USA Today* (October 11, 1994), 4D.

[5] Donald C. Wildmon, "Protect the Right to Boycott Pornography," *USA Today* (April 25, 1990), 10A.

[6] Joseph W. Grigg, "'Peter Rabbit' banned from London schools," *Atlanta Journal/Constitution* (April 7, 1988), 1A.

[7] Peggie R. Elgin, "Hardy Boys banned from Cobb libraries," *Marietta Daily Journal* (January 13, 1988), 1A.

[8] "Residents want 'Playboy' out of library," *Marietta Daily Journal* (October 18, 1994), 4A.

[9] Willmar Thorkelson, "Book Ban Considered," *Washington Post* (September 1, 1990).

[10] Reported in "Texas Report," a supplement to the *Christian American* (July/August 1992).

[11] PAW evaluation reported in Andrew Mollison, "Group says efforts to ban schoolbooks focus on alleged satanic, occult content," *Atlanta Constitution* (August 29, 1991), A11.

[12] "PAW Cries Censor-Wolf: Attempt to Keep Parents Out of Schools, Says FRC," Family Research Council Press Release (August 31, 1994), 1.

[13] Quoted in "The great 'censorship' hoax," *Citizen* (September 19, 1994), 8.

[14] David Shaw, "Abortion Bias Seeps Into News," reprinted from *Los Angeles Times* (July 1–4, 1990) and Al Knight, "School races turn nasty," *Denver Post* (October 10, 1993), 1D and 5D. Knight writes: "The term religious right, in the hands of PFAW and other groups, has become one of the most elastic political labels in memory. It is routinely stretched to include nearly anyone who might be motivated either by conservative or by religious or moral concerns" (1D).

[15] John W. Whitehead, *The Rights of Religious Persons in Public Education: A Complete Resource for Knowing and Exercising Your Rights in Public Education*, rev. ed. (Wheaton, IL: Crossway Books, [1991] 1994), 112–13.

[16] Barbara Reynolds, "Religion is Greatest Story Ever Missed," *USA Today* (March 16, 1990), 13A.

17 Paul C. Vitz, *Censorship: Evidence of Bias in Our Children's Textbooks* (Ann Arbor, MI: Servant Books, 1986), 1. Emphasis added.

18 Vitz, *Censorship*, 3.

19 As reported in Carey Quan Gelernter, "The Real Thanksgiving," *Seattle Post-Intelligencer* (November 23, 1986), L1.

20 As reported in Gelernter, "The Real Thanksgiving," L2.

21 "Squanto and the First Thanksgiving," Rabbit Ears, *Atlanta Journal/Constitution* (November 27, 1994).

22 William Bradford, *Bradford's History of the Plymouth Settlement: 1608–1650*, original manuscript entitled *Of Plymouth Plantation* rendered into modern English by Harold Paget (Portland, OR: American Heritage Ministries, [1909] 1988).

23 Edward Winslow, *How the Pilgrim Fathers Lived*, 2:116. Emphasis added. *CD Sourcebook of American History* (Mesa, AR: Candlelight Publishing, 1992). Also see *Mourt's Relation: A Journal of the Pilgrims of Plymouth*, ed. Jordan D. Fiore (Plymouth, MA: Plymouth Rock Foundation, [1622] 1985), 67–69.

24 Diana Karter Appelbaum, *Thanksgiving: An American Holiday, An American History* (New York: Facts on File Publications, 1984), 9.

25 This editing was exposed in *Education Update*, Heritage Foundation, 10:3 (Summer 1987). Quoted in Robert P. Dugan, *Winning the New Civil War: Recapturing America's Values* (Portland, OR: Multnomah Press, 1991), 149–50.

26 Kendall Hamilton, "No Red Faces, They Hope," *Newsweek* (November 21, 1994), 61.

27 Whitehead, *The Rights of Religious Persons in Public Education*, 41–42.

28 Henry Steele Commager, "Preface," *McGuffey's Fifth Eclectic Reader*. Quoted in Whitehead, *The Rights of Religious Persons in Public Education*, 42.

29 John H. Westerhoff, III, "The Struggle for a Common Culture: Biblical Images in Nineteenth-Century Schoolbooks," *The Bible in American Education*, eds. David L. Barr and Nicholas Piediscalzi (Philadelphia, PA: Fortress Press, 1982), 32.

30 Westerhoff, "The Struggle for a Common Culture: Biblical Images in Nineteenth-Century Schoolbooks," 28.

31 Charles B. Galloway, *Christianity and the American Commonwealth; or, The Influence of Christianity in Making This Nation* (Nashville, TN: Methodist Episcopal Church, 1898), 15.

32 O. L. Davis, Jr., et al., *Looking at History: A Review of Major U.S. History Textbooks* (1986), 3. Quoted in Joan Delfattore, *What Johnny Shouldn't Read: Textbook Censorship in America* (New Haven, CT: Yale University Press, 1992), 85.

33 This is also the conclusion of the editorial writers of the *Marietta Daily Journal*: "History needing revision" (October 30, 1994), 2D. *The National Standards for United States History* has called for the restoration of the role religion played in the founding of America while pushing a "politically correct" agenda in nearly everything else. See Lynne V. Cheney, "The End of History," *Wall Street Journal* (October 20, 1994), A24.

34 Warren A. Nord, "Taking Religion Seriously," Social Education, 54:9 (September 1990), 287. Quoted in History Textbooks: A Standard and Guide, 1994–95 Edition (New York: American Textbook Council, 1994), 32.

35 *History Textbooks: A Standard and Guide*, 1994–95 Edition, 32.

36 *History Textbooks: A Standard and Guide*, 1994–95 Edition, 33.

1. What is censorship and when it is appropriate?

2. What kinds of books are usually singled out for banning?

3. What are some areas in which an anti-Christian bias is apparent in censorship and selective editing?

4. Censorship isn't just a current problem; it reaches into the past. Can you cite examples of how our history is being rewritten to minimize or exclude the role of Christianity?

5. Should religion have a place in public school textbooks?

Warren Smith of The Colson Center expounds on the message of his book, *Restoring All Things*: The world is changed by ordinary people because God uses the least and the most broken to do his greatest work. To become a restorer requires four things:

1. We must become known by what we are for, not what we are against.
2. We must recover the art of storytelling.
3. We must learn to tell the complete biblical story.
4. We must be reconcilers by relearning how to care for the victims of anti-Christian ideologies.

Smith suggests the kind of questions Christians must ask and answer to restore God's story in a broken world:

- What is good in our culture that we can promote, protect, and celebrate?
- What is missing that we can creatively contribute?
- What is evil in our culture that we can stop?
- What is broken in our culture that we can restore?

To access this video, go to www.summitu.com/utt and enter the passcode found in the back of your manual.

▶ **"RESTORING ALL THINGS" VIDEO OUTLINE**

The world is changed by ordinary people. God uses the least, the lost, and the broken to do his greatest work. God loves "re-" words: redeem, renew, resurrect, reconcile, regenerate, restore. There are four key points to becoming restorers:

1. **We must become known by what we are _____, not what we are _____ (Philippians 4:8).**

   Christians should devote themselves to the good, the true, and the beautiful. This can happen in the arts but also in any vocation done well for the glory of God.

2. **We must recover the art of storytelling.**

   There is real power in storytelling. Stories help us remember abstract ideas. They do this by providing relevance and context. We need to recover the art of biblical story-telling. Biblical storytelling illuminates the meta-narrative of God's work in the world. It is telling the truth about the world and God's redeeming and restoring work in it.

3. **We must learn to tell the complete biblical story.**

   We often forget to add the fourth truth to the biblical story: Creation, Fall, Redemption and _____. The gospel is not just the story of what we are saved *from*; it's also the story of what we are saved *for*. We have been reconciled to be reconcilers.

4. **We must be reconcilers by caring for the victims of anti-Christian ideologies.**

   Examples of bad ideas that have resulted in the deaths of millions:

   - _____
   - Sexual revolution
   - Radical _____
   - Faux Christianity that inoculates many to the true gospel message

   How can we restore God's story? By asking and answering these questions:

   - What is good in our culture that we can promote, protect, and celebrate?
   - What is _____ that we can creatively contribute?
   - What is evil in our culture that we can _____?
   - What is _____ in our culture that we can restore?

1. Can you identify some issues Christians are known to be "against" and suggest what we could be known "for" in these areas instead?

2. What makes storytelling so powerful and why is it important in a postmodern world?

3. What part do Christians tend to leave out of the biblical story?

4.   What are some bad ideologies whose victims need care and restoration?

5.   What does it mean that Christians should "run toward the plague?"

Key Questions:

1. What is history?
2. How do the six dominant Western worldviews approach history?

Key Terms:

1. Bourgeoisie
2. Capitalism
3. Communism
4. Cosmic Evolution
5. Cyclical Conception of History
6. Redemptive Narrative
7. Deconstruction
8. Determinism
9. Evolutionary Godhood*
10. Fact
11. Free Will
12. Historical Materialism*
13. Historical Revisionism*
14. Historicism
15. Historiography
16. History*
17. Islamist
18. Jihad
19. Linear Conception of History
20. Nihilism
21. Pan-Islam*
22. Proletariat
23. Redemptive Narrative*
24. Social Progress*
25. Socialism

Key Verses:

1. Acts 17:31
2. 1 Corinthians 15:14
3. Galatians 4:4
4. 2 Peter 3:13

Key Players:

1. Caesar E. Farah
2. Michael Foucault
3. G. W. F. Hegel
4. Herodotus
5. John Lukacs
6. Karl Popper
7. Thucydides
8. Howard Zinn

Key Works:

1. *A People's History of the United States* by Howard Zinn
2. *The Histories* by Herodotus
3. *History of the Peloponnesian* War by Thucydides
4. *Metahistory* by Hayden White
5. *Power/Knowledge* by Michael Foucault

Short answer or essay question on the exam

Greetings!

Your last letter helped me out a ton when writing my economics paper. Thanks a lot! Now I just have to focus on surviving these last few weeks of the semester. Elections are held next week, and finals are held the following three weeks. Surprisingly, this week will be relatively low key, like the calm before the storm. My professors have been helpful with supplying extra office hours in preparation for finals. In fact I met with my History of Western Civilization professor yesterday to talk about some questions I had concerning next week's studies on the French Revolution. He is an interesting old man with a British accent and a penchant for wearing tweed coats and bow ties.

During our conversation, I mentioned how his class has me considering perhaps majoring or minoring in history. He described what it was like to be a historian, digging in archives and spending long hours poring over forgotten texts. He also related his favorite travel memories while researching his latest book. Apparently historians travel the world and learn many languages. An overwhelming topic of our conversation was the method of viewing and analyzing history. Essentially, he was explaining how historians view the overarching theme of history. He views history through the lens of progression. He related it to evolutionary theory. History is always changing, or progressing, as human beings evolve. When I asked him what the end goal of the progression was, he merely chuckled and replied, "progress." Evolution has no purpose, only direction.

The professor's view of history doesn't seem to align with what Christianity says about human depravity and God's redemptive plan for humanity. I told the professor I believed history had meaning and purpose to it. He challenged to me prove it. I told him I was a Christian, but he didn't seem to accept that as an answer. He gave me several books to read on the topic by authors he described as leading humanist and Marxist scholars of history. I assume he means Secular Humanists. I want to be able to speak with him further on these topics, but I need your help understanding the subject better. **What is the Secularist view of history?** Also, **what is the Marxist view of history?** He has mentioned in class before that some historians promote the idea that history is only the interpretations we impart onto the subject. This sounds like something Paige, as a Postmodernist, would say. **How does Postmodernism approach the discipline of history?** Nathan is taking this class with me, so I want to be prepared to talk with him too. How does New Spirituality view history? I also wonder how similar Islam is to Christianity with regards to history. **How do Islamic and Christian views of history differ?**

Thanks again for all your help. I appreciate how much time you spend aiding my understanding of all these different topics. You rock!

See ya!
–Doug

UNIT

18

CONCLUSION

CHAPTER 18 LEARNING OBJECTIVES

Students will be able to:

1. define a worldview. [18.1–18.2]
2. define the key tenets of Islam's worldview. [18.3]
3. define the key tenets of Secularism's worldview. [18.4]
4. define the key tenets of Marxism's worldview. [18.5]
5. define the key tenets of New Spirituality's worldview. [18.6]
6. define the key tenets of Postmodernism's worldview. [18.7]
7. define the key tenets of Christianity's worldview. [18.8]
8. describe how to evaluate different worldviews. [18.9]
9. explain how different worldviews approach the discipline of theology. [18.10]
10. explain how different worldviews approach the discipline of philosophy. [18.11]
11. explain how different worldviews approach the discipline of ethics. [18.12]
12. explain how different worldviews approach the discipline of biology. [18.13]
13. explain how different worldviews approach the discipline of psychology. [18.14]
14. explain how different worldviews approach the discipline of sociology. [18.15]
15. explain how different worldviews approach the discipline of law. [18.16]
16. explain how different worldviews approach the discipline of politics. [18.17]
17. explain how different worldviews approach the discipline of economics. [18.18]
18. explain how different worldviews approach the discipline of history. [18.19]
19. identify how Christians should respond to the truth of Christianity. [18.20–18.22]

1.   What is a worldview and what questions does it answer? [18.2]

2.   What are the six worldviews studied in this book? [18.2]

3.   What are some of the key distinctives of Islam? [18.3]

4.   What are the three main groups in modern Islam? [18.3]

5. What are some of the key distinctives of Secularism? [18.4]

6. What are some of the key distinctives of Marxism? [18.5]

7. What are some of the key distinctives of New Spirituality? [18.6]

8. What are some of the key distinctives of Postmodernism? [18.7]

9. What are some of the key distinctives of Christianity? [18.8]

10. What are four tests that can be applied to worldviews to see if they are valid? [18.9]

11. How is Christianity different from other worldviews? [18.9]

12. How do the different worldviews view theology? [18.10]

13. How does Christianity answer the two main questions of theology? [18.10]

14. How do the different worldviews view philosophy? [18.11]

15. How does Christianity answer the three main questions of philosophy? [18.11]

16. How do the different worldviews view ethics? [18.12]

17. How does Christianity answer the two main questions of ethics? [18.12]

18. How do the different worldviews view biology? [18.13]

19. How does Christianity answer the main question of biology? [18.13]

20. How do the different worldviews view psychology? [18.14]

21. How does Christianity answer the main questions of psychology? [18.14]

22. How do the different worldviews view sociology? [18.15]

23. How does Christianity understand sociology? [18.15]

24. How do the different worldviews view law? [18.16]

25. How does Christianity understand law? [18.16]

26. How do the different worldviews view politics? [18.17]

27. How does Christianity answer the main question of politics? [18.17]

28. How do the different worldviews view economics? [18.18]

29. How does Christianity understand economics? [18.18]

30. How do the different worldviews view history? [18.19]

31. How does Christianity view history? [18.19]

32. How should Christians live in today's world? [18.21, 22]

33. America is a pluralistic society that guarantees freedom of religion. Does this means Christians have to accept other worldviews as valid? Should people be allowed to live by their own rules, whether shariah Law or their own subjective sense of right and wrong? How can Christian citizens get along with others without giving in to other worldviews?

Chapter 18 Key Points

Key Questions:

1. How does Christianity compare to other worldviews?
2. Which worldview offers the best answers to life's ultimate questions?

Key Verses:

1. Matthew 28:18–20
2. Romans 2:15
3. Romans 5:6–10
4. Romans 8:20–22
5. Romans 12:1–2

Key Terms:

1. Atheism
2. Bourgeoisie
3. Collective Consciousness
4. Communism
5. Consciousness
6. Deconstruction
7. Dialectical Materialism
8. Economic Determinism
9. Epistemology
10. General Revelation
11. Islamist
12. Jihadi
13. Karma
14. Legal Positivism
15. Materialism
16. Metanarrative
17. Metaphysics
18. Mind/Body Problem
19. Naturalism
20. Pantheism
21. Poststructuralism
22. Proletariat
23. Proletariat Morality
24. Self-actualization
25. Shariah Law
26. Socialism
27. Special Revelation
28. Sphere Sovereignty
29. Spiritual Evolution
30. *Ummah*

Short answer or essay question on the exam